REUTHER:

A Daughter Strikes

*To our sacred earth
and all her children.*

ELISABETH REUTHER DICKMEYER

REUTHER:
A Daughter Strikes

SPELMAN PUBLISHERS DIVISION
SOUTHFIELD, MICHIGAN — SAN 692-8803 — (313) 355-3686

FIRST PRINTING 1989
UNION PRINTED BY ARCATA IN THE UNITED STATES OF AMERICA

LIBRARY OF CONGRESS NO. 88-050769
Dickmeyer, Elisabeth Reuther
     REUTHER: A Daughter Strikes
     Includes foreword, contents, appendix, bibliography, index
     54 illustrations
     Non-fiction 1. Union/Labor 2. History 3. Biography

ISBN Hardcover: 0-933803-11-7
ISBN Softcover: 0-933803-10-9

3 9082 04826856 2

PUBLISHED BY:
Spelman Publishers Division, Spelman Inc.
26941 Pebblestone Road
Southfield, MI 48034
313-355-3686

SAN 692-8803
Imprints:
Thirty-Three Publishing
HealthProInk Publishing
Spelman Productions (Video and TV)

CONTENTS

FOREWORD

I knew Walter Reuther for more than a quarter of a century, at work and at his home. I found myself observing and learning as he personally led millions of Americans to a better, more just life. Walter was a man of ideas. He not only originated programs. He also had the capacity to take the ideas of others and develop them into practical gains for the human family. And in the back of Walter's mind was always what kind of impact these plans would have to strengthen our democratic system.

When I first met Walter, I was fairly rigid. His example taught me how to be flexible. At the first contract negotiations dealing with the pension plan for older workers, Walter insisted that these gains be tied to Social Security. Since Social Security had not been raised in over a decade, he calculated correctly that the employers would go to Washington and ask for a Social Security increase in order to decrease their own payments into the Pension Fund. That is exactly what the employers did. Walter always thought ahead; in broad terms. There was nothing narrow about him.

Walter saw the union as an instrument for social change. More than any other one person, he is responsible for formulating the ideals and principles of the UAW. He became recognized as a great communicator. He had the capacity to reduce the most complex of issues and translate them into understandable terms for the membership.

Walter was a demanding leader. But he never expected more than he was willing to give himself. He had an unswerving commitment to America's greatness. His enthusiasm rubbed off and touched others who shared in this dream of America's promise. Indeed, the potency Walter had to lead others is a rare ability.

As a bargainer, he was brilliant. He was a marvelous strategist with a terrific sense of timing. The unprecedented gains for the common man under his leadership are legendary.

I knew Walter as a caring, considerate person. And what many people did not realize — he had a wonderful sense of humor. During bargaining, there are always "ups" and "downs." When things weren't going as hoped, we would get depressed. And then Walter's sense of humor would suddenly take over. Often he'd have us laughing at our own dilemma. And he'd always have a plan to lead us forward.

After some of the negotiating victories with Walter, I would feel absolute exhilaration. It was a wonderful sense of accomplishment. And it is the best of all feelings because you did it for others; you didn't do it for yourself. Actually the feedback of appreciation from the uncountable families that were benefited was in and of itself the greatest reward.

It is true that Walter was disliked by some; those who disagreed with his principles and those who were envious of his success. But beyond a doubt, he was respected by all.

I have visited Walter at his Paint Creek home. I also became close to the family. I have known Lisa since she was a little girl. This book is a long-time dream for her, to share the inside story of one of America's most controversial and favorite sons.

When I have the opportunity to travel the country and speak at different universities, I often conduct a test to see how many of the students are familiar with the name Walter Reuther. It's absolutely shocking how few students recognize his name and what he did for the betterment of America and the world.

Hopefully, this book will bring to life in your mind one of the Twentieth Century's greatest leaders. The newspaper columnist Murray Kempton once remarked that "Walter Reuther is the only man I have met who could reminisce about the future." I think his quote is most appropriate today as we struggle with that "future." Many of Walter's ideas and programs are as relevant in this hour as they were twenty years ago.

Doug Fraser

PROLOGUE

It was the spring of 1970. My parents were organizing a world ecology seminar in Northern Michigan. Ecologists from 17 nations were to meet that summer at Black Lake, the UAW's Family Education Center, to discuss how to save the environment. For a long time, my father had sensed the spiritual vacuum at the heart of the century's technological revolution. The destruction of the earth's resources carried the gravest of messages: Mankind was committing suicide.

My parents did not live to attend the seminar. The mysterious plane crash that took their lives that spring cost the earth two good friends and broke a lot of hearts. Especially their daughters'.

Growing up with May and Walter Reuther had never been easy, but it had always been an education. They not only believed in the dignity and kinship of all people, they lived it. As with any life worth living, that brought great risks. The assassination attempts, the extreme security measures, the utter loss of privacy, all left their mark on my psyche. But they also taught me a lesson. Something was terribly wrong with the world and it was my duty to help make it right.

But how, now that my parents were gone? They had been everything to me. I wanted to continue their vision of possibility and hope. Should I write a book? I wasn't ready. I needed to heal and to find out who I was. My search carried me around the world and took years of spiritual growth.

Father's concern for the earth was the ripened fruit of his humanity. For 35 years he had been the conscience of the American labor movement. "The labor movement is about changing society," he said during the last days of his life. "What good is a dollar an hour more in wages if your neighborhood is burning down? What good is another week's vacation if the lake you used to go to, where you've got a cottage, is polluted and you can't swim in it and the kids can't play in it? What good is another $100 onto your pension if the world goes up in atomic smoke?"

Today, the problems father confronted 20 years ago are all but suffocating us. Our seas are dying. Our forests are dying. In the last decade, the so-called greenhouse effect has produced five of the hottest and driest years in modern history. Rain, when it comes, often brims with acidic pollutants. Every year we pump over five billion tons of carbon dioxide into the atmosphere. At this rate, within 40 to 60 years temperatures will rise to fluctuations exceeding those of the Ice Age.

Progress without wisdom is a cruel hoax. Why do we continue to buy it? Greed. Suicidal greed. The profit motive must be restored to its natural place, below intelligence and compassion. If we can slip the bonds of earth in a space shuttle, then why, for example, can't we ply her surface more cleanly (and without saber rattling over foreign fuel) in an electric car? The appropriate technology is at hand. As father used to say, "It is not a lack of know-how, it is a lack of will."

Yet it was the people's immense capacity for good that drove the dreams of May and Walter Reuther. The potential of the human spirit. Can we, at this eleventh hour, rise above our fate and solve our problems as human beings? I hope the story of my parents' lives inspires you, dear reader, to positive action. Nothing is impossible. We hold the future in our hands. As our friend, Eleanor Roosevelt once said, "What one has to do usually can be done."

Elisabeth Reuther Dickmeyer
November 1988
Detroit, Michigan

CHAPTER ONE

THE
SHOOTING

"My God, May! I've been shot!"
— Father to mother, April 20, 1948

"I am my brother's keeper." That was father's philosophy. He was driven by a dream, a vision of truth. And to many, that made him dangerous.

He felt tremendous changes were needed in the American capitalist system. The real strength of America, he believed, is that all citizens share in the wealth created by her industry. Father viewed the labor movement as "an instrument for social change, a vehicle with which we can improve the quality of the whole society." This was his reason for living. It was also his reason for dying.

In mid-April 1948, father received threatening letters at the United Auto Workers headquarters in Detroit. As new president of the UAW, he was then consolidating his power, eliminating the die-hard Communist elements. It was a critical time for the union.

On April 20 that year, father met with the UAW Executive Board at the Book Cadillac Hotel. Discussions were running late. He phoned mother: "Keep supper warm, May." After the meeting, father went to his office at UAW headquarters with Jack Conway, his administrative assistant. From there, he drove alone to our home at 20101 Appoline in northwest Detroit. The house was a little brick-and-frame bunga-low with a big birch tree out front. My parents had moved there in 1941 just before my older sister, Linda, was born.

Father always parked his car on the side street and entered the house through the back yard. But this particular night, he fortunately broke habit and used the front door. It was 9:40 p.m. Mother greeted him and they went into the kitchen, where leftovers were waiting. After father had finished his stew at the breakfast nook, he walked to the refrigerator to get a bowl of peach preserves. Mother was at that moment voicing concern over a slight defect she had noticed in Linda's walk. As father reached into the refrigerator, he turned his body to watch mother demonstrate Linda's problem. There was a deafening blast, "like a bomb," mother later recalled.

Father was thrown to the floor in a pool of blood. "My God, May! I've been shot!"

Mother screamed in horror, then rushed to the phone to call the police and an ambulance. Returning to father, she carefully placed his bloody, shattered arm on a bread board in the panicked hope it could be reconstructed. Father had received a full blast from a double-barreled shotgun. Four slugs of the type used to kill large game had splintered his right arm into 150 pieces of bone. Another had pierced his back and exited out his stomach.

Neighbors came running at the sound of the blast. One saw the gunman run from the back yard, jump into a red Ford sedan and speed away. Another neighbor, Dr. Angelo V. Lenzi, rushed to father's side and placed his arm in an emergency splint. Father was in excruciating pain, but conscious.

"Those bastards shot me in the back," he whispered. "They couldn't come out in the open and fight!" He looked at Dr. Lenzi: "Please Doc, don't let them cut off my arm."

An ambulance rushed father to New Grace Hospital, mother at his side. Father's brothers, Roy and Victor, soon arrived. They pressed close and urged him to fight for his life. After blood transfusions and three hours of surgery, he was placed in a body cast and his arm in traction. Electric shock therapy kept that arm from stiffening.

Back at home, police and detectives were everywhere. Had father

4

parked his car on the side street and entered through the back yard as usual, he would have been an easy target for a gunman waiting in the bushes. Had he not turned at the instant the shots were fired, his chest would have been blown out by the blast.

Neighbors moved in to stay with Linda and me. I had been asleep in a downstairs crib when the shotgun shell exploded. Those violent and terrifying moments are my very earliest memories. It wasn't the first attempt on father's life; nor would it be the last.

Word of the attack spread swiftly. Senators, congressmen, supreme court justices, President Truman and many world leaders expressed outrage. Police posted round-the-clock guards at father's hospital room and even at our home. The UAW, suspicious of the Detroit police, assigned its own guards as well.

Sightseers and the curious converged on our house. Popcorn vendors worked the growing crowd! Linda had to be escorted to and from school by a bodyguard. "Why can't I be like the other kids?" she asked.

Mother wanted to protect us from the anguish of the attack. "Daddy fell against the kitchen window and cut his arm," she told us. "It was an accident." But we sensed it was something more. Though I was only nine months old, the terrifying violence of that night went deep within me. I felt my mother's fear. Something terrible had happened to daddy.

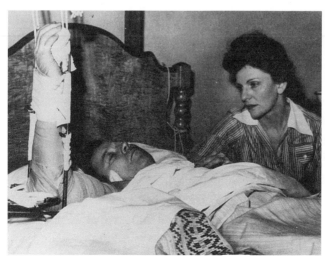

Mother sits pensively as father fights for his life after the shotgun attack by a would-be assassin, April 20, 1948.

5

CHAPTER TWO

THE
COVER-UP

"You see, Lisa, when you are fighting for human dignity, it is inevitable that you have enemies. And sometimes your enemies are those people who are supposed to be upholding law and order."

— Father

2—3 -01

Father's parents, Valentine and Anna Reuther ("Grossvater" and "Grossmutter" to us) read the terrifying headlines and rushed from their West Virginia home to father's bedside.

Grossmutter begged her son to give up his union work and take up a safer profession. "Maybe you could resume your tool and die work, or write books." Father pretended to think about it, but Grossmutter probably knew what her son was going to say. He knew he was marked, so he wanted to accomplish as much as he could in whatever time remained.

"I'm all tied up in this work," he explained. "It's much bigger than I am, and I can't run away from it."

Father was hospitalized for several weeks. Flowers filled his room. Hundreds of letters and telegrams wished him well and encouraged him in his slow and difficult recovery. Encased in his body cast, father suffered from cold chills and high fevers. When he caught malaria and hepatitis from the blood transfusions, mother declared the hospital "a nightmare."

Father's radial nerve, which controlled movement in his right hand, had been critically damaged. Dr. Barnes Woodhall advised him to decide in what position he wanted his arm permanently fixed. Father refused.

"I admire your determination, but I think little of your medical judgment," the doctor scolded. The odds against recovering use of the arm were enormous. But anyone who knew father knew he would probably try — and bet on his success.

With his left hand, father constructed a system of weights and trusses which worked better than the one the hospital had given him.

"Here was a guy who knew design and he knew mechanics," said Uncle Victor. "He was flat on his back, in a cast from his waist up, yet he was designing these trusses. The doctors even used some of his designs at Henry Ford Hospital. And all the while he was working on a medical care plan for the whole nation. This is the kind of character he was."

Father's medical plan later developed into the Kennedy Health Care Bill. His conviction was that health care was a birthright. He wanted the best medical coverage for the lowest possible price. So he thought about it while recovering in his hospital bed. He never wasted his time.

After father came home, he received daily physical therapy and massage from a visiting nurse. His injuries required constant rest, so he was bedridden for months. Too young for school, I was home during his recuperation. Often I sat at the end of his bed, mother by his head, reading him the newspaper or letters he had received. Seeing father disabled disturbed me, but it also increased my love for him. I came to understand that he had enemies. His courage and dedication would teach me much about the potential of the human spirit. A pact developed between us, communicated not by words but by the heart.

After 18 months of therapy, he was able to move his right thumb for the first time. It twitched a fraction of an inch. He shouted for joy and told the nurse: "I have overcome the greatest obstacle."

Father worked to strengthen his withered arm by squeezing a hard rubber ball for several hours a day. I would sit on his lap as he opened and closed his hand around the ball. I could almost feel the pain he felt during this exercise. That was my first lesson in tolerance. His drive compelled him to overcome his physical limitations. In later years, he regained his strong, self-assured handshake. "People can be understood by their handshake, Lisa," he would say. "You should always be decisive and look the person right in the eye."

Deeper than the scars on father's arm was the fear that at any time disaster would again strike our family. Our house on Appoline was on a corner — too vulnerable, said the security experts — so we moved to a mid-block house on Longfellow, closer to UAW headquarters. The union installed bulletproof glass in all of the downstairs windows. A 10-foot barbed-wire fence surrounded the back yard. Floodlights illuminated the property at night. After consulting with George F. Boos, then head of the Secret Service's Detroit office, the UAW provided father and our family with practically the same protection given the president of the United States. Two full-time bodyguards stayed with father, while two guard dogs watched the yard. Our home was a fortress.

The UAW purchased a $12,000 bullet-proof Packard for father. But he never liked it. It was too ostentatious, he said, too impractical. A heavy car already, the armor put even more strain on the engine. When it finally broke down one day, father was delighted. He got out and gave it a kick: "I'll never ride in you again."

The German shepherds were trained to attack on command. Father had to spend hours with the trainer, teaching the dogs to respond to his voice. I sat on the basement steps, watching. When father gave a particular command in German, the dogs lunged at the make-believe assailant. Another command and they stopped. I was struck with the power and violence of these animals, their jaws fearsome weapons with which to defend us.

Father would chuckle after a training session. "Just see, Lisa, these dogs speak German."

The dogs became my best friends. I loved animals, and these dogs and I had a lot in common. As they were confined to their pen in the back, so I too lived in restricted surroundings. I spent hours inside their cage playing with them, yet outside I also felt like a caged animal. With me, they were gentle as pups, but to an attacker, they were ferocious beasts — pitiless, implacable death.

The neighborhood children liked to tease the dogs. With sticks through the fence, they poked the dogs' faces. "Get out of here!" I

Meeting my new-found friend, one of the attack dogs.

screamed, tears rolling down my face. "Don't hurt my dogs!"

I felt the dogs' pain as my own. I couldn't understand why the children were so cruel. My short life had been filled with violence. I wanted to protect the dogs. I wanted to protect my father. But I was just a small girl.

The Detroit Police made a token attempt to solve the shooting, but were unable to discover who did it. The City Council, some churches and numerous labor organizations raised $117,000 reward money for information leading to conviction of the gunman or gunmen.

Congressmen and cabinet members urged the FBI to enter the case. After all, father was a world figure; his name appeared on at least one list of the 10 most influential people on earth. He had personally expelled the Communists from the UAW. And this was one of the FBI's keen interests — stopping the Communist movement in the United States.

Attorney General Tom Clark approached J. Edgar Hoover with the request. Hoover's response was, to say the least, strange: "I'm not going to send in the FBI every time some nigger woman gets raped."

Thirteen months after the shooting of father, violence again struck our family. This time, Uncle Victor was the target. As he sat in his living room reading *The New York Times,* a blast from a double-barreled shotgun ripped through the front window and hit Victor in the face, throat and chest.

Victor: "As I fell to the floor, I remember thinking, 'Dear God, no, not yet. Please don't let me die. I have so much more to do.'

"The attack on me was a way of serving notice to Walter. 'We didn't get you yet, but we're still around.' The attack was really on him."

Victor was rushed to Henry Ford Hospital. Father was returning from a meeting when he heard the report of the shooting on the radio. He told his driver to rush to the hospital. As Victor had done for him the previous year, father held his brother's hand and encouraged him to fight for his life. Victor did, although his right eye had to be removed. "There was no eye," he explained. "It had been shot out."

Grossmutter again made the tearful trip to Detroit. Now a second son lay wounded, felled by an assailant's bullet. She talked to her three sons, Walter, Victor and Roy. "Mothers throughout history have had to wrestle with the problem of losing their sons," she began. "Too many mothers have lost their sons to wars. I haven't. But you boys have made a decision to give your time and energy to the labor movement. That's what you believe in. You must be prepared to give your life for it."

Grossmutter's commitment inspired her sons. Said father later: "I came out of that meeting feeling like I could lift a mountain with one hand."

After the attack on Victor, the FBI received an avalanche of demands to investigate the Reuther shootings. But again, Hoover was obdurate. "We must resist being jockeyed into this," he wrote his staff.

Then the United States Senate took an unprecedented action. It adopted a resolution requesting President Truman to direct the FBI to investigate the shootings. The UAW posted an additional $100,000, increasing the reward money to $217,000. The FBI was forced to enter the case.

It was Sam Henderson, an investigator hired by the UAW, who

finally cracked the case. Henderson found hit man Donald J. Ritchie, whose signed confession then linked five underworld figures to the shooting of father. Ritchie's statement read:

I was in the car the night Walter Reuther was shot. For about four or five years I had been working for Santo (Sam) Perrone. I made about $400 to $500 a week.

In the occupation I was — well, it just wasn't what people would call work.

Clarence Jacobs approached me for this particular job. He told me I would get five grand. I was approached about five days before it happened and asked if I wanted to go. This conversation took place in Perrone's gas station. Perrone asked me several days before the shooting if I was going on the job. I said I was.

I didn't ask a lot of questions, these people don't talk things over very much. All I knew was that Perrone had once said: 'We'll have to get that guy out of the way.' Did he mean Reuther? 'Yeah.'

The night of the shooting, I was picked up in the gas station. The car was a red Mercury. I don't know who it belonged to. I sat in the back seat, Jacobs drove and Peter Lombardo was in the front seat with Jacobs. I was there in case there was trouble. If anything happened, I was to drive the car away.

Jacobs did the shooting. He was the only one who got out of the car. I don't know how long he was gone. It's hard to remember time. I heard the report of the gun. Then Jacobs got back in the car and said: 'Well, I knocked the bastard down.' We took off in a hurry.

After the job they dropped me back at the Helen Bar, about 200 feet from the gas station. I don't know what they did with the car. I heard later it was demolished and junked. I haven't any idea what happened to the gun.

I had some drinks at the bar and then went and saw Carl Renda. Why? I always went to see Renda. He said: 'I have something for you.' He got a bundle of cash and handed it to me.

I went downtown and met a girl. I stayed with her until four in the morning. Then I took a taxi to Windsor. I didn't count the money until I got to Canada. It was exactly five grand."

So the mystery had been solved (no thanks to the FBI). Ritchie was turned over to the Detroit Police. Being the star witness, he was kept under surveillance in the Statler Hotel. He told the detectives he wanted to take a shower, turned on the water, and disappeared. He emerged later in Canada. His confession had pointed to hit men from the mob — just the sort of investigation the FBI would normally pursue — but Hoover refused to seek extradition. Without Ritchie, the prosecutor did not have much of a case.

Hoover golfed regularly with Harry Bennett, Ford Motor Co.'s shadowy boss of security and labor relations. Hoover had many ties to big business and father was challenging big business on behalf of millions of workers.

Said Victor: "The 8,000-odd pages of FBI documentation that I read show they (the FBI) exerted more energy to cover up the traces than to find out who did it. They had censored so much of the documents, there were not six words on a page you could read."

Besides the legal cover-up of the shootings, a kind of psychic cover-up took place right in our home. My parents never discussed the attempt on father's life with Linda and me. They would refer to it only in passing as "the accident." Yet the sound of that shotgun continued to haunt my psyche. The watchdogs, bodyguards and barbed wire fences bespoke the danger lurking everywhere. Horror grew in the depths of my imagination.

When I was five or six, I took my 47 stuffed animals from the shelves and placed them in my bed. For hours, I would shelter them from danger. I imagined the bed as an ark surrounded by a turbulent sea. There were sharks everywhere. The waves were beating against the boat. My pulse beat frantically. There was no room for me to lie down in my little twin bed. I could not sleep.

Mother and father did not express their own fears and frustrations. And there was no acknowledgment of mine. I accepted the bodyguards but hated the loss of privacy. I was angry and afraid and, unable to share my dreadful feelings, became consumed by guilt. I was a bad person. Desperate, I resolved it was up to me to protect my parents. But that was unbearable. I was just a little girl.

Years later, when asked to comment on the 1948 shooting, father replied: "I think there's no question there was a period in the history of the UAW when disposing of me by assassination or some other way was a common denominator a number of people could somehow share. I think the Communist party shared that, because in their judgment I was the only thing which stood between them and seizing the power of this union. I think the underworld figured that I was the kind of person who would do everything that I could to try to keep them from taking control of this union and using it for the rackets.

"And I think there were still a small group of diehard employers who were also willing to work with the underworld and who thought they could weaken the union if they got me out of the way."

While father, in pursuit of his goals, was able to detach himself from all this, Linda and I could not. The danger was too close. Mother wanted to shelter us and she tried vainly to create an illusion of normalcy. But ours was not a normal father. There had been detailed plans in place to have him killed. He had been attacked. Perhaps mother's own experiences were too painful. I don't know; she never expressed them to us.

One day, when I was older, I approached father while he was building a table and haltingly asked him about the assassination attempt. He explained that the investigation afterward had been partially successful, but that the witness had disappeared.

"You see, Lisa, when you are fighting for human dignity, it is inevitable that you have enemies. And sometimes your enemies are the very people who are supposed to be upholding law and order."

My heart sank. How could this happen? Why would the Detroit Police Department fail to guard the main witness? I realized now that the system was limited, often corrupt. I was frightened. The would-be killers were still out there. They had tried to abort father's work and they might well try again. As father drew the sandpaper back and forth over the cherry wood, my eyes grew wider. "But daddy," I cried, burying my face in his chest, "I don't want you to get hurt."

I was both terrified and furious. Life wasn't what it appeared to be. Beneath the show of stability lay a society of cheaters and cheated. The greedy and powerful often stepped on others as they climbed. Moral men and women were not always welcome. Whoever challenged the system was in trouble. My father was marked.

CHAPTER THREE

ROOTS

"A man should always fight for freedom and brotherhood."
— Father's grandfather, Jacob Reuther

Father was born on Labor Day eve, 1907, in Wheeling, West Virginia. Destiny had placed him in a family that celebrated the next day as the most important of the year. Little Walter shared his mother's breast with a tiny girl whose mother was unable to nurse her. That must have been the first lesson he learned in life. To share.

His grandfather, Jacob Reuther, had migrated to the United States from Germany in 1892, fleeing from the repression of Rhinelanders by Prussian soldiers. Oppau, the town where the Reuthers had their roots, had a long-standing reputation for rebellious behavior. Grandfather Jacob was a vegetarian and a pacifist, who believed it was a sin to kill any animal or any human being. And he possessed a strong sense of social justice. He was disappointed in the church's apparent lack of interest in bettering the conditions of the people.

Father's own father, Valentine, was 11 years old when the family arrived in New York Harbor. As they sailed past the Statue of Liberty, Jacob put his arm around the boy and said: "A man should always fight for freedom and brotherhood."

Jacob put a down payment on some farmland in Illinois and built a log cabin for his family. He quickly became discouraged with the local Lutheran church. They did too much talking about the hereafter,

*Great-Grandfather
Jacob Reuther,
a pacifist and a vegetarian.*

*Grandparents
Valentine and
Anna Reuther.*

*Young Walter
Reuther with elder
brother Ted at
home in Wheeling,
W. Va.*

he complained, and not enough about the present. He started holding his own Sunday services in his house along with like-minded social activists.

Young Valentine nearly entered the ministry, then surprised everyone and became an agnostic. Like his father, he could not accept contradictions in the church's philosophy. "God says you should love and forgive your enemies," he would say. "How then can this loving God send erring humans into a life of perpetual damnation and hell?"

Valentine left Illinois to join a brother in Wheeling, a bustling industrial town where the infant labor movement was making headway. In all, there were 4,000 union members in that town. Valentine got a job in a steel mill earning $1.40 for a 12-hour day and before long he found a job driving a team of horses delivering beer for a local brewery. Seventeen-hour days were common. He then organized the brewery workers into a union and acted as their chief negotiator. This was practical help for the poor. The union became his virtual religion.

Anna Stocker had come to Wheeling from the Swabian region of Germany. Her mother would not allow her to marry her first love, so she left her homeland for Wheeling, where she stayed with her brother and worked in a local beer hall. The beer hall offered a free lunch, so Valentine often stopped there. He was strongly attracted to the beautiful red-haired girl of 18. They began attending the Beethoven Singing Society together, found the harmony excellent, fell in love and married. Ted was born in 1905, Walter in 1907, Roy in 1909, Victor in 1912 and, 12 years later, Christine arrived.

Father was a rambunctious boy and once attempted to parachute from a local water tower with his mother's new umbrella. The umbrella was ruined, but Grossmutter made him a shirt from the cloth. When schoolmates teased daddy about his umbrella shirt, he said: "I am so lucky I have a rainproof shirt." Grossmutter was thrifty. Father was independent. Both traits ran in the family.

When a new pastor at Zion Lutheran Church began to preach against the union because it had struck a local steel mill, Grossvater challenged his sermon. There was a brief argument in which Grossvater stressed the need for workers solidarity. The congregation applauded him. He stalked from the church, never to return. He allowed Grossmutter to take the family, but every Sunday when they returned he would ask the boys what the preacher had said. He didn't want his sons to accept anything blindly. Sometimes he would agree with the preacher, sometimes not. In this way, he kept in touch with the church. But he never returned.

Sunday afternoons were set aside for debates. Grossvater wanted his sons to be aware of the issues of the day. The topic would be selected a full week in advance, and the boys spent time at the library preparing their positions on child labor, yellow journalism, women's suffrage, and others. The boys then took turns playing devil's advocate, arguing points of view opposite of those they held. Debates were loud and intense. Purposely or not, Grossvater was preparing his boys to be spokesmen for millions of workers, instilling in them the skills and values they would need later in life.

The boys were also learning outside the home. "The auto lords used to bring blacks up from the South in open railroad cars like cattle to work in the plants up North," Uncle Victor recalled. "They would pass right through Wheeling. There was a glass factory with a big clay bank that formed a hill next to the railroad tracks.

"It was common sport for kids we played with to gather rocks on that huge clay bank as the train pulled through town and throw them at the 'jigaboos,' as they called them. The auto companies wanted those blacks because they would work for lower wages, and because the old AFL union would not accept blacks. So the blacks hated the unions and were brought north to help break strikes.

"One day, Dad (Grossvater) saw the boys throwing stones at the blacks in the cattle cars, and he came home white with rage. He gave us a tongue-lashing and said he had better never catch any one of us down there doing anything like that. We never had. But he gave us a tongue-lashing just in case."

Grossvater took young Walter and Victor to the Moundsville Penitentiary south of Wheeling to meet one of his heroes, a close friend, Eugene V. Debs. Debs was serving a 10-year sentence for his vociferous opposition to America's entry into World War I. Debs ran for president in 1920 on the Socialist ticket while still in prison. (Campaigning from his cell, Debs got more than a million votes.)

"I had the feeling we were in the presence of an extraordinarily warm and affectionate person," Victor recalled. "I cannot forget the moment we said goodbye. Dressed in prison garb and looking quite gaunt, he had a twinkle in his eye and my father was hard-pressed to find words. That was most unusual. When the heavy iron gate slammed shut, tears were running down my father's cheeks. I had never seen him weep before.

"On the way back to Wheeling, there was no conversation until my father broke the silence. '*How* can they imprison so kind and gentle a man?'"

Father's working days began when he was only nine years old because Grossvater lost his sight when a pop bottle accidentally exploded. He was blinded for two years. Father worked odd jobs after school and on weekends. "Everyone helped out," he told us later. "Mother held us together largely, as I look back on it, by sheer faith in God." As a 10-year-old, father himself had molten glass spilled on his right eye and part of his nose at the neighborhood factory where he worked. Safety wasn't on the minds of many employers in those days.

Father later quit high school in order to bring in needed income to the family. He got a job as a tool-and-die worker at 11 cents an hour. At 17, he and three other men were lifting a 400-pound die when it slipped.

"It had oil on the underside," he told us. "When we got it nearly out, our hands started to slip in the oil and we knew we were going to lose control of it. I tried to hold onto it. I was afraid if I let go it might kill one of us."

As the die fell, it just caught father's right foot, crushing and severing his big toe. Carried on a stretcher to a waiting ambulance, he called to a fellow worker: "Bring me my toe! I'm not leaving without my toe!" The worker picked up the bloody mass that had been father's toe and placed it on the stretcher next to him.

Father later explained that he was afraid he wouldn't be able to play basketball without that toe. The smallest member of his team, father was a good jumper. Without the toe, he figured he wouldn't be able to jump high enough to play. "Sew my toe back on," he told the doctor when they reached the hospital.

"That's crazy," said the doctor. "I can't save your toe; it's been completely severed, bone, vessel, everything. I can't sew it on."

"I won't let you work on me until you sew that toe back on," he insisted. "That toe is very important to me." Seeing how determined daddy was, the doctor gave in. He sewed the toe back on.

"Of course, the doctor was right," father said later, laughing. "In a few days they had to drive me to the hospital and amputate it."

Father was determined not to be a cripple, determined he would not walk with a limp. "I forced myself to walk upright, no matter how much it hurt, and I was determined that toe or no toe I was going to play basketball again. It slowed me down, but I did play again. In fact, when I was at Ford, I organized the Highland Park basketball team and I jumped center. We won the championship."

Father's right foot bothered him the rest of his life. He wore soft, flexible shoes and hated to break in new ones. I was a tall girl and my foot was almost as big as his. "I'll break them in for you," I told him. Once in a while he took me up on that, and I would wear his new shoes around the house for a few days before he started wearing them to work.

Grossvater and Grossmutter noticed father didn't seem to have time for girls. "He said they were too much bother." He was a good student and his appetite was always good. He ate everything, "just like a little goat."

Grossmutter encouraged father to stay in high school when he was just a year away from graduating. It was more important, she said, than taking an apprenticeship at a Wheeling factory. "I can't wait," father told her. "By that time my chance will be gone. I've got to get started."

After three years of work at Wheeling Steel, Walter decided he wanted to go north to Detroit to work in an auto plant. The pay was good, he reasoned, and it was a big, growing, exciting industry.

He heard they were hiring at Ford, so he and a friend left home to seek their fortune in Detroit. He was 19. Grossmutter worried for her son. "You'll be proud of him some day," Grossvater assured her.

CHAPTER FOUR

DETROIT INITIATION

"The average worker wants a job in which he does not have to think."

— Henry Ford

Father arrived in Detroit in February 1927, at the height of an economic downturn. Jobs were hard to find, but he finally got work at Briggs Manufacturing, a body-building company which later became a part of Chrysler Corporation. It was backbreaking work with 13-hour shifts and heavy dies. But it gave him a foot (less one toe) in the door of the auto industry. Soon he heard there were job openings at Ford Motor Company.

Hiring practices of the day followed a certain pattern. "The boss' relatives came first," remembered Russell Leach, who worked in production at Briggs. Then came the applicants who had brown-nosed the foreman, "cut his grass, painted his kitchen, repaired his garage."

Younger women had to put up with a certain measure of harassment to get and maintain a steady income. Ann Shafer worked at Motor Products in those days. "We would all mill around the gates like so many cattle," she said, "and the foreman would come out and say, 'I need you, you and you. . .the rest of you can go home.' Many put up with pinching and patting in order to work."

Ford had ended production of the fabulously successful, but now outdated, Model T, the "Tin Lizzie" that more than any other car had put America on wheels. The automotive world was changing. General

Motors and the new Chrysler Corporation were designing more sleek and modern cars with fresh new styling and were cutting the big sales lead that Ford had enjoyed. So, after 19 years and 15 million cars, the Model T production run had ended. Ford was hiring die leaders for development of the Model A.

"I went home and slept on it," father recalled. "I was 19, but I looked 16 with my red cheeks, red hair, and the complexion of a 13-year-old girl." The job he wanted "required" 25 years of experience. He decided to go for it.

After 21 days on the 13-hour night shift at Briggs, he took the bus out to the Ford plant. At the employment office, he noted a guard.

"Good morning," he offered. "I understand you're hiring die leaders. Well, I'm a tool and die maker."

The guard was well aware that 25 years experience was a requirement. "Get out of here, you're a kid."

"Are you a die leader?" father asked.

"Of course not. Would I be here guarding the door if I was?"

"Then you must be an extremely valuable man to your organization if you can tell just by looking at me whether I'm a die leader or not."

Bewildered by the young man's persistence, the guard allowed himself to be drawn into a debate over whether father was qualified. After two and a half hours, the guard called the hiring manager to get rid of the youth. But the hiring manager was also drawn into the debate.

"Look, there's one thing a young man can do nothing about, and that's his age," father reasoned. "I can't do anything about the fact that I'm 19, but I don't see how you can look at me and say I'm not a die leader."

He finally wore the hiring manager down and was shunted to the foreman, a tall, thin man who looked remarkably like Henry Ford himself. He had blueprints rolled up in his hand.

"Why don't you roll out those blueprints? See for yourself how much — or little — I know," father suggested. "And if you're not satisfied, I'll leave quietly. Honest."

The foreman went along with that, seeing a golden opportunity to brush the kid off. But the pink-faced youth read those blues like a seasoned die maker.

"OK, I've proven I can read a blueprint," father said. "But you'll never know how much more I can do unless you hire me! Hire me and find out."

The foreman was intrigued by this brash kid. "Tell you what I'll do," he began. "If you'll work here for two days without knowing how much you'll be paid, I'll watch you. Then I'll decide. That's my offer. Take it or leave it."

"I'll take it."

Father rushed back to Briggs to get his tools so he could report for work at Ford's in the morning. He needed a clearance to take his tools out of the plant. His supervisor stalled, not wanting to lose the boy, who really was a good die maker. He offered to raise his pay from 75 cents to 80 cents an hour. Father refused. The two argued throughout the night and at 6 a.m. he got his clearance.

Father grabbed his tools and took a taxi to the Ford plant. It was an unheard-of extravagance for the thrifty young man, but he didn't want to be late on his first day. With no sleep he reported for work, and the foreman watched him like a hawk during the entire eight-hour shift. Things went well, and the next day, also.

"Well, young man, you have certainly surprised all of us," said the foreman at the end of the second day. "You haven't done anything wrong yet. The job is yours at $1.05 an hour."

Henry Ford's historic offer of up to $5 a day for a job on the line seemed unbelievable to many workers trying to support a family on $12 to $15 a week. Like a giant magnet, the $5 day drew people to Detroit from all parts of the country, including many whites and blacks from the middle and deep South. They brought with them a way of life that routinely included segregation of the races. Racial tension was already building in Detroit.

Father was rooming with a Southern family who continually pressured him to attend their Sunday religious services with them. He kept declining, feeling there was too great a discrepancy between how these whites treated their black brothers and the Christian teachings of their church. The invitations continued. Father posed this question to his landlord and family:

"Do you believe a Negro who lives his life according to the same Christian values you do will also be rewarded and go to the same heaven?"

"Of course not!" was the reply. Father was final: "That is why I do not join you at church."

The foreman who had tested father on blueprints for the die leader job became increasingly fond of him. The man and his wife kept inviting him to dinner. Once, the man took him aside after the meal and said: "My wife and I think you should come and live with us. It would be to us just like having a real son of our own."

"I was afraid it might change my relationship with my boss in the factory," father later confided. "I was afraid that I might be getting something I wasn't earning, or even if that weren't the case, that fellow workers might *think* I was. It would have been awkward." He declined the invitation. A mistake? Father didn't think so.

Father continued sending a big portion of his check home to help his family in Wheeling. After his 21st birthday, however, father Valentine began returning his checks. "We can't accept more money from you," he wrote, asking Walter to keep the money for his own needs and future.

Father finished high school while working at Ford. He decided to continue his education at Detroit City College (now Wayne State University). A question on the college admission form required a brief statement on factors influencing his development.

"I have always felt that one is more or less a product of his environment, his association, and his reading. Securing employment in the die room of the Ford Motor Co., I began to study my fellow workmen and soon learned to choose the men who were of better moral and mental qualities. It was the result of conversations with some of these men that the desire for a better education was kindled inside me. I began to realize that my usefulness to mankind was limited only in proportion to my education."

This ambitious freshman, who also had written he "would like to be able to fill the position of former Supreme Court Chief Justice

Charles Evans Hughes," registered for a full load of classes during the day, while working nights.

He was active in forming the Social Service Club, eventually serving as its president. He also used it as a base for his first picket line. The college had arranged for its students to use the swimming pool of a nearby hotel. When father learned that black students were excluded, he organized a student protest. Students surrounded the hotel, carrying signs charging both the hotel and the college with discrimination. They attracted the attention of the press, and soon hotel and college were receiving letters from indignant citizens.

Finally the hotel closed the pool to all students. That didn't make father universally popular, to say the least. But discrimination had been publicly challenged and defeated.

Father's position at Ford put him among the working-class elite, but it didn't improve the plight of thousands of his co-workers who were less skilled and not as persuasive. The changeover from the Model T to the Model A in 1927 left more than 100,000 men out of work. Many were living in holes dug into the sides of hills or in cardboard boxes by the railroad tracks. There was little to eat; frostbite was common. At every factory, thousands would line up in the morning, desperate for a day's work. Some wore burlap potato sacks on their feet, as they waited in line half a day for a piece of bread or a cup of coffee.

Inside the factories, workers suffered from a different kind of cruelty: the speedup. Assembly lines were run faster and faster to increase production, regardless of the ability of individual workers to keep up. When a worker was physically or emotionally unable to keep pace, factory security men put him back on the street where hundreds were waiting to take his place.

There is a story of one wealthy English industrialist who was showing his daughter through one of his factories when they walked near a worker whose hand had just been mangled in a piece of machinery. He cried out in pain. The embarrassed owner tried to comfort his daughter: "Don't worry, dear, they're too dull to feel the pain the same as you and I."

Henry Ford himself is reputed to have stated that "the average worker wants a job in which he does not have to think." Assembly-line work was inherently boring and dehumanizing. In 1913, in order to maintain a work force of 14,000, Henry Ford allegedly had to hire a total of 52,000. Men were quitting shortly after starting work; many complained they didn't like a job where no skill was involved.

Once Ford started the $5 day, department head William Klan recalled, top management was called in and advised that since the workers were getting twice the wages, management wanted twice as much work. "So we simply turned up the speed of the lines," he said.

As far as safety was concerned, it was every man for himself. In 1916, workers at Ford's Highland Park plant suffered 192 severed fingers, 68,000 lacerations, 2,600 puncture wounds and 5,400 burns.

In a short time, Walter Reuther worked his way up to become one of the highest paid mechanics in the Ford organization. He was also the youngest. But his conscience would not let him enjoy his newly found social position. When Norman Thomas, an avowed socialist, ran for president in 1932, father campaigned hard for him.

Henry Ford's influence in Dearborn was such that it was forbidden to speak or hold a rally for Thomas there. Having put a down payment on a corner lot in Dearborn, father decided a man should be able to speak his mind on his own land. Climbing on the back of his Ford coupe, he began talking to hundreds of unemployed workers about the changes that would be made if Thomas were elected.

The Dearborn police observed the crowd, then intervened and demanded a halt to father's campaigning. "Hey, bud!" screamed an agitated cop. "This is private property. You can't speak here."

Father's face lit up as he reached in his pocket for a copy of the deed: "I know, officer. I own it."

The police put up stakes at each of the four corners of the property and limited the crowd to that space. No listeners were allowed to stand outside the boundaries. It was an unusual scene for Dearborn, and Ford took notice. Father was soon summarily and unceremoniously fired. Perhaps, he said to his visiting brother Victor, it was time for the European trip they had talked about since childhood.

CHAPTER FIVE

EUROPE
IN
TROUBLE

*"I'd rather rot in a manure pile than become a Nazi like you
and the other weak-willed rats!"*
— Father's Uncle Peter to Nazi policeman.

In 1931, when Henry Ford discontinued the Model A in America, he sold the tools and designs to the Russians. The Russians also needed skilled men who knew how to use the tools to produce those cars, and one of father's friends, John Rushton, was already building the Model A in the Soviet Union. When father wrote him about his proposed trip, Rushton guaranteed both Walter and brother Victor employment at the Gorky plant.

Father withdrew $800 from his account at a local bank. (None too soon. The Depression-hit bank closed a week later.) The excited brothers went to Wheeling to say goodbye to their parents, then on to New York to spend a night with Norman Thomas and his family. Soon they were crossing the Atlantic on the S.S. Deutschland.

Arriving in the port city of Hamburg, the brothers looked up a German businessman whose address had been given them by a professor at Wayne University. What they didn't know was that this contact had become a fanatical follower of Hitler. After a 10-minute encounter wherein they told the wealthy gentleman what they thought of his racist propaganda, they were back on the street.

Fortunately, the brothers had another contact in Hamburg, the uncle of a Detroit auto mechanic. They spent a sleepless night in his home listening to Nazi storm-troopers rushing up and down the streets, shooting out windows of homes that had anti-Hitler slogans on them. The next day the young men left for Berlin by train. They shared their compartment with a worried union official. He had reason to worry. They learned later he was shot the following day.

Berlin was stunned by the burning of government buildings and the threat of imminent takeover by Hitler and his supporters. "The circus atmosphere around the ruined Reichstag building," Victor recalled, "the swastika flags flying in the smoke, the barkers shouting to the crowd to buy the Nazi papers — all would have been ludicrous had they not been so tragic."

Norman Thomas had put the brothers in touch with socialist university students living in a housing cooperative on the top floors of an old warehouse. "On the eve of Hitler's election," Victor remembered, "we found our friends barring the windows and doors with furniture. A night watch was assigned, to be changed every two hours; we all slept in our clothes. A back window was left unlocked with a rope ladder near it. We could hear the police marching back and forth beneath the front windows. But that night passed without a raid."

The following evening, after it was announced that Hitler had won 44 percent of the vote, the main door of the warehouse was broken down by brown-shirted troopers. "Our greatest concern was to get the most well-known activists safely out the back window," Victor said. "I remember an emotional farewell with Emil Gross, certainly a marked man in the Nazi book. He was the first we saw down the rope ladder and away into the darkness. The troopers looked at our American passports and warned us that we should find other lodgings. Political and civil rights, as of then, were dead in Germany."

Shocked, Walter and Victor traveled to Dresden and Nuremberg, only to find more storm troopers and swastika flags at every stop. They decided to visit relatives in Swabia. In Scharnhausen, their mother's birthplace, they found swastikas on almost every home. Two uncles had taken opposing sides in the growing Nazi controversy. Adolph, caught up in the Nazi spirit, shouted at doubting Ernest: "When we march on Moscow, I hope I shall have the privilege of shooting you down if you oppose me!"

Father and Victor had hoped to receive their Soviet visas in Scharnhausen, but when the papers didn't arrive, they decided to bicycle through Europe. Starting off for France via the Black Forest, they stayed in youth hostels as they traveled to Marseilles. They then pedalled along the French Riviera. The brothers were wide-eyed through Cannes, Nice and Monte Carlo, through the azaleas and vistas of the blue Mediterranean at the base of the rocky cliffs. They made their way into Italy to Milan, Pisa and then to Rome.

Victor: "I had never realized the measure of the gift the Church made to the world by safeguarding the art of many centuries. The scale of the architecture alone is soul-stretching." But their spirits were dampened by the Fascist rule of Mussolini. They heard him speak from the balcony of his palace and turned away in disgust. The two young men were learning first-hand that Europe was in deep trouble.

Father and Victor were favorably impressed with the Socialist-run government in Austria. A worker in Vienna could move into a very nice apartment for only 5 percent of his monthly wage. And the rest of life's necessities — from health care to schools and food — were easily within the reach of every citizen. Yet, in the Austrian villages, swastikas were thick as measles.

They traveled into Switzerland's Alps. Victor wrote about their first attempt at mountain climbing: "The fact that school children in the area found the mountain easy to master bolstered our self-confidence, and we were soon at the tree line, admiring the splendid view. Soon we came upon rocks that were covered in fresh snow. We walked along a ridge where the sun was melting the snow and the path was narrow. Walter stepped too close to a soft edge, lost his balance, and began sliding over. By happy chance, there was a small shrub on the side of the slope, and he hung on to it with determination as we watched his alpenstock turn and tumble down the thousand-foot drop. I inched myself over and held my staff down to where Walter could grab it and gradually helped him back over the edge. We sat in complete silence and a cold sweat for a while, leaning against the mountain with our hearts pounding."

The brothers returned to Swabia, hoping to find their visas waiting, but their hearts fell; there was still no word from Russia.

One evening they accompanied two cousins to a Goebbels movie in Stuttgart. When the Nazi propaganda film was over, a huge swastika appeared on the screen. Everyone rose to sing the Nazi anthem. Everyone, that is, except Victor and father. The frenzied crowd roughed them up. Father showed them his American passport, but to no avail. The brothers were pushed and shoved out into the street amid catcalls and threats.

They resumed their travels, passing through the Rhineland to the village where their father, Valentine, had been born. There they discovered their Uncle Peter, scowling at a local police officer: "I'd rather rot in a manure pile than become a Nazi like you and the other weak-willed rats!"

"Rot in a manure pile" was close to what happened to Walter and Victor one dark night in France. The French were not happy about wandering youths sleeping in their haystacks; they were fearful of cigarettes setting them ablaze. So father and Victor turned off their bicycle lights before heading for a haystack. "It was very dark this particular night, and we thought we clearly saw the outline of a haystack," Victor recalled. "Dead tired, having cycled more than 100 kilometers that day in rather bad weather, we stretched out our tarpaulin only to discover the next morning that we'd indeed been sleeping on a manure pile!"

They bicycled to Paris where they attended an International Social-ist Conference and toured an automobile factory. Father said the working and safety conditions there were just as bad as in Detroit.

In England they attended a British Trade Union Conference and visited automotive operations where they found children as well as adults working long hours on speeded-up lines. The air pollution from the factories was terrible. They saw that the industrial revolution — intended as a servant of humanity — had become a terrible master. In Scotland they toured textile mills and mines and saw thousands of unemployed dock workers. They were dismayed to find the English and Scots so unconcerned about the demonic Nazi power at large in Germany.

They traveled to Amsterdam, where they met friend Emil Gross, last seen scurrying down the rope ladder in Berlin, moments ahead of the Nazi storm troopers. Gross led a large underground anti-Nazi youth movement; he had asked father and Victor to contact seven members working within Germany. The two brothers had memorized specific instructions so that no papers could be seized. Usually they had to make a number of contacts, giving certain code phrases before they could meet one of Gross' associates. "When we finally reached the right person," father later said, "it was a most curious experience. It was amazing the instantaneous bond that seemed to spring up between us, what we felt for him and he for us. It resulted, I suppose, from the fact that we were both engaged in a desperate business, with our lives at stake if we were caught. This gave us a feeling of solidarity."

Although the brothers were never arrested by the Nazis, they were objects of suspicion. Usually tourists stayed in nice hotels; these two Americans lodged in youth hostels. The two were shocked when they heard Gross had been captured by the Gestapo and sent to a concentration camp. They assumed he was a dead man.

A quarter of a century later, in 1958, Victor was in his Washington office when the telephone rang. A distinguished German publisher was downstairs and wanted to meet with him, he was told. "Send him up," Victor said. It was Emil Gross.

Victor: "I embraced him, tears streaming down my cheeks, and exclaimed, 'My God, I thought that you had been lost!' A flood of questions followed. Then I picked up the phone and called Walter in Detroit. 'You'll never believe who's in my office.'"

Finally, their visas to the Soviet Union arrived. They boarded a train for Poland, bound for Russia.

CHAPTER SIX

"THE WORKERS' PARADISE"

"We have never given humanity a chance. The chance to live and work together in peace with the same dedication we give to war. When that happens, there's no limit to what we can achieve."

— Father

When they arrived in Gorky, it was 30 below. They discovered that their jackets had inexplicably been slit open and the contents removed. Fortunately they had kept their money and passports in money belts, but other important papers were gone.

They found a streetcar that took them in the direction of the automobile plant, but they had to walk the last mile and a half through heavy snow and bitter cold to the "American Village," where many technicians from the U.S. were staying. Father headed a brigade of workers in an unheated factory. "It was my introduction to the workers' paradise," he remembered.

Victor, who taught peasants how to use precision instruments, still shivers at the memory of the cold. "The only heat in the whole building was in the small heat-treatment department where metals were tempered. Otherwise temperatures were 30 to 35 degrees below zero at the workbench. We found those early weeks very difficult. We'd work for half an hour and then go into the heat-treat room for a few minutes, then return to work."

They learned that Henry Ford's motive in helping the Soviets industrialize was not blind profit. Ford felt that if less industrialized

31

nations were only exporting raw materials to the U.S. and then buying back expensive finished products, they would become rebellious and uncooperative. So in the interest of "international peace," he showed the good intentions of the U.S. for Russia's welfare by helping her develop her own industries. There could be no profit without peace.

The Reuther brothers had gone to Russia with open minds to find out for themselves what that "classless workers' paradise" was really like. What they found was a very inefficient system bottlenecked at the top with no representation for the common worker.

Father became a regular writer to the Moscow Daily News. "The shortcomings responsible for the greater percentage of inefficiency in the Gorky automotive plant are administrative in character... The administration seems to be under the illusion that safety measures are entirely divorced from efficiency."

Father and Victor noticed that while the English had been rather unconcerned about the German military buildup, the Soviets were very concerned, to the point of paranoia. An excerpt from father's Russia memoirs reads:

Several times while I was there, one family or another would appear for breakfast without the husband or father. They would sit at an isolated table, eyes red from weeping, faces distorted with anxiety and fear. Nobody asked them what was wrong; we all knew. He had been arrested in the middle of the night by the Russian secret police and taken away for imprisonment or to be sent to a work camp in Siberia or even to be executed. The others knew that any gesture of comfort to the stricken family, even just asking what happened, would be interpreted as sympathy, and they might well be the next victims.

During a brief summer vacation, the brothers traveled down the Volga River to the Black Sea where they stayed with an enclave of German farmers living in Russia. Later they learned these immigrants were deemed a threat to the Soviet government and shipped to Siberia.

For nearly two years, father and Victor worked at the auto operation in Gorky. Soviet officials did their best to persuade them to stay, but the brothers were anxious to be on their way. They gave their tools to friends, but were unable to exchange their rubles for foreign currency, so they spent them on travel — 18,000 miles by bicycle, bus and train.

They traveled along the borders of Turkey, Iran and India. They traveled through mountains and deserts, living among the common people. Peasants, steelworkers, coal miners, and farmers took them in and gave them a place to stay. Their travels restored their belief that "the good in man is so much more overwhelming than the bad." The horrible events taking place in both Nazi Germany and the Soviet Union worried them, but did not discourage them.

"We have never given humanity a chance," father would later tell me. "The chance to live and work together in peace with the same dedication we give to war. When that day comes, there is no limit to what we can achieve."

The brothers arrived in China with a letter of introduction to the president of a university about 13 miles outside of Peking. Boys with rickshaws surrounded them as they headed for the school. They were uneasy about being pulled by another human being, but there was no other way to get there. After a while, they insisted the rickshaw boys change places with them.

"They thought we were nuts, but we persuaded them, pulling them down the road at a fast pace for a while," father recalled. Soon, however, the adventuresome Americans grew weary and much to the amusement of the boys, suggested they trade places again. Their principles were stronger than their legs and backs.

To get to China's coast, the brothers took a steamer down the Yangtze River. Recent flooding had destroyed local crops and there was mass starvation. Believing there was food on the ship, desperate men were trying to jump aboard as it left port. Before the horrified eyes of the brothers, husky deck hands were clubbing the starving men, who fell into the river.

Later, a crowded junk happened into the path of the steamer. The helmsman appeared to make no effort to steer around it and rammed the junk, throwing its passengers into the Yangtze. Father shouted to the captain: "You must do something to help these people!" To which the captain replied: "You Americans have no concept of life in China."

After crossing the China Sea, father and Victor finished their tour of the Far East biking through Japan. They had $7 between them and were living on raw fish and seaweed, when they sought help at the American Embassy. An official directed them to the steamship President Harding, where they found work and passage to San Francisco. Father reported to the engine room, Victor filled in as a deck hand.

When they crossed the International Dateline, father asked what day it was. "Wednesday," he was told. And what day was yesterday? "Wednesday." A born negotiator, he sought out the chief engineer and inquired if they would be getting paid for both Wednesdays. He was told they would get the extra day on the return trip.

"But we'll not be on the return trip," he explained.

"Then, you worked that extra day for the Lord," was the answer. "No extra pay."

Hawaii welcomed the President Harding with beautiful beaches and graceful palm trees. The brothers requested a day ashore. That would be impossible, they were told. The ship would only be there one day, and no one was allowed leave.

Father thought for a moment, then again called on his negotiating skill. "Remember that extra Wednesday we worked for the Lord? Well, I talked it over with Him, and He said it would be all right if we spent that day seeing Hawaii." They did.

In later years, the brothers reminisced about all they learned during the three-year tour. Father recalled:

"It gave us a chance to see firsthand the way people in faraway countries work and live and to understand that despite language barriers and cultural differences, all people long for the same basic human goals of a job with some degree of security, greater opportunity for their children, and, of course, freedom.

"We returned to the U.S. with a far greater understanding and appreciation of the importance of a great democratic heritage provided by the words of the Declaration of Indpendence and the Constitution. We felt we could make a contribution by helping American workers build strong and democratic unions. That's why we went into the labor movement."

CHAPTER SEVEN

STRIKE!

"We've had enough of this speed-up!"
—Uncle Victor calling a strike

In late 1935, father and Uncle Victor returned to Detroit. News of several labor strikes in their absence surprised them. Uncle Roy, while walking a picket line, was shoved against a metal grate by the police with such force that his back was gashed and he bore a scar for the rest of his life.

New Deal legislation nurtured the growth of the labor movement by curtailing open shops and other attempts by the auto industry to control its labor force. The Depression had increased the workers' dependence on their jobs. Employers pushed their people, paying them less for more work. Long lines of unemployed filled the streets.

In a broadcast, Detroit's famous Royal Oak-based radio priest, Father Charles Coughlin, told some 30 million nationwide listeners: "We are actors in one of the most unique tragedies that has ever been chronicled. Abundance of foodstuffs, millions of virgin acres, banks loaded with money — alongside idle factories, long bread lines, millions of jobless and growing discontent."

A physician from Detroit's Receiving Hospital told newsmen an average of four persons a day were brought in "too far gone from starvation for their lives to be saved." Evictions for the unemployed averaged 150 per day.

Father, it seemed, had been blacklisted. He could not get a job anywhere in the auto industry, even under the alias Walter Philips (his middle name was Philip). He had applied at Murray Body Co., which sold most of its parts to Ford. It was said that every new hire had to be approved by Ford's labor boss, Harry Bennett.

"Murray was just starting a major program for a new model," father recalled. "They were hiring a lot of tool-and-die makers. I applied for a job as Walter Philips, was interviewed and hired, conditionally. I still had to pass a physical exam. By the time they were through interviewing me, the company doctor had left for lunch. I was told he'd be back about one o'clock.

"I was sitting in the employment manager's office reading the paper when four big strong-arm guys from Harry Bennett's private army — apparently on the lookout for me — came swaggering in, picked me up, and threw me out into the street.

"Years later, our union got a contract with Murray Body. While we were waiting for some typing to be done so that we could sign, I was chatting with the vice president and asked him if he recalled the incident. He flushed and said he remembered it well and that it had always been a source of embarrassment for him. Nobody on the blacklist could be hired, he said, no matter how much they needed your skill."

Although father couldn't find a job, he never missed an opportunity to get signatures on the union cards he always carried with him. Based on his previous work at Ford, he was given membership in the union's Ternstedt Local 86. They knew he was dedicated to helping the young UAW get on its feet.

That winter, father met mother one evening on a Detroit streetcar.

"I was as interested in the labor movement as your father," mother later recalled, "and I was very active in the teacher's union. I had helped raise funds for strikers as early as 1932.

"Usually I was shy and aloof, but that Friday on the streetcar I was so tired that my defenses were down. Walter and I got to talking and that was the start of our six-week courtship."

Father also admitted the romance was brief, and added with an exaggerated wink: "I think I was pursued."

Slender and fair with auburn curls, mother had graduated from Teacher's College at the age of 18. She was a bright student and, though very shy, had been promoted ahead of her class in school. When she met father, she was already teaching and was very involved in organizing a teachers' union in Detroit.

One day in March, 1936, father grabbed her hand on an uncharacteristic impulse, and they hurried to the justice of the peace to be married. On the way, they asked two surprised strangers if they could spare a few moments to serve as witnesses. It was Friday. Friday the 13th.

An unusual honeymoon portended their future together. "We drove out of town to where your father was making an organizing speech," mother would tell me, "but I was happy. We were doing what we felt was most important. And I was so very proud of him."

The newlyweds had high hopes for organizing labor, but no money. Dave Miller, an early union stalwart, reminisced: "I remember the day the three of us — May, Walter and I — stood on a windy corner in the city, 1936, and Walter told us he had found a room that could be rented for $10. Imagine, $10 a month for a headquarters for the organizing drive on the west side of Detroit.

"Among the three of us we didn't have $10! I remember the day I went home with Walter to ask May to give $2 from their meager household budget to buy some gas for his car, so that he could call on some workers and talk to them about the union. And she gave it to him, although it was sorely needed for other things."

A month after his "honeymoon," father, still without a job, was selected to represent Local 86 at the UAW's second annual convention in South Bend. "One of the brothers made a motion that since Reuther was unemployed and was devoting all of his time to the union without pay, he should receive whatever money there was in the treasury to help finance his trip to Indiana.

"Our financial secretary said she thought we were getting a bit reckless, so she modified the motion to read that upon my return, I would give back to the treasury any money that was left over. With

37

that, she opened her handbag which was the treasury, and gave me five dollars. That was all the money we had!"

The representative from Local 86 hitchhiked to South Bend, where he was elected to the union's Executive Board. It was at this convention that the UAW broke all ties with the American Federation of Labor (AFL), which father regarded as socially stagnant, and joined the more progressive Congress of Industrial Organizations (CIO). Francis Dillon, the UAW president appointed by the AFL, was ousted and Homer Martin was brought in.

At the convention, father broached the idea of electing three vice presidents, one to concentrate on each of the Big Three auto makers. Father criticized one local for paying up to $52 a day expenses for an officer, demanding that daily expenses be limited to $8. He spoke out against the Hearst newspaper chain, claiming it had been distorting the facts in reporting the convention. Then he urged the Hearst reporters to join the Newspaper Guild, which brought a great round of applause.

Working in Detroit with an old desk, mimeograph machine, typewriter, and mother as his volunteer secretary , father received no salary or staff as a member of the Executive Board, although other members did. But he waded in with enthusiasm, holding organizing meetings in back rooms of saloons, in workers' homes — anywhere he could. Gatherings often included spies hired by the auto makers, and new recruits often found themselves out of work the next day.

"The groundswell was there," father recalled, "and I knew it. I could sense their frustration, their resentment at the way management was treating them. It was only a matter of time. All they needed was encouragement, support, leadership."

Mother was making $60 a week teaching and was turning almost all of it over to the union for organizational purposes. She was taking a shorthand course at night so she could help father as his secretary, a job she eventually did full time for $15 a week, giving up her teaching career.

Father became president of the newly expanded UAW Local 174. He was anxious to bring more workers into the union. The Kelsey-Hayes brake drum and wheel plants in Detroit employed 5,000 workers—all potential union members waiting to be organized.

Father knew he'd never get inside personally, so he sent a telegram to Victor, who was attending a Quaker conference in Philadelphia with his bride, Sophie. "If you are interested in organizing the auto workers, come immediately back to Detroit."

By the following morning, Victor was at the Kelsey-Hayes employment door and, within a few hours, had been added to the payroll as a punch press operator. Sophie soon joined Local 174 as a secretary. Her knowledge of Polish proved a great asset in dealing with many of the Kelsey-Hayes workers of Polish descent.

The automotive supplier was notorious for its low pay. Victor was hired for 37-1/2 cents an hour. Many of the women doing the same type of work were receiving only 22-1/2 cents. Plant speed-ups added to the tension. It was time to strike.

Every detail was carefully planned. Frank Winn, a friend experienced in publicity, was brought in. A woman who had fainted from fatigue during a speed-up was asked to faint again on a signal from Victor.

It was a December day in 1936. Less than a dozen people knew the exact plan. At a sign from Victor, the woman fainted. Victor pulled the main switch, shutting down the line. "Strike! We've had enough of this speed-up!"

Victor jumped up on a crate and urged the workers to join together with the union to break the shackles of an unconcerned employer. "Every plea for slowing down has fallen on deaf ears."

The personnel director rushed over and began pulling on Victor's pant leg. "What the hell's going on here?" he demanded. "Get them back to work *now!*"

"Walter Reuther's the only man who can do that," responded Victor, giving him the telephone number where father could be reached. Victor continued his speech into the next shift.

Father was pacing the floor at Local 174. The telephone rang. "Is your name Reuther?" asked the man's voice. "I'm Paul Danzig, personnel director at Kelsey-Hayes. I want you to get these men back to work!"

"Where are you?" father asked.

"I'm inside the plant."

"Well, I'm outside and can't tell anybody to get back to work as long as I'm out here. Send a car over to pick me up and take me into the plant. I'll talk to the guys."

When he arrived, father relieved Victor, continuing to tell the workers the importance of organizing. Victor circulated, passing out UAW leaflets.

Danzig grabbed father's pant leg. "Hey, you're supposed to get them back to work." Father answered with a grin: "I can't tell them to do anything until they join up."

Victor was passing out union membership cards to hundreds of excited workers on the factory floor. The company agreed to talk with the organizers if the workers would return to the line. A meeting was scheduled for the following morning.

"As president of 174, I was there with the shop committee," father recalled. "We sat waiting from 10 in the morning until 3 in the afternoon, but nobody came near us. Of course, we knew what had happened. Ford, the company's largest customer, was telling them what to do. So we called a sit-down strike and left."

Kelsey-Hayes officials tried to enter the plant to remove the machinery, but thousands of workers and sympathizers were blocking the doorways, protecting the sit-downers inside. The machines remained in the plant, silent. An important supply of wheels for the Ford assembly lines was cut off.

Father finally began negotiations. Uncle Roy was also involved in a sit-down strike at General Motors in Flint. Just as the Kelsey-Hayes meeting was to begin, company president George Kennedy glanced at the morning paper . The headlines proclaimed Roy Reuther as one of the chief negotiators of the Flint strike. "Jesus Christ," he barked, "is there another Reuther?"

Just then Victor's voice was heard coming from a sound truck encouraging workers inside the plant. "Who the hell is out there?" Kennedy demanded.

"Victor Reuther," replied an aide.

Kennedy glared at father, who was seated for the meeting. "My God, how many of you Reuther bastards are there?"

An agreement was reached Christmas Eve. "That was a strike that didn't have to happen," father reflected. "And but for Henry Ford and Harry Bennett, it would not have. It wasn't a long strike — only about ten days. Ford must have needed those wheels pretty badly. Kelsey-Hayes was released from the squeeze, we negotiated and signed a contract."

This was the first major UAW victory in its struggle with the automotive giants. At father's insistence, women won equal pay for equal work, 75 cents an hour. The speed-up was stopped, and the company was not allowed to fire anyone for joining the union. Membership in Local 174 jumped from fewer than 200 before the strike to 3,000. By next Christmas more than 35,000 had joined.

"Union dues were $1 a month," mother would tell me. "Usually I would be collecting and members in the crowd would be reaching forward with their dollar bills. Often I would be handed a quarter or a 50-cent piece, with the sincere message, 'Look, I know it's not enough, but I'll get the rest to you in another week. I want to join up immediately. Please let me.'"

Mother would tell me this with a great deal of emotion. She recalled this time as the blossoming of their dream, and she was grateful to play a leading role.

Father and mother at the time of their marriage in 1936.

Lovers on a mission: the early days of organizing the UAW...

...And lovers at play.

CHAPTER EIGHT

BATTLING GM

"She'd go to the union hall
When a meeting it was called,
And when the company guards
Came 'round
She always stood her ground.
　　　　Oh, you can't scare me,
　　　　I'm stickin' to the union
　　　　...'til the day I die."
—From Woody Guthrie's "Union Maid."

In the 1930s, as today, General Motors was the world's wealthiest and most-powerful corporation. Eighty percent of the population of Flint, Michigan, depended on GM for their livelihood. Flint was the home of Buick Division, AC Spark Plug Division, Fisher Body and key Chevrolet assembly plants. The city's judges, mayor, police, newspapers and even clergy were pawns in GM's mighty hands.

Uncle Roy had been trying for two years to make headway in Flint organizing the workers, with little progress. GM stooges had infiltrated the union and attended every meeting. As soon as a worker showed some interest in joining, he or she would suddenly be out of a job.

"The foreman could fire you at will," observed University of Michigan labor historian Sidney Fine. "If a worker wouldn't let the foreman sleep with his wife, he'd lose his job."

Larry Jones, retired Chevrolet worker and a veteran of the early days in Flint, recalled: "We had no security then. Conditions were so vile, so inhumane. I'm 76 years old and I'd have been dead years ago without the union. They used young, strong men the way you used any other commodity, and when you could no longer produce you were finished."

Plant speed-ups had become intolerable. In December 1936, when five union spokesmen were fired for appealing to the company to slow the line, fellow unionists at Flint's Fisher Body No. 2 sat down. They didn't walk out, they just sat down.

The following day, workers at Fisher Body No. 1 did the same. GM was preparing to move the dies out of the plant for transport to a place without union sympathizers, so the 1,000 workers voted to sit down to block the removal of the dies and save their jobs. A couple of days earlier in Cleveland, the Fisher Body operation that manufactured turret tops for GM cars also was hit by a sit-down. For the first time, the General Motors empire was being seriously challenged.

CIO President John L. Lewis had planned to organize the steel industry before getting seriously involved in the automotive plants. But circumstances changed his agenda. His actions could make or break the new UAW.

"The sit-down strike is the fruit of mismanagement and bad policy toward labor," he declared. "Employers who tyrannize employees with the aid of labor spies, company guards, and the threat of discharge, need not be surprised if their production lines are suddenly halted."

President Franklin D. Roosevelt took a neutral position on the sit-down strikes. "It's illegal," he reportedly told Secretary of Labor Frances Perkins, "but what law are they breaking? Trespass? Why can't these fellows in General Motors meet with the committee of workers?"

But that was the last thing GM wanted. Instead, management asked for and got from Circuit Judge Edward D. Black an order that the strikers abandon the plants at once. The sheriff, with 160 armed officers, tried to carry out the order. The workers would not budge.

Then union lawyers discovered that Judge Black owned $219,000 in GM stock. GM was embarrassed and dropped its request for the injunction.

Father, along with the rest of the UAW Executive Board, rushed to Flint to evaluate the situation. GM was conducting a tremendous campaign against the union, hiring the slickest public relations people in Detroit and New York. "It was now or never for us," father recalled.

The Board gave permission for every GM plant in the country with

UAW membership to call a strike as a show of support. Corporate muscle would have to face the workers' muscle. Thousands of union supporters started pouring into Flint from Akron, Cleveland and Toledo. Father led a large contingent from Detroit's West Side. The big strike was under way in Flint, and everyone sensed history was being made.

One of the early problems was feeding the workers. Local merchants contributed food. Soup kitchens sprang up, and the hundreds of sit-downers in Fisher 1 and 2 ate. GM shut off the heat in No. 2, considered the weaker of the two plants. Uncle Victor, Uncle Roy and Bob Travis moved most of the pickets from No. 1 to No. 2 to give support to the shivering workers. Upon their arrival, Victor learned that GM had also ordered the food supply cut off. Union leaders challenged the plant guards, threatening to break down the door to get their "brothers" something warm to eat. The guards stood to the side and allowed the food trucks to pass. The head guard, however, told GM "we are being held captive by the sit-down strikers," then led his men into the downstairs ladies' room, where they spent the rest of the night.

Meanwhile, a large contingent of Flint police had been gathering just across the bridge from the plant. A barrage of tear-gas shells erupted from beyond the railroad tracks, shattering the plant windows. Squad cars crossed the bridge, forming a moving shield for more than a hundred marching policemen. Many wore gas masks and attacked the pickets with blackjacks. More rushed the plant to hurl in additional tear-gas bombs.

Victor manned the sound truck father had brought up from Detroit. He encouraged the workers to stand and fight. The workers had barricaded the second-floor doors of the plant with steel dollies, and they had fire hoses connected and ready. On the roof, they had made large slingshots out of stretched inner tubes and had piled metal hinges as ammunition. David was ready for Goliath.

"Defend yourselves with everything you have," shouted Victor over the loudspeaker. Hinges started flying toward the tear-gas guns. Many hit squad cars and the police themselves. The pickets and police fought hand to hand. Then the workers turned on the fire hoses. The force of the water plus the 16-degree weather compelled the police to retreat across the bridge.

Strikers cared for their wounded. Thousands of onlookers had massed at the end of Chevrolet Avenue to witness the confrontation. Many now joined the workers, picking up whatever they could find to fend off the police, who were launching a second attack.

This time the police concentrated on the pickets. They were especially interested in silencing Uncle Victor in the sound truck. A tear-gas shell landed directly under the vehicle. Victor soaked his handkerchief in coffee and covered his face as he continued broadcasting to the workers: "We wanted peace. General Motors chose war. Give it to them!"

Sheriff Thomas Wolcott arrived, only to have his car overturned by angry pickets. Helpless on its side, its flashing lights lit the full-scale battle scene. Frustrated, the police retreated again, but this time they opened up with their guns, firing parting shots. Thirteen men lay wounded.

Sensing a third offensive, Victor directed the pickets to overturn their cars as a barricade. As he returned to the sound truck, Victor noticed an open window in Chevrolet No. 2 across the street. A double-barreled shotgun was pointing directly at him. He shouted to the men with slingshots on the roof and a barrage of hinges crashed through the window where the gunman was stationed. He never reappeared.

The third attack came just after midnight. This time the police used long-range tear-gas missiles, firing them over the barricade of cars into the midst of the pickets. Genora Johnson, one of the union women, rushed to the sound car and persuaded Victor to let her speak. "Cowards! Cowards! Shooting unarmed and defenseless men!" she shouted at the police, imploring the women in the crowd to stand by their husbands to hold the line.

Then Mother Nature intervened. The wind shifted, blowing the tear gas back into the faces of the police. For the third time, the police retreated over the bridge.

The fighting had lasted most of the frigid night. Dawn's light revealed the battle scene in the street. Dozens of cars were overturned, pieces of shattered glass shimmered in the bloody debris. But public opinion had been swayed. Newspapers reported the brutal force initiated by GM. Thousands had witnessed it. The use of guns against the unarmed pickets would never be lived down.

Newly elected Governor Frank Murphy poured 2,000 National Guard troops into Flint, not to force the strikers out of the plants but to keep the peace.

In Detroit, father led a sit-down strike at the Cadillac assembly plant to show solidarity with the strikers in Flint. There were also strikes in Pontiac, St. Louis, Oakland, California, and Anderson, Indiana. GM was hit hard.

Weeks passed. Finally Governor Murphy negotiated a truce. He had been elected with a heavy labor vote. Union members trusted him. The UAW agreed to leave plants if GM agreed to negotiate and promised not to resume production until an agreement had been reached.

But things were not as they seemed. William H. Lawrence of the United Press wandered into the office of the "Flint Alliance," a company union, where he discovered a press release stating that General Motors was going to negotiate with the Alliance rather than the UAW. Lawrence notified the UAW just before members were to evacuate the plants. Angered, the union sent reinforcements into the buildings.

The workers, who had been inside the plants since the strike began, were starting to show signs of depression. They had been away from their families for a month. It appeared the UAW could not win. The union's resources were dwindling. In a brainstorming session with Bob Travis, Uncle Roy came up with a plan. It would be fraught with risk, but time was running out. There was a feeling of desperation among the union leaders and general membership as well. If they didn't pull a master stroke now, all would be lost.

Roy grabbed some paper and started drawing. He made two squares, one at each end of the paper. One represented Chevrolet No. 9, where ball bearings were produced; the other was Chevrolet No. 4, the only plant in the country that manufactured Chevrolet engines. If the workers struck No. 4, then they could effectively shut down GM by cutting off the flow of engines to the assembly lines. They knew No. 4 was heavily guarded. If they could leak the story that a strike was planned at No. 9, perhaps GM would increase its security there and leave No. 4 more vulnerable.

On February 1, at 3:30 p.m, the union men in No. 9 threw the switches and declared a strike. Roy, with Bob Travis, arrived outside with a large contingent of pickets. As they had hoped, GM had pulled a number of its guards out of No. 4 to protect No. 9. Again there was tear gas. A band of women UAW supporters wearing red berets smashed windows to let in fresh air. In hand-to-hand combat, GM forces were winning control.

Roy signaled union activist Ed Kronk, who pulled an American flag out of his shirt, a sign for 50 Detroit union men to head for No. 4. When they reached the entrance, they were met by father and 50 more Detroiters. Entering the plant with ease, they signaled waiting workers to pull the switches on this second front. The men barricaded the entrances, a job they performed so well, father recalled, that "it took them three days to tear down what we had built up in a few hours."

When word of the No. 4 takeover reached the workers at No. 9, they were jubilant. Some headed for No. 4, singing union songs and even dancing in the streets. Women supporters formed a human barricade at the entrances to No. 4 and told the police: "Nobody gets through but our boys."

Woody Guthrie's "Union Maid" put to music the stories of the brave women who banded together to support organizers:

"There once was a union maid
Who never was afraid
Of the goons and ginks
And company finks
And the deputy sheriff who made
The raid.
She'd go to the union hall
When a meeting it was called,
And when the company guards
Came 'round
She always stood her ground.

Oh, you can't scare me,
I'm stickin' to the union
. . .'til the day I die."

Wearing red berets, wives and other family members of the strikers took turns joining the picket lines. They canvassed local merchants for donations of food and medicine for their strikers. They would cook in improvised kitchens, pass out leaflets, and deliver food and clothing to the homes of needy striking workers.

The National Guard was ordered to surround the engine plant. Howitzers and machine guns were trained on the doors. Soldiers with fixed bayonets dispersed or arrested pickets. No food was allowed in. A court ordered the strikers to be out of the plants within two days or the UAW would face a $15 million fine. The court also said that picketing of any kind was illegal in Michigan. UAW leaders feared the National Guard would be sent in to shoot the workers out. GM, the mayor and the chief of police were urging Governor Murphy to do just that.

The men inside the plant drafted a letter to Murphy: "Governor, we have decided to stay in the plant. We have no illusions about the sacrifices this decision will entail. We fully expect that if a violent effort is made to oust us, many of us will be killed and we take this means of making it known to our wives, to our children, to the people of the state of Michigan and the country that if this result follows from the attempt to eject us, you are the one who must be held responsible for our deaths."

Thousands of sympathizers streamed into Flint from all over the Midwest. They came to urge the workers to fight for their rights, for all workers' rights. They gathered at the gates of the struck plants singing union songs. I grew up with these songs. One of my favorites is "Solidarity Forever," sung to the tune of the Battle Hymn of the Republic:

"When the union's inspiration through the workers' blood
shall run,
There shall be no power greater anywhere beneath the sun.
Yet what force on earth is weaker than the feeble strength of
one?

But the union makes us strong.
Solidarity forever,
Solidarity forever,
Solidarity forever,
For the Union makes us strong."

The court injunction was effective at 3 p.m., February 3. The hour came and passed. The workers shouted cheers. President Roosevelt urged Governor Murphy to practice restraint. John L. Lewis, president of the CIO, wired the Governor that if the National Guard was used he personally would join the workers in the plants and his "breast would be the first that the bullets would strike." Murphy made no move.

An accord was reached February 11. The strikes in Flint, which have been called the Lexington and Valley Forge of American industrial unionism, were over. GM agreed to allow the UAW to bargain on behalf of its members inside the corporation's plants; those who joined the union would not be fired and they could discuss union activities during lunch breaks.

Uncle Roy later wrote: "When the boys came out of the plants, I never saw a night like that and perhaps may never see it again. I liken it to a country experiencing independence. We had a procession down to Chevrolet and Fisher No. 2. Women came greeting their husbands — some of the families reunited for the first time since the strike began, kids hanging on to daddy with tears of joy and happiness. It was a sea of humanity in which fears were no longer in the minds of workers."

Father described the Flint victory as "a great social and economic revolution. Tens of thousands of workers who had never had any of the privileges of collective bargaining suddenly stood up and wanted to be counted. We merely facilitated their coming together."

CHAPTER NINE

BATTLING
FORD

*"We'll never recognize the United Automobile Workers, or
any other union."*

— Henry Ford

Professional criminals flocked to Detroit in the 1930s. Gangs formed
along ethnic lines. There were Polish gangs, Italian and Jewish gangs,
black gangs, and the mostly Sicilian Black Hand. The most famous
Jewish mob was the Purple Gang. Its members were flashy dressers
who terrorized the automotive capital with apparent impunity.

The city — practically a stone's throw across the Detroit River
from Windsor, Canada — was known as the nation's "funnel" for
illegal liquor during Prohibition. The Hiram Walker distillery was in
Windsor. Bootlegging nationwide was a $2 billion business. Walker
sales hit record highs during those "dry days of temperance."

With the repeal of Prohibition, Detroit criminals simply switched
from bootlegging to extortion, kidnapping, and beating and terroriz-
ing union organizers. Some social reformers observed that, in the
1930s, it was difficult to tell the difference between Big Business,
with its thugs, and organized crime.

The UAW victory in Flint sparked sit-down strikes throughout the
nation. The union's next target was Detroit's Chrysler Corporation. In

March 1937, 60,000 Chrysler workers went on strike. They were so enthusiastic that one of the union's biggest problems was persuading most of them to stay out of the plants. When local police intervened and began roughing up pickets and strikers, the UAW attracted 150,000 citizens to Cadillac Square in downtown Detroit to protest. Four weeks after the strike began, Chrysler signed its first agreement with the union.

It was two down and one to go for the young UAW, but the remaining one was not going to be easy. Henry Ford had publicly stated: "We'll never recognize the United Automobile Workers or any other union." And he had an army of 3,000—largely ex-convicts, thugs and underworld characters—whose job was to keep the union out. *The New York Times* referred to Ford's force as the "largest private quasi-military organization in the world."

In charge of the "Service Department" at Ford was Harry Bennett, J. Edgar Hoover's golfing partner, who was second only to Ford himself in the corporate hierarchy. Keith Sward, a cautious writer, gave this description of the Bennett operation:

> For years after Bennett came to power, it was the proud, undisguised aim of the Service Department to blot out every manifestation of personality or manliness inside a Ford plant. Bennett's mercenaries finally mastered every tactic from the swagger of the Prussian drill sergeant to outright sadism and physical assault.

Golf was not all Bennett and FBI Director Hoover had in common. "Bennett sat on a parole board and used to parole people, up to five a day, from the state penitentiary directly to Ford's payroll," Uncle Victor recalled, "with the warning that 'You carry out my orders or back you go.' And I have a strong feeling that most of the skill of the FBI in breaking underworld cases was buying information by having your own people in the mob. If you put enough mobsters on the FBI payroll, you'll know what's going on in the underworld, right? Anyway, it is nothing short of a miracle that the union ever survived the combination of J. Edgar Hoover and Harry Bennett."

To most Americans, Henry Ford was the poor farm boy who had achieved the American Dream. With his assembly-line technique, he had developed a successful line of cars and become America's first billionaire. By the late 1930s, however, he was slipping into senility and losing control of his empire. As his eccentricities occupied more of his energies, Harry Bennett made himself the heir apparent.

"Ford was a jungle because of one man," father recalled, "Harry Bennett. His gangsters ran that company. Harry Bennett was a mean man, a neurotic man, a man with a gangster mentality. It was absolutely fantastic that a man like that could reach the position he did with a great company like Ford. If you read it in a book or saw it in a movie, you just wouldn't believe it. But I was there and I believe it, because I've still got the scars."

Working conditions in Ford factories were notorious. Every worker was identified not by name but by number. The number appeared on his time card and a badge worn on his shirt. Conversation was not allowed in the plant. A worker could be fired for talking with the man next to him on the line. Although in other automotive plants a worker who needed to use the restroom or get a drink of water could be relieved by a stand-in, this was not the policy at Ford.

A visit to the employment office usually included a shove or two from Bennett's men. And night-shift workers might be startled by a flashing light shoved in the face and a Ford service man yelling: "Who's your boss?"

Workers were not allowed to sit down. One of the workers' favorite stories was about an executive who spotted a man sitting on a barrel of nails, humming (also not allowed) and splicing some wires. The executive kicked the barrel out from under the man and sent him crashing him to the ground. The worker jumped to his feet and decked the Ford boss with a vicious right. "You're fired!" screamed the unbelieving executive. "The hell I am!" the worker retorted. "I work for the telephone company!"

Outside the factory, social criticism of Ford included Aldous Huxley's nightmarish *Brave New World* (1932), which satirically dated the modern era from "the year of our Ford." Upton Sinclair's novel, *The Flivver King,* (1937) wove the story of Ford's life with that of a fictitious auto worker, who knew the ambitious inventor from his early days. Father distributed thousands of copies of this book at UAW organizing drives.

The River Rouge Plant, known among workers as the "butcher house" or "sweatshop," was under the geographical jurisdiction of the UAW's West Side Local, where father was president. Father's first attempt to reach the workers failed when he and Victor hired a plane to fly over the plant during a shift change. They spoke through microphones about the importance of organizing. But the plane's engine drowned out their voices and the wind carried what might have been heard far down river. But the press reported the effort and Henry Ford had his notice that he was next.

Father's next approach was to pass out pamphlets explaining that under the recently passed Wagner Act workers had the right to join a union and engage in collective bargaining with management. In accordance with local laws, he went to the Dearborn city clerk and obtained a permit to pass out handbills headlined "Unionism, not Fordism" at the Ford Rouge Plant on May 26, 1937. The union was given permission to pass out the leaflets on an overpass workers used to cross the roadway to and from Gate Four. It was a public bridge, not part of Ford property.

Two days before the event, *Detroit Times* photographer Arnold Freeman visited the overpass. To his surprise he met a hoodlum he had recently photographed at a police station. When asked why he was there, the hood told the photographer he and others had been hired "to take care of these union men who are going to pass out pamphlets. They hired four of us for every one of them."

By the afternoon of May 26, quite a crowd had gathered: newsmen, representatives of the Senate Civil Liberties Committee, and a Chicago clergyman and human rights activist who had come at father's request.

Father, Richard Frankensteen, and a few other UAW leaders arrived at the overpass shortly before the change of shifts. They would be followed shortly by a number of women via streetcar to help distribute the handbills. As father and his colleagues climbed the stairs and walked to the center of the bridge, one of the some 150 toughs-in-waiting shouted: "This is private property. Get the hell out

The setting of the "Battle of the Overpass": Harry Bennett's thugs approach UAW organizers (from left) Bob Kanter, Walter Reuther, Dick Frankensteen and Jack Kennedy.

Father, eyes swollen almost shut, and bloodied Richard Frankensteen after the battle, May 26, 1937.

of here!"

The advancing UAW men quickly found themselves surrounded by the hoodlums, who proceeded to kick and beat them before throwing them down the steps and off the bridge. The attackers followed, dragging their victims in and out of parked cars to continue the beatings.

Father had gone down when he was hit on the head from behind with a blackjack. "Seven times they raised me off the concrete and threw me down on it," father later told a National Labor Review Board hearing. "They pinned my arms and shot short jabs to my face. I was punched and dragged by my feet to the stairway. When I grabbed the railing they wrenched me loose. I was thrown down the first flight of iron steps. They kicked me down the other flight until I found myself on the ground where I was beaten and kicked." Freeman, the photographer, picked up father, Frankensteen and another wounded UAW man, Bob Kanter, and drove them to a doctor. He described father's head as swollen on both sides over his eyes. "Frankensteen was bleeding from the mouth and nose."

The thugs then attacked the women who had arrived to help pass out pamphlets. As they got off the streetcar, they were grabbed by the hair, called "bitch" and "prostitute," and knocked to the ground. One woman, kicked in the stomach, vomited at the feet of the Rev. Mr. Stanford, the Chicago cleric who had come at father's behest. Mr. Stanford pleaded to a mounted policeman to stop the men from beating the women. The man on horseback said he had no authority. "Let her get out of here the same way that she came in. We didn't ask her out." Even the police were owned by Ford.

William Merriweather, who had escorted the women on the streetcar, was attacked with cries of "Kill that union sonofabitch!" and "Kick his brains out!" After taking a severe beating, Merriweather rolled under a parked car for protection. He had a broken back. Many of the terrified women threw their leaflets into the air and jumped back on the streetcar.

Reporters and photographers on the scene were beaten and chased away as notebooks were grabbed and cameras smashed. But at least one photographer had already taken shots and tossed his camera into a waiting convertible, now speeding to the press.

That week *Time* magazine carried a complete report of the event which came to be known as "The Battle of the Overpass." Photographs showed the assaults on the union organizers. One story was accompanied by a photo of father being dragged down the overpass steps feet first by a number of thugs.

Henry Ford retaliated by withdrawing Ford advertising from *Time*, *Life* and *Fortune* magazines for a year and a half. But public opinion swung to the workers. His well-paid public relations staff could not erase the impact of the stories and photos.

Father continued to lead volunteers in the distribution of leaflets at the Ford plants. He also arranged for the printing of 200,000 additional copies of *Flivver King*. The book was having great impact on workers' decisions to join the UAW.

On the night of April 9, 1938, less than a year after the Battle of the Overpass, the Reuther brothers, their families and a few friends were gathering at mother and father's apartment to celebrate Aunt Sophie's birthday. They had sent out for Chinese food to be delivered from a local restaurant. Uncle Victor later wrote:

"There was a knock on the door, and Sophie and I, who were closest, opened it. Instead of the delivery boy, there stood two toughs with drawn revolvers. They pushed their way into the room shouting, 'OK! Back against the wall!' At first it was as unreal as a clip from an old silent movie. The shorter gunman wore a dark hat with the brim turned down to conceal his eyes; he was obviously the trigger man. The other gangster spotted Walter immediately, put his gun in his holster, and drew out of his rear pocket an enormous blackjack with a leather strap, which he twined around his wrist. 'OK, Red, you're coming with us.'

"Only gradually did we realize this was no joke. 'Let's just plug him here,' one of the intruders suggested. 'If you do, you'll never get out alive,' Roy retorted. The shorter gunman kept his .38 pointed at us and toyed with the trigger. The other thug was hitting Walter, who was deflecting the blows with his legs. Then the thug broke a glass floor lamp over Walter's head.

"During the commotion, little Al King, who had been standing near the kitchen door, slouched down, backed into the breakfast nook, and jumped out an open window into the concrete alleyway two flights below. Sophie, meantime, decided to distract the killer. She reached her hand into the kitchen and as Al jumped out the window a pickle bottle sailed toward the trigger man. We all felt there would surely be shooting now, but after Al's 'Help, Help!' had gathered a group in the street, the two professional hoods decided they had better retreat before they got caught and abruptly fled the apartment."

The police were called. An hour passed before they arrived. And when they did, the family wouldn't let them in until they passed their identification papers under the door. They were dressed in dark clothing and wore wide brim hats pulled down to cover their eyes. When they asked for a description of the thugs, Aunt Sophie cracked everyone up: "They looked very much like you."

A couple of days later, father received a telephone call from a man who said he could deliver the names of the two attackers for $5,000. He instructed father to meet him in a dirty, run-down bar in a bad area of Detroit. Expecting a double cross, the UAW placed several of its biggest men in the bar. Father was unfamiliar with bars since he did not drink, but he insisted on going. The informer gave him the names of two of Harry Bennett's men.

The case came to trial, but it was a joke. After the defense rejected over 80 prospective jurors, it was decided the jurors would be picked at random off the street — another ruse, as the jury was stacked. The hoodlums admitted working for Bennett, breaking into my parents' apartment and working over father in an attempt to "take him for his last ride." But then they said father had hired them to do this as a publicity stunt. The jury acquitted them.

Ford's next move was to have Bennett convince the Dearborn City Council to make it illegal to distribute leaflets on the sidewalks leading to the River Rouge complex. So other more ingenious ways had to be discovered for getting the message to the workers. By far the most enterprising — and daring — was that of a union stalwart who worked on the assembly line putting radios into the cars. The UAW-CIO had its own station, but the frequency was so low that it was practically unknown. This worker was putting an extra button in each car that would tune the radio to the UAW station. Because all of the Ford workers who owned cars were required to drive Fords, the company rule and its assembly line were contributing to the union cause.

One day Ford's young grandson, Benson, asked Bennett if he ever listened to "those CIO fellows." Bennett said they didn't have a radio station. "Oh yes they do," Benson assured him. "You ought to listen to them sometime; I get a kick out of them." It would have been impossible to recall all the Fords with the additional radio button. The best management could do was send its service men into the plant and kick the culprit installer out into the street.

In late 1940, it was ruled unconstitutional to deny the union the right to distribute literature on public property. Within two days, union supporters distributed over 35,000 leaflets. And every two weeks they handed out 50,000 copies of their *Ford Facts* newspaper.

The union's big break came when the Supreme Court demanded that Ford Motor Company appear before the National Labor Relations Board to answer charges of unfair labor practices. Ford was found guilty of such practices in nine factories. The company was ordered to recognize the right of its workers to organize.

Reluctantly, Ford began making small concessions at individual plants, but still would not recognize the UAW nationally. It tried to interest the workers in "company unions," controlled by management. The UAW branded them "make-believe unions."

On April 1, 1941, Harry Bennett cut off all negotiations and fired eight union men who had worked on a grievance committee. Workers walked off their jobs, refusing to go back until the fired men were reinstated. Over a hundred Dearborn police swiftly moved into the area, then just as hastily retreated as they saw thousands of workers marching out of the plants. The union leaders themselves were astounded. They had not called for a strike, but the men, bitter with frustration and fear, struck on their own. Father and the Executive Board met and the next morning backed up the workers with an official strike. Mighty Ford was shut down. That night, thousands of workers marched to a union hall less than a mile from the Rouge, where they held a get-it-off-your-chest session. They talked without fear of reprisal. They were beginning to feel the strength in their numbers.

The following morning the Executive Board carried out its strike strategy. Six major roads met at the Rouge complex. The assembly plant was circular with a high wall surrounding it. The Ford service men were inside the wall waiting to attack the picketers when they arrived. They did not realize that thousands of union men had spent the entire night parking their cars on the roads leading into the Rouge, making it impossible for anyone to get in or out. No police or strikebreakers would be able to get through. A solid line of cars ran for blocks in both lanes.

Bennett's attack force comprised hundreds of black workers armed with knives and metal clubs. Blacks were the only men who had not walked out of the plant. They did not trust the union, since it had been the policy of the AFL to bar Negroes from membership.

The pickets were taken by surprise. Thirty-six of them were stabbed and beaten so severely that they were rushed to the hospital, and the picket line was momentarily broken. But within a few minutes, thousands of men waiting around the cars blocking the road rushed to the front. They came armed with whatever they could get their hands on, from tire irons to sticks and baseball bats. When Bennett ordered a second offensive, the strikers fought back and forced a retreat.

Machine guns were trained on the pickets, but after the negative publicity from the Battle of the Overpass, the company knew it couldn't use them. Bennett went to Michigan Governor Van Wagoner and even President Roosevelt for help, but to no avail. The *Louisville Courier Journal* reported: "It is strange for Henry Ford to call frantically for government help, because no American industrialist has so often defied government in connection with labor disputes. He has asked for what he is getting."

For days the fighting continued. Usually Bennett used blacks on the front lines, to engage in hand-to-hand combat, while his own elite band of toughs climbed on the roof to hurl nuts and bolts at the pickets. Seeing that their assaults on the pickets were failing, Bennett turned on the black workers, charging they were strike sympathizers and beating them. By this time, my father and a number of prominent black civic and religious leaders were taking turns on the loudspeaker outside trying to convince the blacks to come out. Eventually, they did.

At last, Governor Van Wagoner intervened with a plan that called for an end to the strike if Ford would honor a National Labor Relations Board election. At issue was the contest between the UAW-CIO and the renegade faction UAW-AFL. If the UAW-CIO won, it would be recognized as the only bargaining agent for the auto workers. Reluctantly, Ford agreed.

The UAW-CIO carried the election by a five-to-two margin, with fewer than three percent of the voting workers opting for "no union." Henry Ford accepted the union. Some said his wife, Clara, threatened to leave him if he didn't. Edsel, his only son, had returned to Dearborn from a Florida vacation when trouble broke out. Henry was reported to have told him to stay out of the whole affair, that Bennett was in charge. Edsel refused, convinced that the decent and proper way to handle the issue was to recognize and negotiate with the workers. Events proved him right.

But even after the negotiations, Ford was furious. In a meeting with Edsel and his production manager, Charles Sorenson, Henry declared: "I'm not going to sign this contract! I want you and Edsel to understand that as far as I'm concerned the key is in the door. I'm going to throw it away. I don't want any more of this business! Close the plant down if necessary."

Although he did acquiesce, Ford didn't speak about the settlement for six weeks. One day he opened up to Sorenson, saying Mrs. Ford had been "horrified" at his threat to close down the plant. "She said she could not understand my doing anything like that and that she did not want to be a part of the riots and further bloodshed." Confided Henry: "I felt her vision and judgment were better than mine."

The man who had negotiated with the union had also been the one most responsible for abusing its workers. "If I had been one of the men in the shop," said Harry Bennett after the contract signing, "I'd have been in sympathy with the union myself."

After the agreement, Victor took a phone call at my father's office.

It was one of the two thugs who had barged into my parents' apartment a few years earlier, threatening to take father "for his last ride." The caller suggested to Victor that since Ford and the union would be working together, perhaps the Reuthers and his boss, Mr. Bennett, should get together for lunch and some friendly conversation. My uncle, not known for vulgar language, let loose with a barrage that shocked the caller. "Gee," the thug gasped, "I was just hired for that job. You guys didn't take it personally, did you?"

About a year after the ink had dried on the first UAW-Ford contract, Henry Ford told father, "It was one of the most sensible things Harry Bennett ever did when he got the UAW into this plant."

"What do you mean?" father inquired.

"Well, you've been fighting General Motors and the Wall Street crowd," Ford said. "Now you're in here and we've given you a union shop and more than you got out of them. That puts you on our side, doesn't it? We can fight General Motors and Wall Street together, eh?"

CHAPTER TEN

"FIVE HUNDRED PLANES A DAY"

*"He's quite a fellow. Three-fourths of the dollar-a-year men
around this place are scared to death of that little fellow."*
— Donald Nelson, chairman of the
War Production Board, on father

By the middle of 1940, most of Europe had fallen to Hitler's army. England was in grave trouble, and the Führer was already peering across the Atlantic toward the United States. Though not officially at war, America was supplying war machinery to its allies. In May 1940, President Roosevelt told Congress he would like to see the United States "geared up ... to turn out at least 50,000 planes a year." Most Americans thought this impossible.

Not my father. A couple of months after Roosevelt's speech, father was driving past the site where federally supported construction had just started on a Packard aircraft engine plant. Noticing that the workmen were still laying the concrete foundation, he remarked to Sidney Hillman, then working with the wartime's Office of Production Management: "This doesn't make sense. Hitler isn't going to wait 18 months while they finish this. He could bomb us off the earth by then."

Father had noted that in Russia they retooled auto factories for producing war machines. With Hillman's encouragement, he outlined a similar plan for high-speed conversion of America's auto plants and suppliers.

Father's report showed how these already-idled auto plants could be quickly turned into aircraft construction sites. His advisors, Eddie Levinson and journalist I.F. Stone, helped him present this plan to UAW President R.J. Thomas, who, they hoped, would place it before FDR at the White House. Thomas glared at father. "Screw you! You're not going to make a horse's ass out of me."

Undaunted, father next approached Philip Murray, president of the CIO, and found him much more agreeable. In December, Murray got in touch with the President, who was impressed with the report, entitled "Five Hundred Planes a Day." Father showed how one factory could make drop forgings for 500 airplane engines a day and still turn out enough auto engines for one million new Chevrolets a year. When GM President Charles Wilson heard of the 500-a-day scheme, he sarcastically remarked, "If Walter is interested in production, we'll give him a job with us."

The plan proposed that the unused potential of the auto industry in men and machines be utilized in mass production of aircraft engines and planes. The plan read, in part:

> England's battles, it used to be said, were won on the playing fields of Eton. This plan is put forward in the belief that America's battles can be won on the assembly lines of Detroit. It is our considered opinion that it would be possible, after six months of preparation, to turn out 500 of the most modern fighting planes a day.

> Unused U.S. plant reserves, according to figures in the Federal Trade Commission's report on the motor vehicle industry, are greater than the total motor plant capacity of England, Germany, France, Italy, Russia and Japan combined. Adapted to plane production, the unused capacity would give us world air supremacy within a short time.

Father hated war. But, as Uncle Victor has noted, "World War II he supported enthusiastically, despite our strong upbringing against wars in general. This was a conflict against a very ruthless regime. It was brutal, anti-Semitic, anti-labor, anti-democratic, anti-everything we believed in."

On January 2, 1941, President Roosevelt met father at the White House to discuss the "500-a-day" plan. "Here's my young engineer," the President smiled, greeting him with a warm handshake. Soon after, FDR turned the plan over to his defense advisors for further analysis. Father was hopeful.

But the automotive moguls opposed the idea, every last one of them! They wanted the federal government, at taxpayer expense, to build them new factories which, they hoped, would then be turned over to them after the war at giveaway prices. The automotive executives also disliked the part of my father's proposal suggesting a nine-member board for production supervision—three representatives each from management, government and labor. They objected to representatives of labor having anything to say about what was done in the auto plants. And anyway, observed General Motors Chairman Alfred P. Sloan, "only about 10 or 15 percent of the machinery and equipment in an automobile factory can be utilized for the production of special defense material."

William Knudsen, director of the Office of Production Management, was also skeptical of the proposal. As former president of GM, he had met father across the bargaining table and resented this "young upstart." Now here he was again, this presumptuous man from labor, with his big plan. Knudsen respected father, though, fully aware of his abilities. In fact, he told father, "Young man, I wish you were selling used cars for us (GM)." When father asked why *used* cars, Knudsen replied: "Anyone can sell *new* cars."

When Knudsen refused to tour an auto plant with father and Sidney Hillman, father told the press: "Mr. Knudsen and I met previously, on opposite sides of the table. I thought on this matter of national defense we might sit on the same side. I was mistaken."

Suddenly, the news headlines announced that only one "Flying Fortress," a key aircraft, had been produced over many weeks. Panic! Father tried to push his proposal again, but once more it was held up because of auto industry objections and influence in high places. Treasury Secretary Henry Morganthau reportedly commented: "There's only one thing wrong with the Reuther program. It comes from the 'wrong' source."

But father pressed on. He wrote and presented a plan to have the Big Three auto makers pool resources for producing 30-ton tanks. That way, he reasoned, they would only need one set of tools and dies instead of three. This idea also interested Washington.

Donald Nelson, chairman of the War Production Board, told a friend: "Reuther's quite a fellow. Three-fourths of the dollar-a-year men around this place are scared to death of that little fellow. And you know, they ought to be—he's smarter than they are."

Whereas the auto moguls objected to father's method of involving *their* industry in America's defense, F.B.I. Chief J. Edgar Hoover was enraged that father was involved at all. Since the Reuther brothers' two-years of work at Gorky, in Russia, Hoover had suspected they were Communists. He initiated an FBI investigation of father that would continue for 35 years until his death.

Whereas the auto barons' motives were financial, Hoover's were political. Father's star in the UAW (itself a threat to Hoover's radical right leanings) was rising. And now, his 500-a-day plan had caught the attention of the President. In memos to FDR and top military advisors, Hoover labeled father a "Communist subversive." How could *he* be involved in America's defense?

Hoover's excuse for calling father a Communist came from a 1934 letter Uncle Victor had written from Gorky to Melvin Bishop in Detroit. Over the years, father's political enemies circulated at least five different versions of that letter, always with the forged last line, "Carry on the fight for a Soviet America." Signed, "Vic and Wal."

The bubble of this fraud was popped when an investigation revealed the original letter, printed in the Young People's Socialist League newspaper *Challenge,* which ends simply with "Carry on the fight." The editor of *Challenge* swore under oath that he had received the letter from Bishop and printed it in its exact form. "Not only would it have been contrary to editorial practice ," he affirmed, "but it would have been contrary to the spirit of the times to eliminate any reference or statement of a political nature, however extreme or exaggerated."

Nevertheless, Hoover accepted the bogus version with the fraudulent words, "for a Soviet America" added; and, for the rest of father's life, he waved it as proof positive that father was a "Communist subversive."

In the summer of 1941, Hoover conceived of a plan to place the three Reuther brothers in "custodial detention" if America entered the war. "I presume we would have been treated as Japanese-Americans were," Uncle Victor recalled, "and locked up in a concentration camp." (Later, First Lady Eleanor Roosevelt would complain to her husband about Hoover and the FBI: "We are developing a Gestapo in this country, and it frightens me.")

In August, the FBI sent copies of the Reuthers' "detention cards" to its Detroit bureau. A month later, however, Detroit Bureau Chief John Bugas (who later became Ford's labor negotiator) submitted the following in a letter to Hoover:

> In view of the recent developments in this country in labor circles, and in view of the stand that WALTER REUTHER has taken against Communistic elements, and further in view of the fact that it is apparent from newspaper articles that WALTER REUTHER is cooperating with the Office of Production Management in certain matters, it is believed that the Bureau would want to reconsider the information submitted, and probably not consider REUTHER for custodial detention at this time.

So, Hoover's detention plans for the Reuthers fizzled—and none too soon. Within four months, the United States was at war.

On December 7, 1941, father was driving to New York City with his advisor, Eddie Levinson, to deliver a Housing Committee report to the UAW Executive Board. The car didn't have a radio. When they stopped and saw newsboys at corners selling "EXTRAS," they learned of the Japanese bombing of Pearl Harbor.

The UAW would now have to act quickly, father realized, to aid the nation. Now was the time to implement his plan for converting auto factories into plane and tank production. "OK, Eddie, let's rewrite the report," he said. His first point to the board was that during the war, the UAW should adopt a no-strike pledge. The UAW was the first union to do so.

The attack on Pearl Harbor prompted FDR to immediately implement father's proposals. Detroit gained recognition as the nation's "Arsenal of Democracy." By 1943, Chrysler President K. T. Keller could report that his company had converted 89 percent of its machine tools to wartime production. That meant, observed *Washington Post* publisher Philip Graham, that father had been "89 percent correct."

"We had a million ideas in those days," father later recalled. "I was just churning and spinning off ideas."

As father had forseen, Detroit's industrial might proved the sparkplug for the Allies' victory. Hoover and the auto barons notwithstanding, the proud UAW seal rolled with the tanks through France, Belgium, the Netherlands, and Germany, and flew on bomber runs over Japan. A 1943 song by Pete Seeger captured the GIs' appreciation:

I was standing 'round a defense town one day
When I thought I heard a soldier say,
"Every tank in our camp has that UAW stamp,"
And I'm UAW too, I'm proud to say.

"Reuther was right on track," reported *Fortune* magazine just as the war ended. "Compared with many industrialists who sat back and hugged profits and the aimless agencies of Washington, the red-headed labor leader exhibited atomic spirit of action. He never let up."

Father and his friend, GM President Charles Wilson, view posters for the Reuther "500 Planes a Day" program, which turned Detroit's auto plants into the "Arsenal of Democracy" during World War II.

CHAPTER ELEVEN

AHEAD
OF HIS
TIME

"I did not fight over there to protect GM's billions over here."

— Anonymous

Japan's surrender in the summer of 1945 brought final relief to a war-torn world. It also brought in the atomic age, with its double-edged promise of progress and extinction.

While factory workers had toiled within tight wage restrictions during the war, many of the corporations had become fat. The workers wanted their share for their loyal efforts.

Historically, whenever a union had won a wage hike, the company would pass the expense on to the consumers. This was the accepted way of doing business. In the economic structure Detroit had built, the laws of supply and demand had been modified. Largely because of the financial controls devised in the 1920s by General Motors, when sales dropped prices did not drop. But the use of labor *did*. The financial risks inherent in the automotive sales cycle were thus shifted from stockholder to worker. When times were bad, shareholders still got their dividends, but workers were laid off.

On August 16, 1945, President Harry Truman — who had recently moved into the Oval Office following the death of FDR — lifted the wartime's 15 percent wage-increase cap. He told the press that further increases would be allowed, *provided they did not force a price increase*. With that statement, the President inadvertently handed father the issue with which he would battle GM and which would eventually propel him into the presidency of the UAW.

Within days of the wage-freeze lifting, father shocked the auto industry by announcing to GM that UAW employees wanted a 30 percent wage increase. What's more, he demanded that GM do this without raising prices. And, he argued, he had the backing of the President of the United States.

Bold indeed, but father's move was thoroughly planned. He had prepared an economic brief with Donald Montgomery (who had recently left a government job in Washington because the Department of Agriculture had rejected his efforts to install a program of grade-labeling products in the interest and protection of the consumer). They filed their brief with the Federal Price Control Agency. Backed by voluminous data, it concluded: "The economic facts of life prove that wages can be increased without increasing prices. Increased production must be supported by increased consumption ... possible only through increased wages ... the industry can pay higher wages out of the high profits it is making."

Father saw how inflation had rendered the workers' pay increases meaningless. While inflation during the war had soared to 45 percent, auto workers' raises were held to 15 percent. He railed against workers being paid by the "wooden nickel of inflation." Father's claims were backed by the director of the Office of Economic Stabilization, William S. Davis, who confirmed that the auto industry could afford up to a 50 percent pay increase without raising new-car prices.

GM was furious that this little "redheaded radical" was once again sticking his nose in *their* business. With negotiations about to begin, father wanted the public to be aware of both sides of the issue. He invited news reporters to the negotiations; GM, however, banned all members of the press.

Labor and GM management met across the bargaining table that October. On one side sat the elderly and dignified Charles E. Wilson, who as chairman of GM drew a salary of close to half a million dollars a year. Across from him was the boyish-looking, 38-year-old Walter Reuther who was making $7,000 a year.

Harry Coen, GM's personnel manager, did most of the company's negotiating. Father once described a company negotiator as "a man with a calculating machine for a heart, pumping ice water." Coen seemed to fit that description. Known for his prejudice against Jews and blacks — and workers in general — his snooty disposition inspired father. While father was speaking of the importance of the consumers' interest, Coen fumed: "Why don't you get down to your size and talk about the money that you'd like to have for your people and let labor statesmanship go to hell for a while. It's none of your damn business what the OPA (Office of Price Administration) does about prices!"

"But unless we get a more realistic distribution of America's wealth," father replied, "we don't earn enough to keep your machinery going." Retorted Coen: "There it is again. You can't talk about this thing without exposing your socialistic desires."

"If fighting for equitable distribution of the wealth is socialistic, I stand guilty of being a socialist."

"I think you are convicted."

"I plead *guilty*," my father replied. He asked his members immediately for a strike vote. Experience had taught him that GM would give no consideration to the union's demands unless there was the threat of a strike. The vote was 70,853 for, with only 12,438 opposed.

President Truman came to the workers' aid when he addressed the nation on October 30:

> I wonder how many of you know that many war workers have already had to take a cut in their wartime pay by one quarter or more. Think of what such a decrease in your own income would mean to you and your families. The corner grocer is going to feel it, as well as the department store, the railroads, the theaters and the gas stations, and all the farmers of the nation. It is a sure road to wide unemployment.

Father wired congratulations to the President and was delighted the next day when Secretary of Commerce Henry A. Wallace reported that the auto workers could receive a wage increase of 25 percent without forcing manufacturers to raise auto prices.

A week later GM made its first offer: 10 percent. Father called it a "bribe" and countered with the stunning proposal that the workers would take as little as 1 percent if GM would open its books to members of an arbitration board to determine whether it was in a position to give the workers a better wage.

Such a request — that GM open its books to show whether it could afford a better pay hike than 10 percent — raised the automotive giant's blood temperature to the boiling point. The company flatly refused. The next day 175,000 auto workers walked off their jobs in 95 GM plants around the country.

A citizens' committee was formed to study the situation. Those leaning toward management as well as those partial to labor were shocked that GM would not even consider the proposal to open its books. What did the corporation have to hide? The committee commended father in a report which included the statement: "The whole matter of collective bargaining has been lifted to a new level by insisting the advancement of labor's interests should not be made at the expense of the public."

On a second level, a three-member fact-finding panel commissioned by President Truman met with representatives of both labor and management. But before the GM spokesmen would even sit down, they demanded to know if they were going to talk about the company's basing employee wages on ability to pay. When the committee replied that this was the intention, the GM people walked out of the room. This gave father the podium before the Presidential panel and members of the press to argue the necessity of tying wage hikes into price ceilings. The panel then recommended a 19.5-cents-per-hour pay increase for GM workers, plus a cap on new-car prices. GM rejected it.

Father created the Citizens Committee to Aid GM Workers, which included Former First Lady Eleanor Roosevelt, Senator Wayne Morse and prominent Republicans Harold Stassen and Henry Luce (owner of *Time* and *Fortune* magazines). Father had also been returning his paychecks to the union ever since the GM strike began. Hundreds of UAW staff and volunteers worked coast to coast educating the public on the importance of the anti-inflationary matter. Father coined a slogan: "We fight for a better tomorrow; I gave to win higher wages — no price increases." This battle cry was seen on buttons worn by thousands of concerned Americans. And he stressed that whatever wage increase the workers won, it would not be at the expense of consumers waiting to purchase a new car after the long, lean years of the war.

This position irritated not only large corporations but also big labor leaders such as John L. Lewis and Philip Murray. Their practice had been to negotiate with corporations for better worker pay without regard to the fact that the companies offset higher wages with price increases. Even UAW President R. J. Thomas, who referred to my father as "The Comet," stated that father's proposal "contained a lot of irrelevancies." Thomas was nervously looking over his shoulder as father was becoming the No. 1 challenger for UAW national leadership.

Father's visionary concepts and growing power in the UAW disturbed another huge labor group: the Communists. Walter White explained:

> Reuther was then emerging as the most vocal and implacable enemy of Communism in the trade union movement generally and in the UAW in particular. Pitted against him was a small but powerful coalition which sought control of the UAW for reasons of political beliefs, personal ambition or honest disagreement with Reuther's opinions and tactics.
>
> It was obvious that some of the members of this opposing faction would gladly have seen the negotiations fail rather than see Reuther, with his anti-Communist views, emerge the victor, and thereby become a more powerful figure in American affairs.

Father continued to lead the rank and file in their strike at GM. In a letter urging retail merchants to support the strikers, he asked: "How many of the Du Ponts do you have as your customers?" He inspired returning UAW war veterans to put on their uniforms, join the picket line, and wave signs reading, "I did not fight over there to protect GM's billions over here." Father was rallying "troops" for a fight which had much more at stake than the benefits of the auto workers. It was a struggle which would ultimately affect every American, then and now.

In the midst of the GM negotiations, the UAW suffered a blow when the Steel Workers accepted an 18.5-cent-per-hour raise — without stipulations on the price of steel. Many auto workers felt Philip Murray, president of the United Steel Workers and the CIO, had stabbed them in the back. Other unions began to follow Steel's example, accepting similar wage-only pacts with no price strings attached. Even Ford and Chrysler locals accepted the 18.5-cent offer! Only GM workers held out.

Then came a stunning blow when 30,000 GM electrical workers, members of the United Radio, Electrical and Machine Workers Union, signed a secret agreement and accepted the 18.5-cents-per-hour increase. Previously, the electrical workers had been committed to the same contract as other GM employees. But that union had many Communist supporters, who apparently felt their move would block father and his growing popularity. Father knew there was little choice but to sign a similar agreement. He told his good friend and colleague Frank Winn: "Well, if this thing falls through, we'll just have to start it all over again; but at least we've made a start."

The long and bitter UAW strike against GM ended in March 1946. It had lasted 113 days. The GM workers signed the same 18.5-cents agreement most of labor had accepted and without stipulation about the price of the new automobiles. It was a great disappointment to father. He had been far ahead of his time. But his concern for the issue of wages and prices had shown the public that labor was not simply interested in its own constituents. Deep down, the industrial giants knew that bargaining with their employees would never be the same. Although the UAW was not able to keep GM from raising car prices, the union had started down the long road to obtaining benefits to be won years later, benefits such as the cost-of-living (COLA) increases and the guaranteed annual wage.

During World War II, American workingmen showed great patriotism. They joined the service to fight or stayed home to work overtime in the forefront of war production.

The major American industries were strong. The auto and steel industries at that time were the most powerful in the world. And, because of their power, they were able to help defend America in her hour of need.

But where is their power today? The rust on American industry mourns our increasing dependence on imports for cars and steel. Must we really count on Japan to sell us steel in the event of a national emergency? How far we have slipped! How old and infirm has the once-vibrant backbone of American industry become.

There was a time when America's corporate captains knew all about making automobiles or steel or ships — and *cared* about it. Since the Second World War, however, control of major corporations has moved to money manipulators who don't care if they make their millions building cars or buying oil wells. Their commitment is not to meeting a market need (or creating one and meeting it), but to meeting stockholder pressure for the fast dollar. Whereas the automotive pioneers built empires with the long term in mind, today the focus is on the next quarterly report, today's closing stock price.

With major corporations becoming multinational, it matters little to them if their products are made in Japan or Korea or Mexico, because they have holdings or have worked out contracts with firms there. The worker may lose his or her job, but the shareholder continues to reap dividends.

Over the years, American auto makers blamed the workers for the industry's decline. American workers were overpaid, management said, and they did sloppy and low-quality work. Workers were told to take pay cuts and lower their standard of living to keep their jobs.

But the Japanese themselves have disproved this theory — right on American soil. They have set up assembly plants in the U.S. and turned out cars of high quality, equal to those built in Japan, sometimes superior to those built by American makers — and all with American labor.

The media and the public then started to get the idea that management was the problem, that there was too much concern for numbers and not enough for a quality product. Not so, said management; then they announced steps to correct the problem that "did not exist."

The corporations had said that if the workers take pay cuts they will be more competitive. But the workers did not design the cars, nor did they have a say in how they would be built.

UNCLE VICTOR: "I could give you a book full of occasions where our shop stewards and committeemen went to the companies and said: 'We can't do quality work at this speed. If you want to minimize the scrap coming off the end of the line that embarrasses you in the showroom, then for God's sake please tell us you want quality.' But the whole emphasis in the past 20 to 30 years in corporate America was volume, volume, volume."

New-car dealers complained bitterly to the factories about the poor quality of Detroit's products. They did not go public with their complaints, but they were the ones who had to bear the brunt of the public's anger. They worked through their dealer organizations to pressure the factories. But the American auto makers paid no more attention to their dealers than they did to their workers, or to the public.

America's love affair with the auto was not over, but there was definitely a lover's spat going on. The public turned increasingly to imported cars, which seemed to be of higher quality and greater value. More expensive, but *greater value.*

The antithesis of greater value is "planned obsolescence," a policy devised at General Motors in the 1920s. Just about everyone who wanted a car had one, so it became a problem of how to sell more cars to the same people. At first, model changes were introduced with gradual mechanical improvements and styling variations each year. Henry Ford didn't like it, but GM was calling the shots now and Ford had no choice but to follow suit. In 1927, the Model T died, the first victim of GM's annual changes.

Sometime after World War II, it became industry practice to build cars that would give two to four trouble-free years. Then the owners were encouraged to trade. Remember, it was not the workers who devised this policy, it was management.

In any competition, leaders must set an example for their followers, be they soldiers or workers. Yet, even as management was telling workers they must take pay cuts, corporate salaries and bonuses were—and still are—at outrageous levels. In Japan, the high-level executive makes about nine times the pay of a worker. In the United States, that ratio is closer to 60 to one. The rich have gotten richer; the poor, poorer; and the middle class, more desperate and dollar-driven. Such is the legacy of corporate greed.

As early as the 1950s, father warned against the merger mania currently plaguing America, calling the multi-national corporations "organized economic power without social responsibility." Perhaps we are ready now to hear what he had to say. I hope so.

CHAPTER TWELVE

BATTLING
THE
COMMUNISTS

*"We won the war. The task now is to win the peace ... Let us
go home motivated by the same spirit that motivated us back
in 1936 and 1937, when all you could get for belonging to
this union was a cracked head."*
— Walter Reuther, accepting the UAW presidency

Since 1939, father had been asked to run for the presidency of the
UAW. He had declined in order to keep harmony within the young,
tumultuous union. But times had changed. The UAW was being led
by R. J. Thomas, a man sympathetic to the Communists. Members
were afraid that if Thomas continued in the UAW presidency many
more Communists would join and gain power. They already had
control of the Executive Board. Before the GM strike had ended, 17
presidents of large Detroit locals had asked father to challenge
Thomas.

For years, father had gone head to head with labor's Communist
faction. Their double-cross of the workers during the GM strike had
only increased his desire to rid the union of their political motives.
The Communists, of course, saw father as their main obstacle to
gaining total control of the UAW.

Shortly after the GM settlement, there was a showdown. The last
week in March 1946, delegates from across the country gathered in
cold and windy Atlantic City for the UAW convention. The UAW had
a reputation for uproarious conventions, but this one still ranks as its
wildest. Every bar and hotel felt its effects. Fistfights were epidemic.
Delegates dropped water-filled balloons from hotel windows onto the

heads of rival delegates. In the lobby of the Chelsea Hotel, a fight mistakenly broke out between two groups which were both pro-Reuther!

Next in line to Thomas, and also pro-Communist, was UAW Secretary-Treasurer George F. Addes. The Thomas-Addes faction employed streetwalkers imported from New York City to solicit the votes of uncommitted delegates. But across town father's supporters wasted the girls' time with the excuse that they were still uncommitted and needed more time and information to be convinced.

At caucuses where father was speaking, he stressed that if Thomas were re-elected, the Communist Party would gain power within the union and the Kremlin would figure in all future decisions. During the war, he reminded them, the Communists had turned on labor by using incentive pay and piecework programs. He exposed their proposed labor-draft law and their betrayal of the UAW during the GM strike.

Father often stayed up talking until three in the morning, slept a few hours, and started in again at 6 a.m. The Reuther backers were confident they had a candidate who was more than the bread-and-butter men of the past. And he was innovative, with the vision to lead during this crucial post-war era.

CIO President Philip Murray arrived to address the convention. Thomas, of course, had deliberately left father off the escort committee. Murray favored Thomas in the election race and his endorsement carried a lot of weight with the delegates. Even though father wasn't a part of the escort, he showed up anyway and walked to the convention with the CIO president. Another member of the party remembered the scene:

> Walking down the boardwalk, I was alongside Phil Murray, and I was getting my heels kicked by Walter trying to get up alongside Phil. As we reached the back of the convention hall, Walter had Phil by the left arm and he walked right up the steps with Phil, you know, right onto the platform. And I overheard the conversation. I guess Phil wasn't sure if Walter was a candidate at that point. I think Phil was probably trying to prevail upon him not to be. And I remember Walter saying, 'Well damn it, Phil, I'm going to run!'

Perhaps affected by father's determination, the respected labor leader did not openly endorse Thomas, as had been expected. He talked around it instead, publicly expressing his gratitude to "Secretary Addes, Vice President Reuther, Vice President Frankensteen, and to this great big guy for whom I have distinct fondness, the president of your union, R. J. Thomas...."

A number of important issues were before the convention. Issues like the recent strike against GM, establishment of a Minorities Department, and the right of women to keep the seniority they had earned while working in factories during the war. To clarify these issues, father pushed for a closed debate between Thomas and himself. He said no newsmen would be allowed in, so "we don't have to pull any punches." Thomas was put on the spot. He was no match for father's forensic skills. Addes saved the day for him when he uncovered a convention rule that required a two-thirds majority vote for a closed session. When the hands went up, many of the delegates thought they saw two-thirds in favor of a debate, but Addes, who was chairing, quickly said it had been defeated, and that was the end of it.

At Murray's request top CIO officials, including Allan Haywood and Sidney Hillman, rushed to Atlantic City to throw their support to Thomas. It was becoming evident that this was going to be a very close race and that every vote counted. In *The Daily Worker*, the Communists had been attacking father for weeks; other anti-Reuther broadsides denounced his "fancy economics."

March 27 was election day. Just before the voting, father went up to President Thomas and offered his hand. Thomas refused. Without a blink, father answered his silence: "Tommy, if you're not big enough to lose, you're not big enough to win."

Edward J. Cote of West Side Local 174 placed father's name in nomination: "The man with whose intelligence, progressive and aggressive leadership we can march side by side to our goal of a stronger, greater and United UAW-CIO... a man who consistently translates the will of the workers into action..."

The first vote was cast by the delegate from tiny Buchanan Steel Products Corporation. With only one vote, the delegate loudly responded: "to Walter Reuther." A snicker arose from the Thomas supporters, but it was drowned out by a roar from the Reuther faction.

One by one the delegates came up to the microphone and the lead see-sawed. Twice the voting was delayed by fistfights on the convention floor. As the final votes were being cast, voices swelled in the Reuther section and suddenly father was raised onto the shoulders of his delegates. He was bewildered; he felt it was premature. He didn't realize this was a trick invented by his loyal follower Brendan Sexton of Local 50 to try to sway remaining uncommitted delegates to their side. Observers felt the ploy didn't really change any votes. Leonard Woodcock, who was keeping score for the Reuther caucus, remembered: "The only change it made was the manner in which the pro-Reuther delegates cast their votes—jubilantly—and the others, the Thomas votes, with a sort of grimness."

Just before the balloting ended, Thomas accepted defeat. Tearfully he told father, "It was a good race." Father replied, "We'll work together, R. J." The final count was 4,444 for Reuther and 4,320 for Thomas. Father had won by a mere 124 votes!

The hall filled with anticipation as father made his way from the shoulders of his cheering supporters up to the rostrum. Standing there with mother, he vowed to work for "the kind of labor movement ... whose philosophy demands that it fight for the welfare of the public at large." He continued:

"I stand before you humble. There is much work to be done in the world. We won the war. The task now is to win the peace.... Let us go home motivated by the same spirit that motivated us back in 1936 and 1937, when all you could get for belonging to this union was a cracked head."

Later that evening father broke custom, sipping a beer and having a cigar, to the delight of cheering blue-collar America.

Father's victory celebration soon sobered. Nearly every pro-Communist member of the Executive Board had been re-elected. Thomas-Addes backers had retained more than two-thirds of the Executive Board seats, from which they planned to make it practically impossible for father to exercise authority. They were determined to push him out of the presidency the following year.

Once back in Detroit, father found Thomas extremely reluctant to give up the president's office. After days of procrastination, the unseated president finally packed up and moved out, swearing under his breath that the Executive Board would never allow Reuther the full

Father's victory celebration upon winning the presidency of the UAW, March 27, 1946. Uncle Roy beams at left.

A kiss from May for the new president!

power of the presidency. Another problem: the UAW national coffers were almost empty. Secretary-Treasurer Addes had concealed the union's bankruptcy from the delegates at the convention. Faced with an inability to meet the payroll, father flew to New York and secured a $250,000 loan from Sidney Hillman and the Amalgamated Clothing Workers Union. Hillman also counseled father on how to consolidate his power within the UAW despite the Executive Board's being against him.

In one of the first board meetings, pro-Communist members passed a resolution saying father would have to pull back his attacks on Communists within the union. Father countered by proclaiming publicly that he would not appoint any Communist to a union position.

The board began to meet secretly without informing father. They brought issues to a vote without giving him a chance to present his position. When father tried to make appointments to key positions, the "mechanical majority" would block them. He would have to find some leverage to force their cooperation.

Studying the UAW bylaws, father discovered that the president's signature was required on any check drawn on the union's account. When he disclosed this to the Executive Board and requested control of the financial records under Addes' charge, the Board swiftly voted against him. Father called the bank and told them to honor no UAW check unless he signed it.

Finding no legal recourse, the board then made a rubber stamp of his signature! When father found out, he simply told them that if they didn't give him some cooperation he would stop signing all Executive Board members' checks. He later recalled: "Those fellows hated my guts, but they loved their paychecks. They came through."

Next, father struck a deal with ousted president R. J. Thomas. Thomas was trying to rebuild his political base, and father pledged to name him director of the Competitive Shops Department, where he could appoint a large number of organizers who would owe him their loyalty. In return, Thomas promised that the board would not block father's appointment of Uncle Victor to head the Educational Department and Frank Winn to manage the Publicity Department. These positions, he felt, were vital for opening up direct communication with the rank and file through publications, summer schools, and seminars.

Then, the Communist-influenced board members came up with what they thought would be the knock-out punch to father. They maneuvered to get a small farm equipment-workers' union, dominated by loyal Communists, to apply for a merger with the UAW. The board moved to give it 500 votes—enough to knock father out of the presidency for good, since they could be sure the votes would all be anti-Reuther. Father proposed they put the matter off until further investigation. The board refused.

Then, John W. Livingston, a Reuther loyalist, said that the rank and file should be allowed to vote on such an important matter. Not wishing to alienate the workers, Addes, who had recommended the merger, agreed. A referendum was set for one month later.

Father swung into action. Here was an opportunity to explain to the rank and file just how difficult the board was making it for him to carry out his presidential duties. Meeting in the basement woodshop of our home on Detroit's Appoline Street, father encouraged his supporters to "go out and beat the pants off them."

The Education Department spearheaded a national drive to expose the Communist proposal as a "Trojan Horse." Father met Addes at a local rally where, before an audience of 2,500 workers and others, they openly debated the issue of merging the farm-equipment workers. The Education Department's campaign and father's debating skills prevailed. By a vote of better than two to one, the Communists' takeover-by-merger failed.

Yet the Communists persisted. The next facet of their "get Reuther" campaign consisted of vicious attacks on father's integrity. They published a small booklet, "The Boss's Boy," depicting father as having sold out to the auto moguls. Copies were distributed in all the factories, but the booklet was so outrageous it became the undoing of its disseminators. Not only did most of the workers not believe the booklet's contents, they were insulted that the Communists thought they were that stupid.

Trying another tactic, the faction fabricated a secret letter over the forged signature of American Nazi leader Gerald L.K. Smith. In the "letter," Smith said that father was an undercover Nazi agent whose work should never be publicly praised, for it would interfere with the great job he was doing driving Jews from the face of the earth. When he learned of the letter, father quickly refuted the lies. His own wife was Jewish, he said, and her parents had fled Czarist Russia where thousands of Jews were being persecuted.

Finally, father's enemies spread the rumor (via newspaper columnist Drew Pearson) that he was going to run for vice president of the United States on the 1948 Republican ticket, with Senator Robert A. Taft as the presidential candidate. Taft's name was hated by the workers because of the anti-labor Taft-Hartley Act, which the Communists started referring to as the "Taft-Hartley-Reuther Act." Again the workers stood by their president. An observer has said of the propaganda warfare of the summer and fall of 1947: "The Commies threw everything but their hammer and sickle at Walter."

In November 1947, UAW delegates met in Atlantic City again for the national convention. The Reutherites had survived and been toughened through 18 months of hard work. Since its conception, the union had been split by factional disputes and self-serving politics. Suddenly, unity became a real possibility. The Reuther slate captured 18 of the 22 Executive Board positions. Father won the presidency by an overwhelming majority: 5,593 votes to the opposition's 339. After CIO President Phil Murray pledged his support to father, the Thomas-Addes group told its delegates to decline from casting their 1,219 votes. Emil Mazey was elected secretary-treasurer, and John Livingston of St. Louis and Richard Gosser of Toledo became vice presidents.

The next day my father introduced Grossvater and Grossmutter to the delegates, who received them with a standing ovation. Standing on the rostrum with his parents, father told the convention:

> "We are the vanguard in America in that great crusade to build a better world. We are the architects of the future, and we are going to fashion the weapons with which we will work and fight and build." He then presented his father saying, "A good pal of mine ... an old fighter in the ranks of labor, a trade unionist from way back when the going was rough, who indoctrinated his boys when they were pretty young and told them that the most important thing in the world to fight for was the other guy, the brotherhood of man, the golden rule."

85

Then father asked Grossvater to say a few words as the delegates had respectfully risen to their feet. "I am extremely happy that the seeds I tried to sow in the minds of our children are bearing fruit, and that they are engaged in the trade union movement that has always been dear to my heart," Grossvater told the unionists. When father presented Grossmuter, he told the story of how he had tried to use her new umbrella for a parachute and how she had fashioned the remains into a shirt for him.

Following his re-election, father went back to work to remove the politically powerful pro-Communists from the UAW. He stressed that "exposure, not repression" must be the solution to the unwanted infiltration. "We must get the Communists out of the political back alleys and walk them up main street in the full light of informed opinion." He encouraged Phil Murray to clean the Communists from the CIO. Eventually, officers were removed from 11 Communist-dominated CIO unions.

My father's dislike for Communist doctrine did not, however, make him an autocrat in the cleaning-out process. He preferred the democratic approach of selection by informed voters. His efforts did not go unnoticed in Moscow. The Soviet newspaper *Trud* reported that Reuther was a "traitor and strikebreaker," and a favorite of the U.S. Chamber of Commerce. The Republican Party, on the other hand, described him as the "most dangerous man in America and a Communist."

Although father's re-election was regarded as a "swing to the right," liberal writer James Wechsler wrote in *Harper's* magazine that he was hardly a "full-blooded Tory who spent his evenings at the Union League Club." Father was pleased to be criticized by the far right as well as the far left. This, he felt, helped keep him properly situated in democracy's middle.

Father's stand against Communism had come at a critical time. *Life* magazine later reported that his victory over the Communists in the UAW was "the biggest setback of all time for the Communists in the American labor movement." Hubert Humphrey later wrote:

> Communist infiltration of the CIO was a direct threat to the survival of all of our country's democratic institutions. The CIO victory over the Communist party was a significant victory

for our nation. It was a crucial defeat for the international Communist conspiracy ... it is a story of American men and women, members and leaders of our trade unions, and their successful struggle against our totalitarian enemies.

By the end of 1947, the auto moguls sensed they would have to continue to contend with this new breed of labor leader. It looked like father might be around for some time. And he brought a different kind of people into the field of labor: young, intelligent, socially conscious individuals, attracted by his dream of labor's role in a free society.

Even Henry Ford II stopped by father's office, eager to chat with him and, no doubt, to size up the man his own grandfather's thugs had beaten senseless. "Our chat was very satisfactory and very pleasant all around," said father of the younger Ford's visit.

Indeed, a lot had happened since the Battle of the Overpass.

CHAPTER THIRTEEN

"TOO OLD TO WORK, TOO YOUNG TO DIE"

"The thug who fired a shotgun through Walter Reuther's kitchen window last April 20 performed one unintended service for the dynamic young leader of a million unionized automobile, aircraft and farm equipment workers. The weary months of convalescence from the assassin's bullet have given the owner of one of the most agile minds in America time to think. This is a luxury that most men in public life are forced to forego because too many things demand their attention and leave them no time for real thought.

"Ideas have always been Walter Reuther's long suit. Author of a score of "Reuther Plans" for solving the problems of war and peace, he has what his friends call a brain with jet propulsion. His adeptness at formulating and dramatizing the ideas that are both novel and challenging has been the principal ingredient in his rise to economic and political power. If the speed of a man's mind could be measured in the same way as the speed of his legs, Walter Reuther would be an Olympic champion."

— A.H. Raskin, *New York Times* labor editor, 1948

Our family's life would never be the same. The would-be assassin's buckshot shattered our peace, our trust and our privacy as surely as it had shattered father's arm. Overnight, the little house on Appoline became a house of horrors. Just walking into the kitchen would make my mother shudder. How could she sweep or wash the floor without remembering her husband's blood on it? For months after the assassination attempt, strangers wandered the back yard, sleuthing, and satisfying their curiosity.

For months, father was in a cast from the waist up. Mother nursed and encouraged him in her tender, conscientious way. She held him, and us, together and was always there when needed. She was trying to protect us, her daughters, from this unspeakable nightmare.

When I reached the age of three, I remember sensing the great strain on mother—her constant fear. She worried about her husband. Would her children, too, be involved in future assaults? For the time being, she carried these burdens alone. Father was absorbed in his struggle for life, and then for the use of his right arm. He had a different temperament than mother. He didn't hold things in. He couldn't; he worried about the whole world.

As I've mentioned, the assassination attempt was always referred to as "the accident." Unfortunately, neither father nor mother ever explained to us what had happened. One day, I remember asking mother why father's arm was smashed. There was a moment of silence. Then: "Someone tried to hurt your father." "Why?" "Because he is helping the workers." She sounded so matter-of-fact. I sensed there was more, yet she dared not say it. And I loved her too much to ask.

During his recuperation, father spent more time at home than he ever would again. A preschooler at this point, I followed him around the house on Longfellow like a small puppy. I sensed he was a warrior, a hero, and that he was fighting an important struggle. His right arm was small and bony from "the accident." With me, he was always gentle and giving. We played ball together, throwing the same small rubber ball he squeezed almost constantly to restore the muscles in his arm. Father would toss it across the room with his left hand, and I would return it to him. I sat on his lap for hours while he read newspapers and squeezed that ball. He squeezed it for years, and sure enough, his strong grip returned.

Woodworking was father's favorite pastime. Once his arm started to respond to the treatments, he resumed his time with the lathe, the saw and the hard walnut with great zeal. I remember that it gave him solace during the tedious full recovery. He constructed a maple bookshelf using no nails or screws. The parts were held together by wooden wedges. He proudly showed me the finished product, pointing out how simply and effectively it was assembled. These times together cemented a very deep and lasting bond between us.

Mother, who played the piano by ear, teaches sister Linda. Father, whose arm is still in a sling, holds me as we attentively watch.

President Truman and father chat at the White House.

In 1948, with his right arm still in a sling, father addressed a crowd of 7,000 Ford workers assembled at Detroit's prestigious Cass Technical High School. It was an elderly group, 60 years old and up. His announcement: while in his hospital bed, he had been working on an industry-wide pension plan, the plan was for those who were "too old to work and too young to die."

Father promised those 60-up men he would not sign a contract in 1949 unless it included a pension clause. They cheered. This was unprecedented. Pensions were management's business and had never been a point for collective bargaining. Reporters at the speech hurried up to Walter afterward. One said he was really "out on a limb" with this promise. Father acknowledged: "I know. I'm hanging on the last leaf of the last twig!"

He then singled out Ford Motor Company for his first pension target. The Number Two automaker's young president, Henry Ford II, had by then "canned" Harry Bennett and more than 1,000 of his hired thugs from Ford, and was busy trying to turn Ford into a moneymaker after years of losses. Many doubted his ability to run such a large business. And he himself was aware that he had the job not because of his managerial talent but because his name was on the building. Awaiting Henry's very first presidential speech were 4,000 members of the Society of Automotive Engineers, many of them giants in the industry.

"Labor unions are here to stay," Ford declared. "We at Ford Motor Company have no desire to 'break the unions,' to turn back the clock. There is no reason why a union contract cannot be written and agreed upon with the same efficiency and good temper that mark the negotiation of a commercial contract between two companies."

Ford's speech was applauded. Newspaper stories called him "sincere, courageous, and a statesman." *Time* featured him on its cover; he quickly rose to national prominence.

Father found it all very encouraging. Ford was interested in his concept of "human engineering" and had even used the exact phrase to title his recent address. Uncle Victor deftly observed the change in policy from the Harry Bennett days: "When it came to points of principle — the first guaranteed pension, supplemental unemployment benefits — we always went to Ford first."

Father and Henry Ford II worked together for "human engineering."

Father preceded his requests and demands with a solid explanation of why the retirees deserved more. For workers 65 and over who had worked for the company at least 30 years, he asked Ford for $100 per month above their Social Security stipend. Henry didn't buy it; the figure was considered too high. Eventually, the two sides agreed on $100 per month total. That one agreement tripled the 1949 retirement benefits of most workers!

Father insisted that the benefits be funded exclusively by the corporation, and that the money be salted away for the workers each year and not be used for anything else. His foresight paid off a decade later when it became apparent that the United Mine Workers pay-as-workers-retire plans did not provide enough money to pay its pension program.

Chrysler took a bitter 104-day shutdown before agreeing to retirement benefits for its workers. Without a fight, General Motors followed suit.

Half the battle was won. Father then went to Congress bent on raising Social Security up from $32 a month. In a later interview with a British newspaper, he related what had happened: "In 48 hours in Washington, we did what could not be done by Congress in 12 years. We took our collective-bargaining process leverage to increase Social Security from $32 to $100 a month for everyone. They say the pocketbook nerve is the most sensitive." Whereas industry leaders had always blocked attempts to increase Social Security, now that government would be paying more of the pension, the legislation sailed through Congress.

Frank B. Tuttle was one of the first Chrysler pensioners to benefit from the agreement. In a letter to father, he wrote:

> On my 65th birthday, I had three important messages. One was from Social Security, telling me that I had an insured life income of exactly $38.69 a month; another from Chrysler Corp. declaring it would never grant the 'preposterous' pension plans of our union; and one from you saying that those demands would be won, either at the bargaining table or on the picket line.
>
> Chrysler managed to reverse the sequence — we went to the picket line first and the bargaining table afterwards, but today I am looking at pension checks of $157.46 a month. And even a little Social Security of $38.69 was due to the action of our union. Without the protection of our union it is highly improbable that I would have lived to be 65 at all, and without the union who would want to? Before our union the best a worker could hope for was to die on the payroll, before he became old enough to be replaced by a younger worker.
>
> In 1830 Daniel Webster said in Congress, "Union and liberty now and forever, one and inseparable." Probably few auto workers would know who said that, or when. But millions of workers in our own and a host of other unions feel in our hearts that union and Reuther are one and inseparable. Today at 76, I have not only an economic competence, but an inheritance to leave to three generations of descendants — and my common stock in Reuther is a large part of it.
>
> Frank B. Tuttle

Father's innovative approaches to benefits for his rank and file and his mastery of negotiating for what he wanted, were translated into gains for non-union workers too. Concerned with keeping their employees, companies hurried to give them something resembling what their counterparts had won. "Human engineering" had arrived.

When I was two years old, another attempt was made on father's life. Two nights before Christmas, *Detroit Times* reporter Jack Pickering received an anonymous phone call: "You did me a favor once.

I want to tell you a story. Dynamite is being planted in the UAW-CIO headquarters. It's for when the big guy is in the office."

Police searched, but the bomb was actually found by the UAW watchman. The *Detroit Times* story gave this account:

> The bomb contained enough explosives, police said, to blow the four-story brick building sky-high and to cause heavy damage and possible loss of life in the second-story General Motors Research Building 25 feet away.
>
> The bomb, planted in an outdoor stairwell leading to a side basement entrance, contained two fuses and detonators showing the dynamiters deliberate attempt to touch off a devastating blast. The dynamite was contained in a cardboard box brightly wrapped in red and white candy-striped Christmas paper.
>
> To add a bizarre touch, a blue ribbon was tied around the box.
>
> The bomb was apparently meant for Walter Reuther, president of the UAW, because the anonymous caller told Pickering: "It was planted for when the big guy was in the building."

The "bomb" turned out to be 39 sticks of dynamite taped together, with two 90-inch fuses attached. One of the fuses had burned all the way down to a defective cap; the other, to within an inch of the explosives where its course had been stopped by careless wrapping of the tape.

Once more, providence had spared my father. But again, we asked: "Why would anyone want to hurt daddy?"

And again mother's reply: "Because he is helping the workers."

That idea was now thoroughly drummed into my consciousness. It had completely changed my life.

CHAPTER FOURTEEN

PRESIDENT AGAIN, POLITICIAN NEVER

"I have no interest in the job. I already have a job to do and I intend to do it. Even if the post were offered to me, I would not accept it."

— Father on a proposed appointment
to a U.S. Senate seat.

In 1948, father's political influence had grown faster by far nationally than at state and local levels. Already UAW presidential endorsements carried considerable weight. On one occasion, when CIO President Phil Murray brought father to a White House conference with Harry Truman, the President told the CIO chief: "Phil, that young man is after your job."

Murray responded with a smile. "No, Mr. President, he's really after yours."

Father felt that Truman had little chance of winning the 1948 presidential race. New York Governor Thomas E. Dewey was expected to unseat the incumbent from Missouri. Later, Jack Conway wrote that father advised the UAW to focus its energies "into those areas where we had the greatest chance of electing congressmen, senators and governors and not to put our limited resources into the presidential campaign."

At election time, father was under anesthesia in a Durham, North Carolina hospital, awaiting surgery on the radial nerve in his damaged right arm. Conway heard the results on a local radio station and hurried to his bedside.

"How did it go?" father asked.

"As far as Congress is concerned, we did pretty well," Conway replied, rattling off the names of the victorious—Humphrey in Minnesota, Kefauver in Tennessee, Paul Douglas in Illinois.

"What about the governors?" father pressed.

Adlai Stevenson had prevailed in Illinois and our home-state friend G. Mennen "Soapy" Williams would occupy the governor's office in Lansing.

"Incidentally," Conway deadpanned, "Truman got elected."

What an uproar! Truman had taken the issues to the people, father noted, and that must have made the difference.

Two years later, the news columns indicated Michigan Governor Williams had father in mind for the U.S. Senate seat of ailing Republican Arthur Vandenberg.

"Two weeks ago I told a conference at a union meeting in Chicago that I have no interest in the job," father commented. "I already have a job to do and I intend to do it. Even if the post were offered to me, I would not accept it."

Shortly thereafter, Vandenberg died of cancer. Blair Moody, Washington correspondent for *The Detroit News*, urged father to run for the seat. "You are the only person I would be willing to support— and not seek it myself," Moody told him.

"I told Blair that I appreciated his friendship," father recalled. "We sat until four o'clock in the morning in my home, eating Swedish coffee cakes and drinking tea and coffee. He was trying to persuade me."

Father declined because he could never give up his position with the union. He felt he could do more as president of the UAW than if he were a senator from Michigan. Henceforth, that became his position on holding any political office. Governor Williams named Moody.

But father did not completely abandon the political scene. One of the men he admired most was Illinois Governor Adlai Stevenson. When, prior to the 1952 Democratic national convention, Stevenson had not joined the race, President Truman started sounding out prospects for his vice president, Alben W. Barkley. Truman advised Barkley he would need the backing of labor.

Barkley invited 16 labor leaders to breakfast at his Blackstone Hotel suite in Chicago. After small talk, Barkley came to the point. The labor men had failed to choose a spokesman and the table fell silent. Finally, father spoke up:

"Mr. Vice President, you know that we all have the greatest admiration and affection for you. That is why it is so painful for us to say what we feel we have to say." The labor leaders were hoping that Stevenson would run and didn't want to commit themselves to another man so early, even though he was the duly elected vice president.

Barkley immediately withdrew from the race, giving the loss of labor support as his reason. One press report stated that the "labor men had convinced Barkley not to be a candidate." The stories castigated father in particular, as he had been their inadvertent spokesman. Actually, gentleman Barkley had quietly accepted the fact that they wouldn't back him. But the story sold newspapers.

In 1951, the UAW purchased land from the Edsel Ford family on Detroit's East Jefferson Avenue in order to build its international headquarters. It had been only a few years since a handful of union men could not raise $10 to rent a single room for union activities. "Solidarity House" was the fulfillment of father's dream.

With the help of friend Oskar Stonorov, the reknowned architect and protege of Frank Lloyd Wright, an attractive angular building with lots of glass arose. The headquarters was dedicated June 9, 1951, with my sister, Linda, cutting the ribbon.

In the foyer of his office, father placed a giant mural depicting children of all nationalities. They were smiling and playing together. It represented the kind of world my parents wanted to help bring about someday.

Father then designed his own solid walnut desk. Stone paperweights would top huge stacks of papers, each one labeled and extremely orderly. He doodled with a pencil while talking on the phone—which was a good part of his day—filling his wastebasket with crumpled papers by evening. Also on the desk: a calendar decorated with a Soapy Williams green-and-white bow tie, a metal paperweight bearing the profile of Phil Murray and a cylinder used to store pencils. These items never changed positions.

Father's office faced the Detroit River. I can recall the many hours I spent watching the ducks bob and search for food as I waited for father to finish his work before leaving for the night. On the wall behind his desk, father stored books about economics and the labor movement, along with a few of the honors he had received from various groups. Photographs of our family, his brothers Roy and Victor, and a snapshot showing him speaking with President Truman were on the walls. He called this office his second home. Rather than drive home, sometimes he would sleep on the sofa. This happened regularly during labor negotiations.

Shortly before the move to Solidarity House, Doug Fraser became father's administrative assistant. Their friendship had developed during the 104-day strike against Chrysler. According to the union, since the issue was only retirement benefits due the workers, the walkout had not been necessary. The Number Three automaker had charged the union with "trying to put their hands in the kitty." Chrysler ran full-page ads decrying the union's demands and had tried to destroy the UAW's public image. At the end of the strike, father made an unprecedented move. When it was time for the traditional hand-shake, he ignored the hand of Chrysler's chief negotiator. Despite the presence of the media and dozens of cameras, despite the pressure to conform to tradition, he felt the whole ordeal had been needless. He just stood there and refused to shake hands with management.

"I was never more proud of him than at that moment," Doug Fraser later recalled. The two of them would laugh as they remembered this scene. Chrysler was flabbergasted. Fraser served as father's assistant for eight years before his election as regional director. "I thought I knew a lot, but he taught me a great deal," Fraser reflected. "I grew more in those eight years than in any other span in my whole life. And we had a similar sense of humor; I don't think the public saw much of that. They perceived him as serious, doctrinaire, rigid. I think all of us were like that at one time. In fact, I was *more* inflexible—one of the things I learned from him was flexibility."

In 1952, there was a heated race for the presidency of the six-million-member CIO. Father was running against incumbent Allen

Haywood, a favorite of MacDonald and his steel workers. On December 2, father won the election by a million votes. He began his acceptance address much as he had six years earlier before the UAW:

"I stand before you humble .... Our enemies have been watching the proceedings of this convention from the cocktail bars of the Union League clubs and millionaire's clubs all over America. Reading the stories in the press of the division in the CIO has filled their hearts with hope, filled their minds with designs to take us on ... drive us back and rob us of our hard-won social and economic gains. I say that the fat men on the plush cushions are wrong. We are going out of here united to carry on this struggle until we win."

A couple of days later father met with George Meany, who had been reelected president of the AFL by a simple vote of the Executive Board. They talked of reuniting the two huge federations, split up since 1935. Both men pledged to work toward a merger.

Although father was a lifelong abstainer from alcohol and tobacco, many of the men who had worked for his re-election did not share these habits. At one of their campaign meetings, father had pledged to

A victory kiss after father won the presidency of the 6-million-member CIO, December, 1952.

smoke a cigar and drink a shot of whiskey if he was elected. His allies did not forget his promise. While taking the oath of office, he was handed a cigar and a glass of whiskey. A puff of the stogie started him coughing; he tossed it aside, then he put the whiskey to his lips. Without taking a sip, he gasped: "What the hell, how can you guys drink this crap?" The guys roared. He posed for a whiskey-and-cigar picture and more or less fulfilled his promise.

Later, while addressing the Brewery Workers, who were also CIO members, father joked about his abstaining from drinking. "It is a hell of a comedown when the son of the former head of the Brewery Workers' Union is a teetotaler." They forgave him.

Grossvater was proud to hear of father's election to the CIO presidency. He had committed his whole life — and his sons — to the cause of social justice. On December 6, 1952, he wrote this letter from his home in Bethlehem, West Virginia:

> Dear everyone:
> Enclosed herewith are some clippings from our local newspapers, the *Morning Intelligencer* and the *Evening News-Register*. The *Register*, you will note, carried an editorial. I thought you all might be interested in what our papers had to say about the Wheeling boy. All is well, only our telephone wires are so hot I'm almost afraid to touch them without gloves (ha-ha). People I hardly remember called to congratulate us on our smart son. Now, though I just had a haircut, my hat seems a little tight. I can't understand why, there is so little in my head; could that be ego causing an unnatural expansion?
> Love to everyone.
> Dad.

As chief of the UAW, father's salary was $11,250 a year, at a time when heads of much smaller unions were receiving up to $75,000. He finally accepted an increase after he was pressured by members of the UAW Executive Board, who could not have a raise unless he accepted one.

Father was uninterested in wealth and his personal habits were exemplary. In fact, he was self-disciplined to the point of asceticism. This gave him a personal power that people quickly sensed. Ironically, it also made him the target of suspicion.

That same year father sat before a Republican congressional subcommittee on foreign policy. Senator Richard Nixon asked father if there were anything in Truman's foreign policy with which the CIO disagreed.

He replied: "Senator Nixon, there are things in the foreign policy of the United States that we in the CIO disagree with, but in essence, on its basic positions, we agree. We believe that we have to do more on a positive basis in terms of helping people to help themselves. The difference between the CIO and the Republicans is that we criticize the Truman Administration's foreign policy for its deficiencies and the Republican Party criticizes it for its virtues."

Father was destined to cross swords many times with the ambitious Mr. Nixon — the last time, just days before his death.

Father and Adlai Stevenson shared the vision of a more compassionate America.

CHAPTER FIFTEEN

PRISONER
OF
FEAR

"What we need is the power of human fellowship, because the differences are only skin deep. Inside, Lisa, we are exactly alike. We are all children of God."

— Father instructing me after racial
incident in our neighborhood

I was never comfortable in our home on Longfellow. We moved there to escape what had happened on Appoline. But it never felt right. There was a foreboding atmosphere about the place. Despite mother's "business-as-usual" pose, I couldn't relax. Fear had followed us to our new address.

I felt isolated from most neighborhood children. I could not freely play with them. They would point to me and laugh among themselves—as only children can do—innocent in their cruelty.

When father drove up to the house in his huge Packard with the bulletproof windows, the kids would stare at him. Perhaps they thought he was some kind of underworld figure. "Why does everyone stare at us, mummy?" I asked, peeking out the window behind the living-room curtains. Once, when father opened the front door, I saw three boys throw stones at the house and then run away. "I hate the way they treat us, and they are cruel to our dogs, too."

Mother didn't know what to say. After all, she never had to grow up like this, either. She did the best she could. "Your father is doing a very important job. Those children do not understand." End of discussion.

The bodyguards were nice to us, and we were nice to them. But they weren't family. They were paid professionals, and I resented their intrusion into our privacy. The UAW had assigned these union members to live with us right in our home. They were with us all the time. I even remember sitting in the basement with them, watching the *Howdy Doody* television show. Maybe I was the only child in the Peanut Gallery with bodyguards.

I had my favorites, though. Peter Bonno and his brother, Joe, were Chippewa Indians. They had worked for the UAW since the early days. It was Peter who taught me to ride my first bicycle without training wheels. Back and forth we went along the sidewalk in front of the house. I remember the older children teasing when I fell down. "Don't pay any attention to them," Peter would say. When father came home from the office, I showed him my progress. Peter was the same age as father. He was a simple man with an enormous heart.

During my preschool days, I retreated into the world of television downstairs. The basement was a small, dimly lit room with a rollaway bed and bath. The guards lived there, too, along with our toys and the TV.

There was a certain ritual to this time spent in the basement. The bodyguards would sit passively on the overstuffed vinyl chairs. Sometimes there were two of them, but usually just one. During our first years of heavy security, there were several turnovers among the guards. It was difficult to find men who could integrate into a family's home life. After extensive interviews with my parents, a likely candidate would move in with us for a trial period. One time in particular, the trial turned out to be mine.

I was four years old at the time. One morning, mother escorted me downstairs to meet the newest member of our household. She had an important meeting with the school board, so I was to stay with the bodyguard. I had seen so many different men in the last year, I had become somewhat numb to their individual personalities. I thought it was stupid that we were all trapped together in this house. The men didn't seem too happy about it either.

Mother turned on *Howdy Doody*. She would return in time for lunch, she said, and kissed me good-bye. I turned my attention to Clarabell, Howdy's clown friend who spoke not a word, but squeezed a little horn to communicate. Out of the corner of my eye, I sized up the new bodyguard. How peculiar to be alone with this stranger!

Soon Clyde came over and sat down next to me on the couch. As we laughed at the show, I felt myself warming up to him. He seemed to be able to enjoy this childlike activity just like me. In no time, his arm was around my shoulder. "You're a very pretty little girl," he told me, as he gave me a hug. Suddenly his hand worked its way between my legs and he started to fondle me. I froze with surprise and terror. Then an inner voice spoke, I jumped and ran upstairs. But where to now? We were the only two in the house and I knew no place to go in the unfriendly neighborhood outside.

"Don't be afraid," Clyde called to me from the basement. I was shaking and didn't reply. My mind was spinning with terror. Who was this man who had violated me? I knew instinctively that what he had done was wrong, but I couldn't understand whether it had happened because I was bad or he was. Then Clyde appeared in the basement doorway. He told me that nothing was wrong, and that I should not mention it to anyone or I would be in big trouble. He didn't want that to happen to me, he said, because I was such a good girl.

I stayed upstairs until mother returned. She opened the door and with her sweet voice called out, "I'm home, Lisa. How was your morning?" Since the incident, I had convinced myself it happened because of my own badness. I was petrified, thinking mother might find out, but I had never been so glad to see her. I guarded the terrible secret, believing I had caused it to happen and that if it were discovered I would be punished.

The thought that Clyde would return for duty the next day sickened me. Would he become a regular guard? The person hired to protect me was abusing me! I felt trapped and helpless.

After a week or two, Clyde was transferred. Before he left, he approached me with seemingly kind eyes and inquired about our "secret." When I couldn't reply, he looked hurt, as if I weren't being fair to him. I was most relieved when this very sick man left our home.

After the Clyde incident, I withdrew from the guards and avoided the basement like a chamber of horrors. Father was away a lot, so I spent most of my time with mother, or playing with the big watchdogs in the back-yard pen.

Feeling forever penned in myself, I withdrew inside to find some-one who could be free. But everywhere loomed the horrors of my early childhood. Even at that tender age, I could see that there were good men like my father—and bad men, too.

It was hard for me to fit in, especially when I was escorted to class every day by a bodyguard. The other children would stare. "Who is that big man?" they would ask. "Are you afraid to walk to school like us?"

Actually, I *was* fearful. But I always thought this feeling was my own weakness. My parents tried to create a stable home life; appar-ently, life was "normal." So I blamed myself for these negative feelings.

My first-grade teacher, Mrs. Muskgrove, encouraged me to ex-press my feelings. Through music, art, and her constant help, I was able to come out of my shell and get along better with the other kids. But I still feared their criticism, their pointing at me as someone different. Because I was different. I would return home from school to a prison—complete with guards, watchdogs, and barbed wire. And so my mind became a prisoner of fear.

While still in the first grade, I had my first encounter with racial prejudice. My closest friends were twin girls who lived several doors down the block. Their father was a doctor. These two girls were identical, except that one wore blue earrings and one wore green. I would often go to their house and play after school. They were younger than I, so I would help their mother dress them and watch them in the back yard.

One day, some older white children came riding past the house on their bikes while the three of us were playing out front. They mocked us and shouted slurs and horrible names at the two black girls. I was stunned. I had never met racial hatred face to face.

I took the girls inside to their mother and ran home crying. That evening, I told father in detail what had happened. I described how the older white kids had been filled with hate, how they had spit and yelled.

These children were ignorant, father explained. Their parents taught them to hate, and that's how hate goes on. "Hatred is terrible, Lisa. It hurts both the giver and the receiver."

"Why do people hate each other because of their skin color?" I asked. "My friends are just like me."

As my father answered me, I felt he was speaking to the rest of the world.

"What we need is the power of human fellowship, Lisa, because the differences are only skin deep. Inside, we are exactly alike. We are all children of God."

I was especially struck by his last phrase. He was not a religious man, but there was a spirituality in his conviction that people were not to be judged by their color but by their inner character. His religion was pragmatism guided by morality. And he practiced what he preached.

Happy days for Linda and me with daddy at home.

106

CHAPTER SIXTEEN

ESCAPE
TO
PAINT CREEK

"Walter P. Reuther, the extraordinarily able and intelligent leader of the UAW, may well become in another decade the most powerful man in American politics."
— Historian Arthur Schlesinger, Jr., 1955

Our family would usually go up north to Higgins Lake for two weeks each summer. After the assassination attempt, it was hard for father to find someone who would rent him a cabin. Everyone was fearful of future attacks. So my parents began to look for property north of Detroit.

Mother found five acres of land with a small, rundown house and took father to see it. The land was beautiful, located between Rochester and Lake Orion, where mother had gone swimming as a girl. A rushing trout stream called Paint Creek ran through the property, forming three horseshoes. The owner was an eccentric doctor who loved trees. Everywhere he had planted evergreens, weeping willows, honeysuckle, forsythia, mulberry, poplars — it was a regular arboretum.

Our first summer at Paint Creek, I felt as if I had been set free from a cage. I spent hours alone in the woods by our house. The trees became my best friends. They did not tease me as the kids in Detroit had. Mother called my sister Linda and me with a high-pitched hoot-owl sound when she wanted us to come home. That was my only restraint; otherwise, I was free. It was a freedom I had never known in the tight environs of our Detroit homes. Paint Creek was, by contrast, a wonderland.

Originally, father had intended to use the property only in the summer. The house had a tiny kitchen and a living room with a cobblestone fireplace. Narrow stairs led to the attic. That was it. We would all "camp out" in the living room. Father made a few changes that first summer. He expanded the living room and built a master bedroom.

As summer was ending, I felt intense anxiety over returning to Detroit. Linda also loved the country. As mother and father sat in the living room one day, Linda and I entered quietly; and, in a very polite voice, I informed my parents that we were not going to return to Detroit. In fact, we did not care if we ever saw the city again. "I hate it there, mummy. It's too scary." Father and mother looked at each other with amusement.

"Lisa, you always have strong feelings," mother said. "But we can't change where we live because of them."

"Why not?" I asked. "Both Linda and I are happier here. So are you and daddy." My parents had been relaxing there for the first time in years.

"Daddy, this is a serious sit-down," I explained. "Linda and I are going to have a strike unless we have our way."

Mother peeked at father. I could see they were pleased with both our determination and our terminology. But they would have to think about this strike threat. When Linda and I went to bed that night, we heard them discussing the situation.

The next day was Sunday. Usually we started to pack around noon for the trip home, but nothing was going on. Then father sat us all down by the fireplace.

"I know how hard it's been for you girls to live in Detroit," he began. "I am very sorry for this. Mother and I have decided to stay in the country."

Wow! We were really going to stay. I couldn't believe it. I jumped up and gave each of them a big hug. This was my happiest day yet. And certainly a turning point in my life.

Monday morning, mother enrolled me in a small country school about a mile away from our new house. The Baldwin School had been a two-room schoolhouse until the previous year, when five additional rooms were built to accommodate the growing community. I was thrilled. Classrooms with huge windows faced the woods. Each class had less than 30 children, much smaller than in Detroit. And, the children welcomed me! They didn't tease me about my father. They probably didn't even know what a labor union was!

Our family's lifestyle changed dramatically after the move to Paint Creek. Our routine settled into regular country rhythms. My parents would rise daily with the sun about six. Father had a cup of tea and a thin slice of whole wheat toast for breakfast. Mother had toast, too, but with coffee and prune juice.

During the school year, Linda had the bathroom first, since her bus pick-up was a half-hour earlier than mine. When it was my turn, mother would help me bathe and watch a pair of cardinals outside the window. They came every morning. They mate for life, she told me. We both felt a strong affinity with all living things, but the red birds were special.

My hair was always long, so mother had to spend ten minutes braiding it. When I was in the fifth grade, I remember one of my classmates saying, "The Orientals believe that a person is carried back to God by the hair. It looks like you are ready, Lisa." I liked this legend, even though it didn't sound practical. Mother would sit with me while I had breakfast, then walk me to the gate where I would wait for the bus to take me to the Baldwin school.

For me, these were carefree days. The ride to school and the ride back home each took a full hour because I was the first to be picked up and the last to be dropped off. I enjoyed the travel because I sat next to my best friend, and every day we would sing songs and play hand games. The bus driver had several stuffed monkeys made out of socks that she passed around to entertain the students. We had the same driver for five years, so she became like a relative.

Living near Rochester, about 20 miles north of Detroit, meant two hours of car-riding each day for father. Sitting in the back of his Oldsmobile, he would bring out manila folders full of proposals that needed consideration. Or he would read the *New York Times* and the

Detroit Free Press. He never squandered a minute. His motto was: "By the wasting of your time, you do yourself the greatest crime."

Mother's adjustment to our new home was perhaps the most difficult. She was separated from her friends who had been especially important to her when father traveled. Rochester was the symbol of status in the 1950s, an upper-middle-class conservative Republican town where mother's broad social values would not easily be accepted. And she was a shy person. But her dedication to Linda and me helped her get established in the community. She introduced a modern dance class in the school system and became very active in the PTA.

When I was in the second grade, I remember a school field trip to the old Wonder Bread bakery complex in downtown Detroit. Mother was one of our chaperones. After the tour, the school bus stopped at a park for lunch. There was a playground with swings, teeter-totters, monkey bars and slides. We marched off the bus for a short recess before lunch.

My play was interrupted by a disturbing sight: Mother, who was sitting on a park bench, was approached by a strange man who walked up and introduced himself. Throughout the entire recess and lunch break they talked. My mind was burning. Why is mother talking to another man? Only seven years old, I wasn't bold enough to ask her right then; so I held back and watched.

When it was time for the class to reboard the bus, mother further alarmed me by declining to board. "Lisa, I'm going to ride back with this gentleman," she began. "He's a newspaper reporter, and he wants to do a story on daddy." She gently guided me back on the bus. I sat by the window, watching as she crossed the park to the reporter's car. He opened the passenger door for her, then circled and entered the driver's side. They drove away.

As a young girl I had formed a very proper idea of how men and women should behave together. My parents' exemplary behavior inspired this pure model. I remember observing conversations between the sexes with curiousity. What was this spell that hypnotized everyone? Why did men become silly? And women so absorbed with their looks and the impressions they were hoping to make? Because mother and father did not socialize in more typical ways — bridge clubs, country clubs, cocktail parties — their chaste relationship became idealized in my mind.

The trip back to school seemed to take forever. I was obsessed with thoughts of my mother and this man. I had never seen her talking alone with any man other than my father — except perhaps a relative, or briefly with the grocer or a repairman. We returned just in time to line up for the final bus ride home. An hour later I remember jumping off the bus with a skip, hurrying over the two bridges, and entering our front door — preoccupied, concerned, and very self-important.

I found mother in the kitchen washing endive for our dinner salad. "What were you doing with that strange man this afternoon?"

Mother laughed at my tone and manner. "He wasn't a stranger," she smiled. "Daddy and I have known him for years. He covered the last UAW convention for the Detroit papers. With negotiations coming up, he wanted to ask me questions about daddy's demands."

I was satisfied. It felt good to be in familiar surroundings and to be reassured by someone I trusted so completely.

When father arrived home that evening, mother related the day's events to him, including my suspicions. When he heard about the discussion concerning negotiations, his eyebrows rose. "You didn't reveal my strategy, did you, May?"

"Now Walter," mother replied with a sweet smile, "I wouldn't tell your secrets! But I must admit," she winked, "Lisa was rather upset by my conversation."

Father smiled. "Don't worry, Lisa, your mother is a real trooper." We all laughed as I realized I had made a mountain out of a molehill.

The decision to stay at Paint Creek put pressure on my father. He had to winterize the simple additions he had built. The new bedroom was not yet enclosed, so we were still all sleeping in the living room.

For better security, the UAW bought the plot in front of ours, with a large house for the bodyguards. Our house was back from the main road, invisible to passers-by. Around the entire parcel, the union built a six-foot, chain-link fence topped by barbed wire. Metal bars extended across the creek bed. The only access to the property was through the front entrance, where the guards checked anyone who came. For the first time in years, we were able to live alone in our own house and share the intimacies of family life.

Despite the pain it caused his hand, father himself worked on the extensive remodeling of our Paint Creek home. He saw it as a means of rehabilitation. He spent hours hammering and sawing. When the pain became unbearable, he would soak his stiffened hand in warm water and stretch his fingers, then resume work. "I got a good house and a good hand, all for the same money," he would later say.

Before the cold set in, father hoped to complete the master bedroom, the living room, a small kitchen, and an upstairs bedroom for Linda and me. Linda was at an age when sharing a room with one's younger sister was "square." We fought a lot, often fiercely. With her five-years-older vocabulary, she usually got the better of me, so I resorted to biting.

Linda really did need a place to call her own. She liked rock 'n' roll and talking to her friends on the phone. These activities meant nothing to me; finally we were separated. There was no other bedroom, so through the winter of my eighth year I slept in my parents' walk-in closet. I loved it. I tucked my bed into a small space between my parents' wardrobes. It was very cozy. And very special to be so close to mummy and daddy.

Sometimes I would overhear them talking at night, or even through the night, especially if father had just returned from a long trip. When it was cold, he would build a fire in the bedroom fireplace, then sit with mother on their Danish loveseat before the crackling blaze. If I awakened, they would let me snuggle between them. The room was elegant and spacious. Its large window overlooked a Japanese-style garden, a treasured spot.

One night, just before Christmas, I overheard father giving mother a report of the day's events, as he often did. But this evening, he was clearly disturbed. "May, a car followed me from Solidarity House tonight all the way to Rochester. Eddie finally lost them on Silverbell Road. I think I'm being watched. And the FBI says there's a contract on my life."

Mother's silence sharpened my sudden flash of fear. I dared not confront my parents; they would be upset if they knew I had overheard them. My mind was swirling; I buried my head in my pillow and tried to fall asleep, but all I could see was a little girl crying, "Why do they want to hurt my daddy?" I had transferred my terror to this image. I could not express these feelings. I had to keep them inside.

While my parents could adjust to the cloistered life with body-guards and a high public profile, Linda and I felt trapped by an existence we had not chosen. (Or had we?) While mother continued to paint a normal, rosy picture of our life, father sympathized with us and tried to accommodate our frustrations. The man who cut the Big Three down to size frequently gave in to his daughters' requests.

One summer, father arranged a homecoming for Linda and me which thereafter became a family tradition. We were coming home after spending several weeks at the FDR Camp in Port Huron. Father greeted us at the door with a twinkle in his eye. As we entered the house, we saw a huge poster with the words, "Welcome Home Dearest Linda and Lisa." Below the message were detailed pictures he had drawn of the whole family, including every animal. Each had a name tag, just in case we couldn't recognize who was who. His drawings were primitive, which made them more dear. I loved those Paint Creek homecomings.

Despite the distances, my parents made a special effort to remain close to our grandparents. Pop and Dora Wolfman lived in Detroit, so we were able to make frequent visits to their small home. Dora would fill our tummies with walnuts and raisins and her favorite Jewish rye bread. I would sit in the kitchen with them for hours playing gin rummy. Dora had an air of melancholy about her that vanished at the sight of her granddaughters. Pop would give us handfuls of silver dollars which he had saved through the years. He liked to pinch my cheeks and say, "How's my sweetheart?" It was sad to watch them grow older. I wanted them to live forever.

Grossvater and Grossmutter Reuther's home was still in Wheel-ing, so our visits with them were less frequent. When I was not yet seven, I stayed with them for several weeks while the rest of our family went to Europe. Being with Grossmutter was like entering a dream-land. I had always idealized her. She was a homebody, probably more because of the times and her circumstances than by choice. She baked her own bread, mended the clothes, cleaned the house, and all the while worked on special projects like beautifully embroidered doll clothes with tiny feather stitches which she gave to her granddaugh-ters.

Grossmutter was famous for the good things from her stove, like cookies and anise cakes. Father would tell a boyhood story about his mother preparing pancakes for her hungry family. Despite her Swabian culinary skills, she was often unable to keep up with consumption. These pancakes were filled with fresh cherries from Grossvater's back-yard trees. When she sensed she was getting behind, Grossmutter would cook a few batches with the cherry pits still in them, to slow down the eating and let her regain the lead!

When Linda was 13, Uncle Earl gave her a pinto pony named Charlie. He was a wonderful pet, gentle yet fast. I would follow them around, watching with great admiration. Occasionally, Linda would allow me to ride him, but he was definitely hers. I was frustrated, so my parents found me a mare said to be a good horse for an eight-year-old. But when my Charlotte joined the family, things took a turn for the worse. Charlotte would intimidate Charlie, not letting him eat or drink. Charlie lost weight and became morose. Charlotte also had the obnoxious habit of "cribbing." She would fasten her teeth to a surface and force gas from her stomach. And when we tried to bridle and saddle her, she would kick and bite.

During Charlotte's first summer, Grossvater came to visit. Father told him about the horse's behavior. Grossvater, who had trained many an animal in his day, considered Charlotte a challenge. Approaching her as she grazed, he placed a lead rope on her halter. Then, without saying a word to anyone, he began to beat her on the back with a huge stick. I was shocked to see the intensity of my grandfather's emotions as he tried to tame my horse. Even father was taken aback. I stood at a distance and watched, afraid to intervene. Grossvater yelled at Charlotte, striking her again and again. Father explained that Grossvater knew how to break her rebellious spirit without hurting her. I had my doubts.

As fall approached, Charlotte continued her anti-social behavior. One day, when my parents were away, my friend Carol and I decided to go riding. We walked slowly toward the two horses, carrots in hand to coax them. Charlie came submissively. Not Charlotte. After five minutes of being chased around the corral, Charlotte changed course and came up to me. I looked up at her, and the next thing I knew she was cribbing my nose! Her enormous mouth around my face, she pressed her teeth to my nose, belched, and ran away. That was the last straw. My parents returned to find my nose under a bandage. Charlotte was sold to a more experienced rider. We all celebrated, especially Charlie.

My friends from the animal kingdom filled my youth with joy and companionship. The animals were regular members of the family. We had birthday parties for them every year. I would make presents for the dogs, like a new collar out of bailing twine. Or a basket of fresh clover blossoms for dear Charlie—with carrots on the top. Even the watchdogs had stockings which hung beside ours every Christmas.

Father took great pleasure in building our Paint Creek home. It was the most ambitious construction project he had ever attempted. He approached it in a mood of "discovery learning" and enlisted the aid as well as the enthusiasm of his bodyguards. He would wake up in the morning, look at a wall, and decide to knock a hole in it for a picture window. It was my job during the summer to serve the work crew ice tea, father's strongest drink.

He called the trout stream circling our home "my moat." At some points, the creek was 30 feet wide, so father built two bridges to connect the guardhouse to our house.

Once, the creek rose nearly two feet over the bridges and threatened to soak the electricity box beneath the house. Mother phoned Solidarity House and father abruptly left a guest in his office and rushed home. The guest he ran out on was Clare Boothe Luce.

Mosquitos that bred along the creek bothered father, so we tried spraying the area with a repellent. The spray kept the mosquitos away, but drove the birds away as well. After discussing the problem, we decided it was worth the mosquito bites to have the birds come home.

Our home blended with nature. The outside was a rich redwood; inside panels were golden maple. The floors were narrow maple boards, partially covered by muted beige wool rugs. Furniture was Danish modern. Not everything blended with nature, though. Heavy panes of bulletproof glass brought from the Detroit house were installed in the living room.

Clerestory windows opened the home to the gentle morning sunlight from the east. On a narrow wooden ledge in the living room, mother displayed pottery from Sweden, Germany, and Mexico. Wide slate window sills made space for artifacts from India, Japan, and Africa.

Father liked large windows. He loved the stream and placed windows so that it could be seen from just about anywhere in the house. The water flowed briskly, so briskly it did not freeze in the winter. Paint Creek was his Shangri-la.

Father's expansion of our home took years and was a valuable outlet for his energies and imagination. He decided to push out the wall on the south side of the house to build a den. He moved the wall about eight feet, then used its redwood panels as one of the den's walls. (Father would spend a lot of time in that den, working on speeches or watching the evening news.) He left the copper downspout inside the wall. When it rained, water would rush down the metal pipe, creating a musical sound. He liked to give visitors a tour of the house, especially when it rained.

Our home was mostly handmade. The wooden beams in the living room were the only visible trace of the original house. Father's friend Oskar Stonorov had drawn up a blueprint at the beginning of the project, but later signed it, "Walter Reuther, architect." He felt it was appropriate since father had changed most of the original plans.

In later years, he built a magnificent guest house, intended to house diplomats and world leaders. A 13-foot ceiling rose above the living area with a whole wall of windows overlooking the creek. The floors were made of wide oak boards. A connecting kitchen integrated the cook with the activities of the house.

Finally, father decided to push out the kitchen of our house to build a dining room, his last, most-beautiful project. The dining room had three large windows facing the waterfall and clerestory windows as well. A large Japanese-style light illuminated the room at night. The room became the scene of many wonderful gatherings.

My parents' bedroom was simple and elegant, with a fieldstone fireplace. Walls were solid maple, with some white plaster for contrast. Father built mother a large walnut desk overlooking the stream and the garden. Later, the garden became my parents' favorite project.

Mother's knowledge of Oriental gardening was extensive. Father hauled in huge boulders to complement the dwarf trees and shrubs. He built a fish ladder by the waterfall, so that the fish could swim upstream to spawn. At night, the lights shone down from the trees, and a small Japanese lantern adorned the garden.

Despite the magical setting, Paint Creek's periphery—with its armed guards, attack dogs, and forbidding fence—served as a stark reminder of the possible dangers ahead.

Another reminder was the pain in my father's arm. He never complained about it, but I had seen him with tears in his eyes.

"How do you tolerate the pain, daddy?" I asked one day.

He thought a while before he spoke. "You know, Lisa, any goal worth achieving has its difficulties. Have you heard of Helen Keller? She is the *real* example of strength in the face of tremendous obstacles. She was born deaf and blind, yet she has not only overcome these handicaps, she has led the way for others born like her and inspired the whole world."

In 1954, father wrote to Helen Keller on the eve of her departure to the Far East as an ambassador for the deaf and blind.

My Dear Miss Keller:

As you undertake your arduous but heart-warming journey, I want you to know the prayers and best wishes of the men and women of the CIO accompany you.

Your courage in the face of adversity, your genuine love for people, your generous service to mankind, have made for you a very special place in the hearts of all Americans.

Good Luck and God bless you.

—Sincerely yours,

Walter Reuther
President

Six weeks later, Miss Keller wrote this reply:

Dear Mr. Reuther:

It is a task both delicate and difficult for me to thank you in words for your most friendly tribute. The only adequate acknowledgement is the invisible, inaudible but nonetheless real heartthrobs of appreciation that accompany these lines.

Your wonderful thought of me on the eve of my departure for the Far East will kindle my courage as I reach out into the unknown and not easily attainable areas of service to the blind and the deaf who await the Light and the Utterance of Life that is God's gift to all men.

Hoping that you may continue to help keep warm the interest in raising the handicapped to the rights and activities of normal humanity, I am, with renewed thanks,

Faithfully yours,
Helen Keller

Another person whom father contacted about this time was Senator John F. Kennedy, who was recovering from surgery in New York. He sent Kennedy a telegram wishing him a speedy recovery, "first because we like you and second because unemployment compensation will be our number one priority, and we need a fit and fightin' Jack Kennedy in that battle." He was working closely with Kennedy on social legislation. Jacqueline Kennedy sent the following longhand reply:

Dear Mr. Reuther:
You will never know what you did for his morale. It means more to him than anything now to know that a friend in the outside world is thinking about him. So I want to thank you, because I saw how much you cheered him up.
Every good wish from both of us.

Very Sincerely,
Jacqueline Kennedy

Only the future knew just how much father's friendship would mean to Kennedy. Historian Arthur Schlesinger, Jr. may have had an inkling, though, when in 1955 he wrote: "Walter P. Reuther, the extraordinarily able and intelligent leader of the UAW, may well become in another decade the most powerful man in American politics."

CHAPTER SEVENTEEN

THE
MERGER

*"It is more than a matter of economic justice to the wage
earner. It is a matter of economic necessity to our nation, for
freedom and unemployment cannot live together in
democracy's house. Corporation executives get paid by the
year—why not a worker?"*

— Walter Reuther, fighting in 1955
for a guaranteed annual wage.

Father was continually appearing before Congress, testifying on
every social issue. In March 1955, his backing of farm price supports
before the House Agriculture Committee led its chairman, Representative Harold D. Cooley, to say: "Mr. Reuther made the best farm
speech I have heard in our committee room during the entire 20 years
that I have served on the Agriculture Committee."

Father's commentary on the President's Economic Report was an
annual event on Capitol Hill. He also contributed significant speeches
on the peaceful uses of atomic energy and the impact of automation.
During his 24 years as president of the UAW, he made close to one
hundred appearances before Congress.

In June 1955, father appeared on the cover of *Time*. He was
negotiating with the Big Three auto makers for a guaranteed annual
wage (GAW). In an article he had written: "It is more than a matter
of economic justice to the wage earner. It is a matter of economic
necessity to our nation, for freedom and unemployment cannot live
together in democracy's house. Corporation executives get paid by
the year—why not a worker?"

A UAW radio program aired a new song written with Henry Ford
II in mind, encouraging Henry to accept the GAW. "Dance With Me,

Henry" included the advice, "You better feel that boogie beat, and get the lead out of your feet." The GAW negotiations kept father away from home even more than usual. Linda, who was used to having him help with her homework, complained, "Father, you've *got* to come home this weekend—I have a test on Monday!"

Father later told union delegates at a closed meeting in Detroit's Tuller Hotel how the UAW strategy had worked for the proposed GAW. "We decided General Motors was the easiest place to get money because it has the most, but GM's the most difficult to pioneer with a principle. Ford is the easiest place to make progress on principle. So we decided on the strategy of implementing the principle we expected to establish at Ford with the money we got from GM."

Following this, father developed his successful one-at-a-time offense. He knew that the competition among the Big Three—Ford, Chrysler, and General Motors—was more crucial to them than their dealings with the union. Each was afraid that a strike would cause a forfeit in market shares to its domestic competition. This pressure helped the union immensely in getting additional benefits for the workers.

When father first presented the GAW to Ford Vice President John Bugas, the former FBI man replied, "This is something that we will never, never do." Father cautioned, "Never say never, John." After rejecting a "trick" GM offer (workers would supposedly put money into GM stocks they couldn't touch until maturity), father remarked, "Hell, that's for the provident! I'm interested in the folks who can't take care of themselves. That plan's a wheel-of-fortune deal."

Then Ford offered the UAW a plan identical to the GM "trick". After hearing only one page of it, father exploded: "It's a very bad policy and it will get you nowhere. You guys have got rocks in your head." Calling the Ford proposal an insult, father shot across the table: "By God, this is the first time I've seen a Chevy coming down a Ford assembly line."

Bugas, who headed Ford's negotiating team that year, said a poll had been taken and the results showed workers favored the Ford plan over father's by a margin of 9 to 1. Father always did his homework with the rank and file, so he knew they backed the UAW position. He

challenged Bugas to put it to a vote, with the winning plan representing the new contract, adding: "Since you say the workers back your
program, you have nothing to lose." Watching Bugas squirm at the
idea, he later said: "Poor John! I thought he'd die."

The outcome was only days away. According to *Time*'s cover
story:

Reuther and Bugas negotiated through the preceding night
and into the morning. As noon neared, unshaved, rumpled
newsmen, who had waited up all night, crammed into the
corridor outside the conference room in the Detroit-Leland
Hotel. Inside, after 26 hours of hard bargaining, Reuther and
Bugas stood up during a brief break and stared silently at each
other. Reuther, who had won his principle, as planned, suddenly grinned and held out his hand. "You've got a deal,
Johnny," he said. As the doors opened, flashbulbs flared and
newsmen were toppled in the rush. Despite 40 hours without
sleep, Reuther radiated his usual brisk, cold-shower glow. He
praised Ford's plan for a modified Guaranteed Annual Wage
and, after a night's sleep, tackled General Motors.

Back at Paint Creek, a family celebration. We were all a little
delirious. The *New York Post* stated:

The agreement between the Ford Motor Co. and the Auto
Workers Union is a landmark of industrial democracy in the
U.S. According to the Marxist cliches, the union's demand
should have precipitated a long and violent class struggle.
Walter Reuther was advancing a proposition that would have
been generally considered revolutionary two decades ago.
There will be diehards who call young Mr. Ford a 'traitor to his
class.' But in the history books he will be remembered for a
contribution to the social engineering of this century as momen-
tous as the mechanical wizardry of his grandfather.

Father's preparation for the GAW negotiations lasted months. For
several weeks before a confrontation, he would sleep only three or
four hours a night. Yet he never seemed to falter. He emanated
confidence and vitality. The tip-off that he had chosen his target came
when father placed his briefcase and toothbrush under a specific table

at home. Then the marathon meetings would begin, often going 40 hours. The corporate negotiating tables were long and brilliantly lit. Switchboards, private lines, and recording devices were available to relay messages to and from the room.

Shortly after the Ford contract was signed, GM and Chrysler followed suit. The Guaranteed Annual Wage benefit provided workers with a new measure of security. Father saw this triumph as his gift to society, a symbol of his love for humanity. It was essential, he said, that the workers share in the abundance created by technology.

Father emerges from Guaranteed Annual Wage negotiations with Ford. Able colleagues Ken Bannon (front) and Irving Bluestone (back) share historic moment.

My father was an effective negotiator for two reasons. First, he realized price increases were not necessarily tied to raises. Advanced production technology enabled the auto makers to enjoy higher profits . They could pay workers better wages and still keep the car prices stable or even cut them.

Second, it was father's practice to start preparing and lining up his troops three years in advance of negotiations. He traveled across the country, talking with members of the rank and file, garnering ideas from and informing them about his plans for new contract demands. When he arrived at the bargaining table, he knew what he wanted and that he had the workers' full support.

Father raised bargaining to a highly-skilled profession. He represented a new generation of negotiators who saw their role in terms of the total community, not merely the interests of the membership. Picking one of the Big Three as his target, he would seek to develop a contract that could also be offered to the remaining manufacturers. A few days before the expiration of a current contract, after hours and hours of negotiations, he would take over as the chief UAW spokesman, and the intensity of the process would increase dramatically. He was known for his ability to apply pressure, or ease off, just at the right times.

When father had decisions to make, he had a staff of 26 officers and 46 technical and legal specialists on the UAW staff whom he could call upon for advice. Doug Fraser and Irving Bluestone were close advisors. Irving was so close he was like another Reuther brother. Father also relied heavily on advice from brothers Victor and Roy. Jack Conway was another confidant. Conway eventually left the UAW to work with the ALF-CIO's industrial union department.

About the time of the guaranteed-annual-wage negotiations, a cartoon appeared in the *New Yorker*. A group of auto tycoons, with worried expressions, were seated around a fancy table in a plush executive board room. One was asking, "Did anybody ever think of offering Walter Reuther a vice-presidency, at a hundred grand?"

While building our family home at Paint Creek, father had also been building a coalition within the American labor movement. After his initial meeting with AFL President George Meany in December of

1952, father was hospitalized for emergency gallstone surgery. The operation was successful, but he had to remain hospitalized for most of the month to recuperate. Upon his release, he immediately met with Meany to continue working on an AFL-CIO merger. For the next two years, they kept at the painstaking task, hammering out the details and presenting them to their respective members for approval.

During one such meeting in New York, Meany and heavy-set William F. Schnitzler, later secretary-treasurer of the AFL-CIO, were walking with father through a hotel lobby. "Look, there's Walter Reuther!" a woman exclaimed to a friend. "Yes, but who's that with him?" the friend asked. "His bodyguards, of course." Meany chuckled to himself. He was all too aware of father's prominence in the public eye.

Arthur Goldberg was the chief designer of the AFL-CIO merger plan. By February 1955, he had it ready for presentation at the AFL Executive Board meeting at Miami Beach. Father's presence was required for the presentation, so the AFL booked him into a fancy suite at the Monte Carlo Hotel. Father was always opposed to conspicuous consumption and hated the luxurious setting for these meetings of the leaders of workers. He quietly rejected the suite in favor of a small room down the hall. He let James Carey of the Electrical Workers stay in the suite. When reporters showed up at the suite—looking for Reuther, Carey told them, "He's down the hall in the linen closet squeezing oranges." Indeed, they found father preparing juice for himself and his bodyguard. Some criticized him for being ostentatiously frugal. He was just adhering to spartan personal preferences.

In December 1955, the merger was completed. Meany was named president and father a vice president; many had assumed father would be offered the number two position of secretary-treasurer, but the AFL wanted to fill that one, too.

After the merger, father and Meany received Social Justice awards at a luncheon given by the National Religion and Labor Foundation. Eleanor Roosevelt attended, then submitted a story that ran in the *Washington Star*:

> Mr. Reuther's speech was an appeal for high ethical standards, which stirred his listeners deeply.
>
> Mr. Meany warned liberals in this country that they should

AFL President George Meany and CIO President Walter Reuther share the gavel at the historic merger of the two giant labor federations. New York City, Dec. 5, 1955.

President Eisenhower, George Meany and father meet at the White House to discuss ways to abolish unemployment.

not fall into the error of McCarthysim in reverse and appear to be too soft in their fight against communism. I agree with him, but ... it is a sad mistake, for instance, to give the impression to the people of India that their prime minister, because he wishes to remain neutral between the Soviet Union and the U.S., must therefore be a communist. Nehru is trying to keep his country a democratic one, and when we consider his neutrality we must remember our own for many years ... As leaders in the world we must not allow ourselves to be frightened into exaggerated statements which can only antagonize....

On several occasions, our family accompanied father to Miami Beach for meetings of the AFL-CIO Executive Board. We would stay in two plain adjoining rooms. Father used one room for discussions with his staff members, so mother would stay with Linda and me during the day. As usual, father had little free time. Occasionally, he would go for long walks with us along the beach. He was embarrassed by these rendezvous in the resort atmosphere of Miami Beach. He would never go swimming in public, or be seen anywhere in public during the day, when he felt he should be at work. At night, if he had a little time, he would take us to a cinema or down the street for an ice cream sundae. Although it was evening, he wore his dark glasses.

My parents were different from the people who daily gathered around the Monte Carlo Hotel pool: wealthy women bedecked with gold; men puffing on cigars, their bellies bulging, staring at the women. No wonder father shied away from the Miami crowds! It was awkward for us, as well. But the pool relieved the long hot days and gave us something to do.

Father sometimes characterized the members of the AFL-CIO Executive Board as discussing a few "meaningless resolutions" in their plush suites in the morning, then adjourning "to spend the afternoon at the race track." In fact, he was so embarrassed by the profligate appearance of these annual Miami Beach gatherings that after the 1958 event he persuaded the organizers to have the next meeting in Washington, D.C. George Meany was upset. To undermine father's efforts, Meany had a private talk with Luis Muñoz Marin, governor of Puerto Rico, and asked him to invite the AFL-CIO Executive Board there for its 1959 meeting. The invitation was forthcoming and the Board approved changing the site from Washington to San Juan. Father was dismayed but went. Meany caught a cold and missed the opening session in Puerto Rico. Father, as president of the CIO, chaired the meeting in his absence and won an OK for a membership march on Washington, to bring the problem of unemployment directly to President Eisenhower's attention.

When Ike was asked by newsmen the next day about the proposed march, he sarcastically remarked that it had come from the "sunny beaches of Puerto Rico," far from the northern cities where unemployment was so high. This was a slap at the labor leaders, and especially at father whose proposal it was.

Father responded: "Mr. President, I have spent no time on the sunny beaches of Puerto Rico, nor have I been with you and your many big business friends on the golf course, the duck blinds, and the quail hunts." We loved father's rejoinder, as did millions who read it in their newspapers.

Meany arrived in San Juan the next day and tried to kill the march, claiming it would be invaded by "peaceniks" and other radicals. Father angrily objected, and a compromise was worked out for a smaller demonstration. Meany despised marches and demonstrations, though an effective way for common people to publicly express themselves.

Shortly after this widely-reported disagreement, Grossvater wrote us a brief letter. He saw George Meany as a childish person in a powerful leadership position.

Dear Walter, May and Lisa,
We suppose by this time you are again settled down in your regular routine, or at least somewhat rested from your hectic meeting at Puerto Rico. We read all about your meetings in the daily papers, where George protested against your opening the meeting before his arrival, thus assuming the position of president. Just how small can some men get? Under parliamentary law, the Vice President presides in the absence of the President; if both are absent, the board members select one of their number to preside during their absence ... Give our Lisa a big hug and kiss for both of us, hope she did not get too homesick for her momma and father, bet she's glad you are back.

Although the Florida trips embarrassed father, I was excited to go, especially since it meant saying good-bye for a few weeks to the cold Michigan winter. When I was nine years old, however, I became obsessed by a fear of flying. For three years, the feelings had been building up. Whenever I traveled with my parents, I would add up the numbers of the flight. If the total were six, it was a bad sign. Five was my lucky number. Once, mother and I were packing our suitcases for a Miami trip with father. I noticed the airplane tickets sitting on mother's desk. I quickly calculated the sum of the numbers on them: six. My mind was paralyzed with fear. All afternoon I anguished. What made matters worse, my favorite teddy bear had been broken that morning by our new and very playful German Shepherd puppy. It all added up to a bad omen.

The suitcases were sitting by the front door. Father was still working at Solidarity House and would meet us at the airport. Mother took Linda and me upstairs to get dressed for the trip. I burst into tears: "Mother, please don't make me fly. I don't want to go on the airplane." Tears streamed down my face. "And look," I sobbed, "my bear is broken, too. How can I go when my friend is sick?" Mother was startled by my outburst. She could see my emotions had been building up to this climax for a long time.

Quietly, mother took action. First, she sewed my torn teddy. I continued to cry as she pushed the needle in and out of his body with the skill of a surgeon. But this mending process was only superficial to me. I still did not want to fly!

Next, mother got on the phone to our close friend Lou Schwartz, a well-known psychiatrist, who instructed her about dealing with this type of anxiety. Mother calmed me enough to get me into the car and to the airport. Once in the plane I was by my father's side, and I felt safe. As the plane swung around and headed for the runway, I grabbed father's arm. Hearing the engines revving in preparation for takeoff, I hid my face in his chest and prayed for our safety. Then I fell asleep. Time passed swiftly. I awoke to the stewardess' voice announcing our arrival in Miami.

CHAPTER EIGHTEEN

MEXICO
LESSONS

"The American Dream is not about gadgets. It's not about the size of our gross national product. It's not about the level of our technological sophistication. The American Dream is about man. It's about broadening the opportunities and facilitating the growth of every human being, so that each person can reach out and achieve a sense of purpose and fulfillment."
— Father, anticipating a spiritually-oriented society

Our family's time together was always limited. Father was sensitive to family needs, and he frequently tried to combine work with family trips.

One such occasion was a Christmas excursion to Mexico, where father was scheduled to talk to labor groups. The labor movement there was becoming militant. In an upcoming election, democratic principles were at stake.

When speaking almost daily, it was father's practice to deliver the same talk to different groups. But here in Mexico, audience responses were only lukewarm. They would applaud, but without enthusiasm. Father thought perhaps it was the lag between his English and the interpreter's Spanish.

But the last speech he made brought people to their feet. There was stamping and yelling. On the way back to the hotel, father told the interpreter, "I don't understand it. I've made the same speech everywhere, and elsewhere the people were polite, but not this enthusiastic." The interpreter looked at him and smiled. "This time I told them what you should have been saying all along!"

Father had told the Mexican workers to press companies for more

129

safety in the factories and a more livable wage. If wages in Mexico and other developing countries remained so low, he foresaw the day when America's big corporations would export their work and cripple democracy's strongest middle class.

Besides the Mexican workers, father's speeches had other listeners. Everywhere he traveled, U.S. legal attachés would monitor his activities and send regular reports to the FBI. Father had spearheaded the drive to kick the Communists out of organized labor. His own union was a model of democracy in action. And even after 185 people interviewed by the FBI confirmed his patriotism and commitment to the American way of life, Director J. Edgar Hoover still insisted that father's "ideology, if I may be permitted to use the word here, is Communist."

As the radical right stepped up the attack, Hoover led the pack. His men trailed my father in the U.S., too, especially in the streets of Washington. Father, Hoover declared, had been "trained at Lenin University in Moscow in street fighting." Was he expecting Reuther to rumble?

Father joined mother, Linda, and me for weekend excursions. Taxco, famous for its weaving and terra-cotta roofs, was a couple hours' drive south of Mexico City. An avid shopper, mother was in her glory amid the corridors and small stalls, each stuffed with things to see, touch, and buy. The weaving and pottery studded the colorful piles of fruits, vegetables, and flowers.

In a country rich with natural beauty, it was sad to see such a poor standard of living. As we turned a corner to enter the town square, a small girl walked up and tugged at my dress. Clothed in rags, she looked up at me with her dirt-smudged face and held out her hands for money. I ran to my father, who was walking a little ahead of our group. "Please daddy, give me some money for this little child." He looked at her sad brown eyes. She had been taught from an early age to appeal to passers-by for money. "Just this once, Lisa. We don't want to encourage begging." I placed a quarter in her fingers and in an instant she was gone. We saw her later approaching another tourist. This was her livelihood. Her parents had sent her out into the streets, I guessed, to help support their family.

As in many poor countries, it was a tradition in Mexico to bargain with the merchants. Mother quickly became an expert at this. Our family would watch as she negotiated for a fair price. I felt embarrassed. After all, we had plenty and these people were struggling to live. Father seemed to share my feelings. So while mother was haggling in the marketplace, he and I decided to sit near the center of town and talk. The peasants start their prices high, he explained, knowing they will have to bargain down to sell their goods.

The second day of our visit to Taxco, I became very ill. My temperature climbed to 105 degrees. I had a chill with the fever and could not keep down any food or liquids. Mother still had hours of shopping planned. Father told her not to worry, that he would take care of me.

Our hotel room was very small and dark. Two cots stood next to each other. There was no other furniture. A tiny window recessed in the thick stucco wall was our only source of air. The cloistered, stuffy atmosphere alone was enough to make me feel miserable. By noon my fever was still high. Father kept forcing me to drink seltzer water; but it wouldn't stay down. He grew desperate. Leaving me alone in the little room, he made a quick trip to the front desk to explain the situation to the receptionist. Our drugstore remedies had proved ineffective against the local bacteria. He asked her to order some suitable medicine.

About a half hour later a young boy knocked on our door. "Medico," he said, handing father a container. It was an old Coke bottle without a label. A dirty cork sealed the chipped top. Father felt we were running out of time; we needed to break my fever. "What do you think, Lisa? Should we give it a try?" I was too sick to reply. Father poured a teaspoon of the medicine, said a quick prayer, and gave it to me. I fell asleep, my first rest in 24 hours.

When I awoke, father was standing at my side. "I wasn't sure you were going to wake up, Lisa. I guess the higher powers were helping us today." My fever had broken and I was able at last able to sip a cool glass of sparkling water. I did not realize the danger I'd been in. I felt safe and sound under my father's protection.

When mother returned that evening, her arms full of packages, father related the events of the day, showing her the dusty "medicine bottle." Mother admitted she was glad she missed the frightening situation. After a full night's rest, I was ready to face a new day.

Then another challenge: tomorrow, mother informed me, we were scheduled to attend a bullfight.

I was a very opinionated young girl and quite set in my ways. Frequently, father would have to pacify me if our plans changed unexpectedly. This news of a bullfight infuriated me. "Mother, how could you sit and watch them tease a poor animal? It's horrible. And I read in school that they kill the bull at the end. I just won't go."

My decision was final. But what could my parents do? They had been invited by a trade union delegation. Father felt it would be an affront if we did not go. But what to do with me? One of the trade union families was having a traditional Christmas party at their home. About 20 children would be going, and I could be included.

Mother dropped me off and I was quickly ushered into the festivities. Everyone thought I looked like a little Mexican girl with my long braids and "Indian" face. I did feel an affinity for their way of life. The evening passed quickly. We played musical chairs and ate pink ice.

Saved from the bullfight! I celebrated Christmas with my new-found Mexican friends.

132

Then everyone was blindfolded and given a chance to hit a huge piñata in the shape of a donkey. After a lengthy beating with a straw broom, the piñata burst, showering us with small prizes. We all scrambled to the floor, filling our pockets with balloons, whistles, and hard candies.

The most fascinating event was the festival of lights, a symbolic ceremony performed every Christmas. We were directed to the outside patio where the children stood, each with a candle. As they began to sing, one of the mothers explained that they were pleading for entrance into the house. "They are standing in darkness and the house represents light."

After 15 minutes of serenading, the patio doors opened. The children entered and placed their candles on a small altar in the corner of the room. "Christmas is a time when we celebrate God's shelter, as represented by Christ's birth," the mother continued. "The children have left the darkness and entered the light of God's presence." Indeed, the children now looked to me like angels.

On the way home I was thinking how much I had in common with these children. Despite our different languages and backgrounds, we had shared a deep experience together. When it was time to go, they had formed a circle of friendship around me, as if to stop me from leaving them. What a special evening!

And then there were the cathedrals. Since it was Christmas time, pilgrims were coming from all over Mexico to these holy places. What a powerful experience to stand inside and behold these magnificent houses of God.

The best was Quetzalcoatl. It had a rich history as old as Mexico herself. The symbolism of the cathedral celebrated the triumph of good over evil. We stood in the courtyard watching hundreds of ragged pilgrims complete their journey to this sacred place. One woman was bowing down every three steps to show her devotion to God. Others had crawled on their knees for miles. One elderly man had to be carried the final distance by his son because he was too weak to walk. He was determined to touch the famous spot which could bestow God's blessings.

My child's mind had thrilled to witness the pilgrims' devotion. These pious peasants had an inner purpose that ran deeper than the humdrum hustle of modern life. One thing puzzled me, though. Why were the churches so rich and the people so poor? Grossvater had criticized organized religion for being rich while the people starved; and so had an old union song, "You will eat bye and bye." Its words told of "long-haired preachers" who offered salvation in the hereafter, but refused to help their fellow humans with the daily problems of survival. Perhaps this was why father never went to church. He was too busy trying to alleviate human suffering in the here and now.

Yet modern culture, with its accumulation of wealth and advanced technology, did not really satisfy the inner person. Father would often speak about this. He felt that our industrial society was moving to a time when working men and women would seek a spiritual culture beyond material goods. The workers had their material benefits. It was now possible for them to consider more sublime goals.

"The American Dream is not about gadgets," father would declare later. "It's not about the size of our gross national product. It's not about the level of our technological sophistication. The American Dream is about man. It's about broadening the opportunities and facilitating the growth of every human being, so that each person can reach out and achieve a sense of purpose and fulfillment."

CHAPTER NINETEEN

JOURNEY
TO THE
EAST

"The best, most sensible and moral place to store food sur-
pluses is in the empty bellies of half-starved people."
— Walter Reuther, in a letter to
Secretary of State John Foster Dulles

In 1956, father visited India. He had been corresponding with his
close friend Chester Bowles, the United States ambassador to India.
Since 1951, Bowles had been urging father to visit the country. He saw
India as hanging in a precarious balance between freedom and
communism.

Father spoke of India as "freedom's last best hope in Asia." Back
in the 1930s, he had wanted to bicycle there with Victor on their
Eurasian tour. Then Roy's letter arrived, recalling them to help
establish the trade-union movement in Detroit, and they had to pass
India by.

Bowles wanted father to write a book about his disappointing
experiences in the Soviet Union, to be distributed to India's trade
unionists. Uncle Victor recalled the events leading to the request by
Nehru and the Indian National Congress that father pay an official
visit:

"The new Indian state had very many internal problems to solve;
it could not afford to become involved with any of the major political
blocs. Nehru's decision to maintain his country's neutrality is even
more understandable when one realizes how close India lies to both

Soviet and Chinese borders. He believed that India's most important contribution to world peace lay in providing leadership for the growing group of developing nations that were interested more in implements of agriculture and industrial production than those of war. Hard-liners in the Pentagon, however, and in Dulles' State Department, and, of course, George Meany, all decided that those who were not with us must be against us."

India had been offended by a Meany statement condemning Nehru as "an aide and ally of communism in fact and effect, if not in diplomatic verbiage." The State Department asked my father to help mend the wounds. The *New York Times* added: "Mr. Reuther can do a great deal to assuage their injured feelings and to correct misunderstandings they may have about American opinion, especially that of organized labor."

Several domestic duties forced father to postpone his visit. He was absorbed in the upcoming presidential election between President Eisenhower and Adlai Stevenson. His mobilization of the workers' votes was critical. Then the steel industry tried to undermine CIO unity, accusing father of moving toward socialism. They criticized his involving labor in social and political reform.

In April, father finally broke away to visit India. The people received him warmly. They knew of his proposals before the U.S. Congress for a United Nations Development Fund to be financed by the big industrial nations and distributed responsibly to the emerging ones. Father believed it was a great blunder to spend so much money on military defense. America should invest in the offensive against poverty, hunger, and human despair. These were the conditions the Communists exploited.

Father had several long discussions with Prime Minister Nehru, with whom he developed a plan for democracy in India. Standing before the Indian Council on World Affairs, he addressed several issues. On Soviet Communism, he quoted Gandhi: "'As I look to Russia, the life there does not appeal to me. It is beneath human dignity to become a mere cog in a machine. I want every individual to become a full-blooded, fully developed member of society.'"

On building world peace, he asked a question: "Why can't we find a way to tap the great spiritual reservoir that lies deep within us and

Father and Prime Minister Nehru, New Delhi, India, 1956.

get people and nations working, sacrificing, and building together in peacetime?"

And on world hunger: "India and America have much in common. Both our nations were conceived and dedicated to the proposition that all men are created equal. They contributed to the world and to the ages two moral giants, Gandhi and Lincoln. In an age of nuclear giants, we need more than ever a rededication to the human and moral values [of those great men]. In the world in which we live, peace and freedom cannot endure with the world half fed and half starving."

Father wasn't just making speeches; he meant every word he said. Immediately upon his return to America, he would write Secretary of State John Foster Dulles: "The best, most sensible and moral place to store food surpluses is in the empty bellies of half-starved people." He stressed his "firm conviction that American interests and the cause of world peace would be better served if our efforts are directed wholeheartedly toward economically self-reliant friends, whether or not they choose to be our military allies."

Unity in diversity, he argued, would strengthen the world's stability and dispel the idea that America was trying to remake others in her image. "The American people will listen, and they will sanction the boldest action geared to those positive peacetime ends. For they will understand that the costs of such a program will ultimately be reckoned, not in dollars or cents alone ... but in millions of lives spared, in nations not devastated by hydrogen bomb attack, in civilization saved from ruin, in humanity freed for action in the never-ending and rewarding tasks of peace."

While still in India my father wrote home and described his hectic schedule, including 16 meetings in one day. The *Hindustan Times* reported that his tour was "a most welcome whiff of fresh air" and renewed India's positive feelings toward the United States. From New Delhi, an Associated Press dispatch stated that one of father's goals—"to heal the wounds caused by Meany's speech"—had been met.

Before leaving for India, father had had a two-hour discussion with George Meany concerning Nehru's position of neutrality. Now he had patched up Meany's verbal insults, but Meany did not appreciate it. Instead, he grew suspicious, misunderstanding father's motives and the values behind his actions. He saw the India trip strictly as a political move to gain power within the AFL-CIO, undermining his own position. Henceforth, the marriage of the two labor confederations started to sour.

Father's India trip was his farthest away from home. Because of the extreme distance, he did not telephone, as he often would have from Europe. To fill the void of his absence, mother regaled Linda and me with fabulous stories. As a young student, she had read much Greek mythology. These ancient fables captured her imagination. She would tell us some of the Greek myths, and other legends as well, describing supernatural beings and the mysteries of nature. She also read to me from a book about the world's great religions.

Much later, I would examine the tapestries of philosophical and religious thought for myself. Mother and I would note parallels between the Eastern and Hellenic views of the world. The Greek myths I heard as a child I later traced to the *Vedas* of India. And now, while father was in India, mother sowed the seeds of curiosity that would one day take me to that faraway land as well.

At last, the day of father's return arrived. When I awoke, I begged mother to let me go to the airport with her to greet him. It was the middle of April. The trees were patiently waiting to bloom. I could not be so patient. Sitting in school that morning, I felt each minute as an hour. After lunch, mother arrived with the bodyguard.

The drive to the airport took forever. I sat alone in the back seat, asking every few minutes, "Are we almost there, mummy?" Why did time pass so slowly when I was waiting to see father? "Mummy, will daddy be able to stay home for a few days? Does he have to go back to work right away?" I knew he would have even more work when he came back; so I learned at a young age to cherish the times we had together.

Mother and I got off at the terminal while the guard parked the car. We checked at the front desk. The plane was 15 minutes late. "That's not so bad," mother assured me. "International flights are often much later."

Soon the passengers started to file through the gate. The second person was father. My eyes filled with tears as I saw his smiling face.

I rushed up to him and gave him an enormous hug. Mother stood by the sidelines until father was away from the portal. Reporters and photographers were on hand. Mother remained composed, keeping her strongest emotions in check. I was glad that was not expected of me.

The drive home was easier than the trip to the airport. I sat in the back seat again, but this time beside father. He was telling us stories about India. He opened up his briefcase to bring out a soft beige garland made from the silkworm cocoons. He placed it over my head, explaining how the Indian people press their palms together and bow slightly to acknowledge God's presence in everyone.

Father had traveled extensively throughout India, meeting with trade unionists, government officials, and the people on the streets, as well. They all sensed his compassion and gave him precious gifts in thanks.

Home at last, father opened the large metal trunk he had brought back. The contents filled the living room with the exotic scents of sandalwood and incense. My mind flew to this magical land. I had heard about India's poverty and disease, but I never imagined these gorgeous treasures: a sandalwood box inlaid with pearl, silver, and ivory; a hand-carved ivory statue of Radha-Krishna standing in a garden; brass vases and silver bowls delicately imprinted with floral designs; and yards of silk cloth, some in the form of saris for "daddy's girls." How could such a poor country produce such wealth? I promised myself I would go to India someday to find out.

After the exquisite saris were distributed (prolonged by my whining when Linda received the turquoise-and-gold one I wanted), father put on his white Nehru hat and marched around the living room. He spoke variously of the majestic Himalayan mountains, the thousands of temples, the cottage industries, and of overpopulation.

The last was one of India's most vexing problems. Her spiritual culture rejected contraception and abortion as sinful. Father made a mysterious proposal. "You know," he said with a twinkle in his eye, "if every village hut had a light bulb, perhaps this burden of population growth could be curbed." Linda and I shrugged while mother smiled at his childlike yet thoughtful humor. Electricity would give the villagers more light to be creative and not merely procreative. The appetites of the flesh would no longer enslave the "enlightened" spirit.

When the trunk was almost empty, father brought out his final surprises. "Close your eyes, Lisa." He placed a set of delicate prayer beads in my hand. "Now keep your eyes closed and smell the wood." My nostrils relished the subtle fragrance of sandalwood. "These are the beads they use for chanting God's names in the temples," he explained. "They are hand carved. Each strand contains 108 beads, something like a Catholic rosary." Thrilled by this gift, I forgot my envy of Linda's sari. "I love them, daddy. Thank you so much."

Throughout the weekend, I followed father around the house. I couldn't hear enough about India and her ancient culture. I begged him for more stories about the temples and the Himalayas. Deeply moved by what he had seen, he described the architectural wonders and the snow-capped mountains. Then he paused and leaned forward. "But I found the most fascinating part of India to be the ascetics." Author William Manchester wrote that father's union associates regarded him as a "true ascetic." He knew that habits like smoking and drinking sapped one's strength and vitality. My early impressions of him squeezing that rubber ball to rehabilitate his arm, defying the pain, transcending the agonies of the body by determination, would teach me that father was the master of his body, not its slave.

Father learned that India's ascetics, through knowledge and renunciation, attain a realm of consciousness unknown to most of the West. Some yogis, he related, lived hundreds of years in the Himalayas where they subsisted just by breathing the air. Others were seen present in two places simultaneously. Some could walk on water and fly in the sky. Others could take an object and multiply it many times before the eyes of amazed viewers. "There is so much more to life, Lisa, than meets the eye. Man has to go within himself to discover his true potential." The more he learned, the more he wanted to learn. And so did I.

Father offers his respects as he receives a turban and flower garlands from Indian villagers.

A joyous air-port reunion upon father's return from India.

Years later (at Putney) I was still wearing the sandalwood chanting beads daddy brought me from India.

CHAPTER TWENTY

THE
VISIONARY

*"His [Reuther's] national role has long transcended the
leadership of an automobile union. Because he is deeply
involved in sensitive issues, and because he moves swiftly on
the advancing edge of the present, he also has a substantial
international following. British Laborites extrapolate from
their own political system—he would be a potential Cabinet
member there—and find him the most exciting man in
America. In India he is a popular hero."*
— Author William Manchester

With the 1956 presidential election drawing near, father came under
attack from the Republican right. Michigan Senator Clare Hoffman
declared:

> In the opinion of many, Walter Reuther, because of his
> shrewdness, his intellectual ability, his adroitness and the
> power he wields, is far more dangerous to the security of the
> republic and the liberty of the individual citizens than is Russia
> or any possible federation of Communist nations.

This about the man who had won unprecedented victories for
millions of private citizens; who had fought Communist infiltration in
his own union, whose belief in the worth of the individual motivated
almost everything he did.

The Republicans were very much aware of father's influence with
the Democratic Party. Vice President Richard Nixon called him "the
smartest labor leader in America" and preached to his GOP workers
that "Reuther is the man to beat," not the Democratic presidential
nominee, Adlai Stevenson. Republican Senator Carl T. Curtis of
Nebraska told father, "You are the man who makes or breaks aspirants
in the Democratic Party."

Yet, my father had no political aspirations of his own. Therefore,
rising Democrats like Hubert Humphrey saw him, not as a rival, but
as a great ally.

Dear Walter:

Don't brush off with false modesty or disinterest any of the congratulations and laudatory comments you might hear on the speeches which you made in Minnesota this past week. Of course, there isn't a Democrat in Minnesota who isn't devoted to you one hundred percent, but at the Bar Association luncheon I noted some of our most hardened Republicans nodding in agreement with practically every word you said. You had them hypnotized, Walter. It was a tremendous speech. I am mighty proud of you.

It goes without saying that your appearance in Minnesota enhanced the Humphrey name, too. I am indebted to you for many things in many ways, but with your two appearances in Minnesota, my debt assumes the proportions of George Humphrey's favorite target—the Truman unbalanced budget. And I'm not as optimistic as the Secretary—I am afraid I shall never be able to balance this budget.

Many, many thanks.

Sincerely yours,
Hubert H. Humphrey

Sherman Adams, President Eisenhower's chief of staff, was convinced that father had presidential ambitions and suggested he might want to be "the [first] Socialist President of the United States." Indeed, father had been encouraged to run for President on numerous occasions. The renowned Reverend Henry H. Crane of Detroit wrote: "I think you and Victor are two of the noblest Christian gentlemen that I know, and I would rather see you president of the United States than any man alive."

In a 1957 interview with Mike Wallace, Eleanor Roosevelt was asked if she thought father would make a good President. "I haven't ever thought of it," she replied, "but I have a high regard for Walter Reuther's intelligence." When Wallace pressed, the former First Lady ventured, "He might."

But my father never wanted to be president. He was deeply committed to his role in the American labor movement. When a few years later, a "Reuther For President" committee appeared in New Jersey and then a "Reuther in '60" shop opened in New York, father sent out a special letter: "I am not in any way interested in running for or holding any office. I have said this publicly many times before and

I repeat it now with all the emphasis at my command."

Like many girls who adore their fathers, I was quite taken by the thought of mine becoming the President of the United States. He would be a great one, I thought. When I was about ten, and probably dreaming of playing on the White House lawn, I asked, "Daddy, could you ever be President?"

"No, Lisa, I don't want to be in politics as a candidate. I can do more through the UAW; that's my life's work."

"But," I pressed, "could there be a time when you might be President?"

Mother chuckled and chimed in like a press secretary: "Your father would only accept this role during a time of global crisis or an economic depression."

Father's involvement in the 1956 presidential campaign centered around his efforts to increase political awareness of his own constituents. As in the past, he worked for Democratic candidates: Adlai Stevenson and Estes Kefauver, both his personal friends. Father viewed Stevenson as a brilliant statesman. During the Democratic Convention, Stevenson waived selecting a running mate, letting the convention decide between Kefauver and Senator John Kennedy. In a room where the candidates could meet the delegates, John Kennedy came up to father and said, "Mr. Reuther, I would like to ask for your endorsement." Father told the senator: "Young man, when you change your voting record, I'll endorse you."

The UAW felt Kefauver was friendlier to unions; its strong lobbying helped the Tennessee senator win a place on the ticket. Father also pushed within the AFL-CIO Executive Board, committing labor to back the Democratic team, overcoming George Meany's opposition to any endorsement.

My normal bedtime was delayed on election night. It was a family ritual to stay up late to watch results on television. I sensed father's emotional investment in the election. Stevenson's 1952 defeat by Eisenhower had been a great disappointment. The task in 1956 of unseating an incumbent President was even greater. As the night turned to early morning, it became apparent that Eisenhower had been re-elected. Father slumped to the floor. As tears rolled down his face, he pounded the carpet with his fists.

Despite this election setback, father recovered enthusiasm, educating union membership about the political positions of candidates and office holders. "The great challenge ahead," he had told delegates at the 1952 CIO convention, "is to lift the level of political morality of the politicians in Washington. But you cannot raise it in Washington until you raise the level of political conscience of the people back home. *This* is the job."

Father's limited schooling made him an avid supporter of increased public education. Before the National Education Association, he proposed a five-year program in which the federal government would make available 1.5 to 2 percent of our gross national product for aid to education. He also proposed that college graduates be given the alternative of teaching to compulsory military service.

America's crisis in education, he felt, was a symptom of a larger moral crisis — her colossal defense budget. We have the resources to educate, he said, but we lack the courage. We should be building more understanding, not more bombs.

"Why is everybody always fighting wars?" I asked him.

Father loved these questions. He answered them the same way he would answer the world.

"The task is difficult. The struggle will be hard, but let us always remember that human progress has never been served to mankind on a silver platter.

"It's strange," he smiled. "There is a lot of talk about brotherhood. But some people kill the brother and keep the hood."

Father felt the UAW should stem from and strengthen American democratic principles. He did not see his role as a one-man show. He encouraged his staff to make their own decisions. And he used their skills to sharpen his own thinking. Said Doug Fraser:

> We built a tremendous staff of professionals. They really came to work for the union because of Walter, the kind of union he formed. People came who were totally dedicated to the union. Otherwise, they would have gone elsewhere and earned twice as much money. A lot of people contributed, of course, but Walter more than any other individual formulated the ideals and principles which safeguarded the democratic workings of the UAW. He formed the institution and now the institution

forms the leadership.

Walter gave his administrative assistants considerable power and latitude. He delegated authority to use. I could not separate myself from the president. I felt comfortable in making a decision. I can't remember a time when he said "you should not have made that decision." I made the decision and it was his decision.

Father's honesty about his own limitations forced him to develop new methods of protecting the union from bureaucracy. He wanted to devise a safeguard against corruptible power.

To ensure fair dealings within the union, father created the Public Review Board. Originally, the Board was composed of seven professionals from the clergy, law and academia. Members had the authority to overrule the UAW Executive Board where justice was not clearly done in inter-union dealings. The Public Review Board was a bold step, unprecedented in the field of labor.

I recall his excitement the night he returned from Solidarity House with the big idea. "You see, Lisa, history is full of examples of power corrupting men."

Father was proud of his union's integrity. To air grievances, members could appeal to the Executive Board, with the UAW delegates voting a final judgment at the annual convention. Since the Executive Board could sway the convention, the Public Review Board provided an alternative disposition of any appeal. The hearings were public, the appellants entitled to counsel, and all expenses paid by the UAW. Results: the Public Review Board has not been shy about expressing itself. Members later ruled against father himself when they felt he was in error. He accepted their ruling and enforced it.

"Watch out for the man who insists he has the perfect solution for everything," he would say. "That is the trademark of a fanatic, and most of the world's troubles have come from fanatics who have somehow or other gotten themselves into positions of power."

Father protected the democratic process and the rights of the individual with great zeal. His firsthand experiences in Russia had taught him the perils of losing this vision. His presidency was a responsibility he accepted with the gravest humility; not an end in itself, but a means of service to his fellow man.

While chairing the UAW convention, father gave the minority the fullest opportunity to voice its position. Columnist Murray Kempton witnessed this democracy in action at the UAW convention, July 1949.

> Always at the end when you watch the auto workers, you come down to the leader who seems so unlike them and yet is so much like them, and you keep coming back to the taut, tired man on the platform, even though there is no exterior symbol in this whole convention to remind you that he exists. There is not even a portrait of Walter Reuther on the backdrop — just pictures of kids and a doctor and two old people. Those are pictures of a program and not of a leader, and it is strange that his command of you and of his union is the fruit of not one small trick of the ham actor. He leans so far the other way that during this convention he hasn't dropped a hint to remind the delegates that he was shot hardly a year ago and still goes every day to the hospital. He had very carefully and conspicuously not done what so many of us thought he would do — turn the UAW into an iron personal machine ....

Father's style of leadership was appreciated worldwide. In 1947, he gave a rousing speech before the British Trade Union Congress, encouraging their own struggles by describing the gains the American labor movement had made in wages and benefits. They received him with enthusiasm and saw him as a hero for the common laborer. The London Daily Express reported: "No overseas visitor in living memory has made such an immense impact by his personality and tempestuous oratory."

Implicit in father's interpretation of power was a strong sense of balance. As president of the UAW, he assumed a strict, ascetic style. With the help of inspired associates, he crafted a constitution that discouraged bureaucracy and encouraged democracy.

Father was always restless in the face of social injustice. He saw the people behind the problems — the starving, the poverty of the masses beneath hoarding by a few; and the cataclysms that come when self-serving leaders ignore the people. Father inspired men and women everywhere, to solve the problems they'd often created themselves. And he saw nuclear weapons as the ultimate expression of man's growing inhumanity. At the very top of his agenda was the survival of the human race.

CHAPTER TWENTY-ONE

THE FIRST
NUCLEAR
PROTEST

"New clear power? It sounds like a good idea to me!"
— Lisa Reuther's assessment as a ten-year-old

Father was deeply committed to the peaceful use of atomic energy. He believed humanity could harness this resource for the benefit of the whole planet. But he also knew that even the slightest negligence could spell disaster. As for me and Linda, nuclear power meant merely another ceremony or two.

In 1956, the ground-breaking ceremony took place for the Fermi Nuclear Power Plant in Monroe, Michigan. No run-of-the-mill nuclear facility, Fermi was to be a "fast breeder"—later labeled at a Congressional hearing "the most dangerous of all reactors." Father was furious at the decision to build such a reactor so near a highly populated area. Only 30 miles south of Detroit and 20 miles north of Toledo, Ohio, Fermi was dangerously close to three million people. And that figure was rising.

Foreseeing a potential nuclear holocaust, father began to act. Backed by the International Union of Electrical Workers, the United Paper Workers of America and, of course, the UAW, he demanded a public hearing on the safety of this reactor. Five months later the hearings commenced, setting historic precedent.

During the proceedings, father requested that the Fermi people build a prototype fast-breeder reactor in an unpopulated area. He cited

British examples as an acceptable approach. "They are building one reactor at Dounreay, on the farthest tip of Scotland, and another in Windscale, in the borderland Lake District, far from the cities and population areas." Rejecting his advice, the Fermi people presented six testimonies from "experts" in the nuclear field. Among them was Hans Bethe, a Nobel laureate and physicist from Cornell University, who stated that the reactor could be built without "undue hazard to the lives and health of the public."

Father refuted his argument. He quoted the Atomic Energy Commission's own Advisory Committee, which had warned the Commission about Fermi's lack of safety. Father stressed that an unproved and experimental reactor was too dangerous to build between Detroit and Toledo. For instance, the Grosse Isle Naval Air Station had at least 36 landings every day. The planes would have to descend directly over the nuclear site. An accident would be catastrophic. He demanded that the construction permit be revoked immediately. Father knew that the more time and money invested in the project, the more difficult it would be to stop its progress.

For two years, the hearings continued—and so did construction. Then, in May 1959, the Fermi people won their first court battle. A month later, father filed a brief before the U.S. Court of Appeals. On March 23, 1960, the court ruled that the construction was illegal and would have to stop within 15 days. It was a victory for public safety and my father was jubilant. I was too young to understand the importance of those hearings.

"New clear power?" I asked father. "It sounds like a good idea to me!"

He smiled at my innocence. To insure public acceptance, the nuclear industry promoted the idea that no serious accidents would ever happen. In a way, everyone was treated like a child, protected from the truth. But the public had a right—and a responsibility—to know the risks. Father was adamant that people should know all about it.

The nuclear interests took the case to the U.S. Supreme Court. While it was waiting for review, a nuclear accident occurred at the SL-1 reactor in Idaho Falls. Three workers died almost immediately from large doses of radiation. But back in Monroe, Michigan, the industry continued to build, confident that the Supreme Court would uphold their right — and their investment.

Father protested the continuing construction. He presented a study of 40 reactor accidents, all potentially very dangerous. He quoted a University of Michigan study stating that, should a nuclear accident occur at Fermi during a steady wind blowing into Detroit, some 133,000 people would meet sudden death. Construction nevertheless continued.

Finally, the U.S Supreme Court voted on the reactor, seven to two in favor of continuing construction. Father was crushed. He had fought long and valiantly. Deciding to make one last effort, he questioned the granting of an operating license to Fermi. Again he was rebuffed.

Although he had lost the legal battle, father had acted as an educator, a responsibility he gave top priority. Throughout his life, he tried to teach by encouraging others in their pursuit of excellence, by his own innovative ideas and by his ability to translate those ideas into practical programs.

Some criticized his involvement in the nuclear issue. Why, they asked, was he meddling in someone else's affairs? But that was part of his vision of the labor movement as a servant of society. In challenging the building of the Fermi nuclear reactor, he was representing thousands of union workers, plus millions of citizens.

Those first public hearings dispelled some of the mystique shrouding the nuclear industry. Nuclear power was touted as being perfectly safe. Father did not challenge the concept of nuclear power. Indeed, he hoped that nuclear fission could help solve society's energy problems. But he condemned the irresponsibility of the AEC.

On October 5, 1966, father's nuclear protest, begun ten years earlier, was vindicated. A meltdown occurred at Fermi. Fortunately, the reactor was operating at a very low level at the time. Despite the extreme care taken to prevent the possibility of a serious accident, a mishap had occurred.

The meltdown baffled the Fermi people. They flew in experts from around the world—who could only respond with theories and guesses. After 18 months, it was determined a small piece of zirconium installed as an added safety feature had loosened and blocked the coolant nozzles. Shelden Novick, editor of the magazine *Science and Citizen*, wrote: "The huge quantities of radioactivity involved and the proximity of Detroit made the prospect terrifying indeed. The actual accident was not only incredible; it might have been far worse."

The meltdown had not been immediately publicized nor was it ever recorded on the sheriff's log of Monroe County. But later, it became the subject of a book, *We Almost Lost Detroit*.

The Fermi reactor never got back on its feet. After ten years and over $130 million spent, it had produced only 52 hours of electricity and not an ounce of plutonium fuel.

The saga continued, but first, some historical background:

Walker L. Cisler, who headed the Detroit Edison Company, had provided the major push behind the development of the Fermi plant. Private enterprise, he felt, should tame nuclear power to serve mankind's mushrooming energy needs. With the blessing of the AEC, Cisler proposed a reactor that would power electrical generators and produce more fissionable fuel than it consumed. Cisler's ambitions were considerable, but so was his misunderstanding of the ramifications of such a reactor. Hence, the meltdown at Fermi.

Enter Fermi II. Begun almost two decades ago and as of autumn 1988 still not in full operation, Fermi II has cost Detroit Edison more than $4 billion, a bill some 20 times the original estimate. Not until the plant reaches 90 percent capacity will Edison be able to charge its customers and start to recoup the enormous expense.

When father had challenged the construction of Fermi, he was challenging Walker Cisler's dreams. And his own. He insisted on testing those dreams in the fire of public scrutiny. He and Cisler fought bitterly during the years of the public hearings. The two men shared a strong social conscience, but the plant issue deeply divided them.

Despite their fierce opposition, Cisler and father emerged as close friends. In 1969, Cisler would travel halfway round the world at his own expense to be present at the dedication of a Walter Reuther Research Chair at the Weizmann Institute in Rehovot, Israel. Appropriately enough, the chair was dedicated to the "peaceful uses of atomic energy."

CHAPTER TWENTY-TWO

BALDWIN
DAYS

"You know, Lisa, few human beings are so wealthy that they can live what they believe. I'm doing what I want to do and that is a rare gift."
— Father, at Paint Creek

Many times I felt I was sitting across from father at the negotiating table. His keen judgment made it an awesome challenge to convince him of my point of view. I soon developed persuasive skills of my own.

While I was attending the Baldwin School, mother was elected president of the PTA. At an upcoming meeting, the school library was on the agenda. In order to encourage parental attendance, each class would receive points if the students' parents attended. One point for a mother, two points for a father. The class receiving the most points would be able to check out books longer at the school library.

The day of the meeting, I jumped off the bus and ran into the house. "Mother, when is father coming home?" I demanded.

"He's returning from Washington later tonight," she replied.

I was determined to have him attend the PTA meeting. It was 7:15 when he reached home. The meeting was at eight. I had little time for my negotiations. As he sat down to dinner, I began with the conclusion: "Father, you *have* to come. You're worth two points."

In my enthusiasm I had forgotten to explain the contest. "Everyone has promised to bring their fathers," I exaggerated. "You have to come."

The three of us arrived at the small country school at exactly eight o'clock. Parents and teachers were filing into the gymnasium. Even a few of my schoolmates were there, probably to see who had succeeded in bringing both parents. I was proud to enter the room with my mother and father.

Mother was chairing the meeting. She stressed the need for a wider range of books in the library. This would require funding, she advised. A plan had to be developed to raise the money. Before voting on the resolution, mother called for discussion. Several parents affirmed their commitment to improving the library. Then father raised his hand. When recognized, he rose from his metal folding chair. He seemed self-conscious and, after a sentence, his voice cracked. He cleared his throat and tried to continue. There was a long moment of silence, then father finished his presentation and sat down, his face flushed with embarrassment. I was sitting on the chair next to his. It was the first time I had seen him intimidated by a group.

On the way home in the car, father explained the difficulty he had experienced at the meeting. "I think there weren't enough people for you to feel comfortable," I offered. Father agreed with my analysis, then laughed a boyish, almost embarrassed smile. The man who could speak for hours before thousands of workers had struggled with shyness at this small PTA gathering. He had just returned from a Congressional hearing in Washington, tired and absorbed in his responsibilities. There had been only a handful of fathers at the meeting. I squeezed his arm: "Thanks for coming, daddy. You're a real friend."

The days at Baldwin School and Paint Creek were simple compared with the strained environment we had known in Detroit. When I was in the sixth grade, I was selected to make a short speech about the importance of trees. To beautify the area, the school had just planted 20 saplings around the building.

Father helped me make an outline of important ideas. We didn't write out complete sentences. "Don't memorize anything, Lisa," he advised. "Just speak from your heart." The night before the dedication we rehearsed for two hours.

On the big day, the Baldwin School gym swelled with children.

Parents had been invited, too; mine were sitting in the second row. I was the second speaker. When I reached the podium, I remembered father saying, "Speak from your heart." My notes only confused me anyway. And now the moment of truth. What should I do? I looked out into the audience and saw my parents smiling. "Trees are an expression of God's wonder," I began. "They shelter us from the sun and rain. Without trees, our planet would be barren. They replenish the atmosphere with oxygen. . ."

The words flowed with ease. I loved nature. The trees surrounding our new home were my intimate companions. My five minutes passed quickly and effortlessly for me. After the assembly, father came up and gave me a big hug. "You're a natural, Lisa, just like your dad!" I blushed. "You know, father, it was fun."

My parents had a passion for planting trees. They received hundreds of tiny seedlings from the forestry department which they scattered around our property. Once, when tornado-like winds uprooted many tall poplars and damaged other trees on our property, father and mother traveled to their favorite nursery in nearby Romeo. They walked through the nursery with Mr. Riemann, the elderly German owner, marking the items they wanted for Paint Creek. The bodyguard would come later with the trailer to pick them up. Although father usually shopped with greater restraint, he did not mind indulging in trees.

With the guards' help, father would dig the holes. Then he and I would carefully place the trees in their designated spots; mother acted as the vigilant supervisor. It was my job to fill the water buckets and add the plant food. Every tree required several buckets of water to eliminate air pockets around the roots. Once we replaced the dirt, father and I would walk around the tree, packing down the earth with our feet.

My parents were nature lovers. Every window of our home overlooked a small miracle. They helped organize the Paint Creek Conservation Committee, committed to preserving Paint Creek as one of lower Michigan's last uncontaminated streams. One Saturday, father helped the local Boy Scouts clean out Paint Creek. In his knee-high rubber boots, he looked like a big kid, grinning from ear to ear as he pulled trash from the rushing stream.

My father's life was highly integrated; there was no separation between work and play. That's why he could live at such a vigorous pace. "You know, Lisa, few human beings are so wealthy that they can live what they believe. I'm doing what I want to do, and that is a rare gift."

Mother shared his dreams. If he were digging the holes for new trees, she would be busy discovering their exact identities. Mother's willingness to make her home his base of operations allowed father to go out into the world. Their lives complemented each other. Planting trees together was an intimate example of their shared values.

Father would often talk conservation with C. Alan Harlan, an affluent electrical contractor from nearby Bloomfield Hills. Despite their diverse occupations, Mr. Harlan and my father were like two young boys together. They compared notes about species of trees and shared cuttings from their gardens. More than once, Harlan brought over his heavy truck and hoist to assist my father in moving large trees.

One day, father was determined to transplant a gigantic maple onto the barren hill by the guest house. The tree carried a root clod weighing over two tons. After several hours of digging the tree's new hole, he, Harlan and four other men carefully maneuvered the enormous maple into position. The men strained to keep control of the tree. It looked easy enough to me—standing at a distance—but afterwards father admitted he had been nervous. The tree had nearly snapped the heavy chain and rolled down the slope.

The transplant was a success and father frequently relived the event. Whenever he gave a tour of the guest house, he would point out the lovely maple tree. Then, with youthful flair, he narrated the drama of its transplant. He often stretched the details just to thrill his audience. Mother and I never tired of hearing that one. He was a good storyteller.

The Baldwin School Minstrel Show disturbed my parents. They detected in its performance a derogatory attitude toward blacks. Nevertheless, it was tradition at the school, and I was to be a part of the show. No black students attended Baldwin, so some of the players had their faces painted. By curtain time, I was quite aware of the piece's racist overtones.

But it was another kind of insensitivity that disturbed me during the show. I stood in the chorus next to a huge weeping willow tree, cut down for the backdrop. While the others sang and danced, I became absorbed in the sad plight of the willow, sacrificed for this silly show.

When the last song ended, I quickly left the others to find father. "Look at this poor tree," I said, bringing him to the stage. "Someone killed it just for this stupid minstrel show. How could they have done such a horrible thing?" Father had often explained how willow trees might be grown from small cuttings allowed to root in water. "Please, daddy, let's bring it home so we can grow baby willow trees." He paused for a moment, then slapped me on the back. "OK, Lisa, you have a deal." After notifying the school janitor, father sent the bodyguard with the trailer to retrieve the willow.

The next morning was Saturday. Home for the weekend, father told me to gather as many bottles as I could find. Mother drove me to the Paint Creek Market where I negotiated for three cases of old pop bottles. We found another half-dozen milk bottles in our basement. I lined the cement wall by the guardhouse with bottles. Adding a pinch of plant food to each, I then filled them with water.

Father was working by the pond. I ran to fetch him and hand in hand we walked to the pasture where the chopped-down willow tree had been placed. After separating the branches from the trunk, he seized each branch and cut off the smaller branches and twigs. "These are the ones we'll use for rooting," he said. "The others are too big." When he finished, we had close to one hundred specimens. I was excited at the thought of creating new trees from these shoots.

The first step took about five weeks. Every day after school, I would check the progress. Soon I noticed delicate hair roots forming at the bottom of the twigs. I watered the cuttings every two days and added plant food to their solutions weekly. Father would also examine their progress when he returned from the office in the evening. Then one Friday night, he told me we would begin our planting the next morning. On Saturday we walked around the property, placing the tiny trees here and there. The larger branches we placed alone, the smaller ones in groups. For years, father and I continued to check their progress. Many of our rooted twigs developed into mature willows.

The Mayfair Festival happened every spring. Bake sales and children's crafts abounded and the highlight was a popularity contest for the Mayfair King and Queen. Every sixth-grader was eligible to enter. Like the other sixth-grade girls, I secretly wanted to be the Mayfair Queen.

Cans lined the windowsill in the school auditorium, each labeled with a sixth-grader's name. The younger children would cast their votes all week by putting change in the appropriate cans. I asked my father for some coins which I intended to put in the can marked "Lisa Reuther." Since the other sixth-graders had done the same thing, I didn't consider it cheating. I brought father a small plastic bag. "I'll cast my vote for you any day, Lisa," he said, filling the bag with silver.

I took the bag to school and asked the janitor to place the contents in my can. He laughed when he saw all the coins. "I guess your father has to have his finger in every election. That was a sizeable sum he gave you." I knew he was joking, but I took the election seriously. My father's change made the difference. I won the throne.

The day of the festival, my friend Alan Hall and I were crowned king and queen. Wearing small plastic crowns covered with gold glitter, we each received a trophy with the inscription "Baldwin Mayfair Festival." Then we were helped onto the back of a horse and paraded around the playground. No U.S. president that my father would help elect could ever be happier!

While I first attended Baldwin, mother had to decide whether I should ride the school bus with the other children. It would be simple enough for the bodyguards to daily drive the short distance. She decided to forgo the special treatment. Following father's example, she tried to detach herself from the anxieties of the decision: I was to ride the bus.

Father instructed the guards to keep a watchful eye on me as I waited with the other children. This time spent with my friends waiting for the bus was great fun. It helped me feel like a carefree kid in the country. I did not realize that the guards stood close by, fully armed and ready to act in case something happened.

One day in my last year at Baldwin, I noticed a man in a dark car parked across from our bus stop. I shrugged him off the first day, but the next morning he was there again. Old fears started to stir.

That same day after school, I was standing in line with the other children waiting for the bus to arrive when I saw him again, sitting in his car. It was definitely the same car and the same man. And again, he appeared to be staring right at me. Suddenly I felt panic. Who was this person? What did he want with me?

The school bus pulled up and the safety patrol mother shepherded us on board. I climbed into my assigned seat, hoping this familiar setting would let me forget that man. An hour later I stepped off the bus. The ride had distracted me from the earlier fear, but as I turned to walk into our driveway, I saw the man again. Pressing my school books to my chest, I ran pellmell down the pavement to the guard-house. I banged on the door. No one was there. Down the stairs and through the gates I rushed, afraid to look back. As I crossed the wooden bridges, my imagination overtook me. The trees were reaching down, grabbing at me. I pushed open the front door and fell inside, weeping.

Mother was in her bedroom. She came to the front door. "What happened, Lisa?" Heaving with sobs, I was unable to answer. Finally, I calmed down enough to tell her about the man waiting at the bus stop and again at school.

"It was just a coincidence," she said softly. "Don't worry." Again, her brushstrokes of normalcy. Maybe she could convince herself, but I knew our life was abnormal.

From then on, the bodyguards stood at the stop with me until I got on the bus; the driver changed my seat to one directly behind her and the safety patrol mother held my hand until I was on the bus each afternoon.

I did not see the man again. But I had that familiar fear that he was out there somewhere. He had moved into my psyche to stay. And sometimes at night, when I was walking across the bridges, I would feel his presence and shivver at the recurring nightmare.

CHAPTER TWENTY-THREE

THE
INQUEST

"Walter Reuther and the UAW-CIO are a more dangerous menace than the Sputnik or anything Soviet Russia might do to America."

— Senator Barry Goldwater

The Republicans were nervous about the strong political influence of the labor movement, so early in 1957 they formed the McClellan Committee to investigate unethical labor practices. Because he helped the Democrats, my father was their main target. Through the committee, the Republicans hoped to link him with the corruption of other labor organizations.

The committee's investigations began with Teamsters Union President Dave Beck. Witnesses testified to a number of corrupt practices in the truck drivers' union— misuse of funds, extortion, embezzlement, rigged elections, and more. Beck hid behind the Fifth Amendment, but eventually was found guilty of grand larceny and tax evasion.

Teamster Jimmy Hoffa, another figure with a dubious reputation, took over Beck's post. Father had known Hoffa from the early days when they battled over their differing visions of the labor movement. Because of the UAW's strict ethical code, Hoffa labeled the UAW people "the squares from Milwaukee Avenue" (the early street address of many of Detroit's union offices). But now Hoffa faced bribery charges. Father, who had publicly referred to Hoffa as a "fast-buck man," advised George Meany to expel the Teamsters Union from the

160

AFL-CIO. Soon the Teamsters and two other shady unions were out.

On the surface, Hoffa and my father had much in common. Both came from small coal towns. Both started organizing in Detroit and now led powerful blue-collar unions. Both had suffered at the hands of thugs and police during the organizing campaigns of the thirties. Both had keen political astuteness and loyal followings. Both were ardent anti-Communists. And neither smoked or drank.

"We knew each other from the rough-and-tumble days," Hoffa said of his relationship with father. "For some reason, (it's kind of inexplicable) we drifted apart . . . Reuther knows what the union business is all about; George Meany don't."

A closer look revealed deep differences. Father had come out of the socialist tradition, while Hoffa was very much a capitalist. Father staunchly opposed organized crime; Hoffa consorted with it. During his reign, Hoffa was the subject of a series of indictments and court trials and finally in 1967 was convicted of mishandling the union's pension fund and jury tampering and sent to prison.

Although many labor leaders feared the McClellan Committee inquest would damage trade unions, father welcomed its scrutiny.

American labor had better roll up its sleeves, it had better get out the stiffest broom and brush it can find, and the strongest disinfectant, and it better take on the job of cleaning its own house from top to bottom and drive out every crook and gangster and racketeer we find. Because if we don't clean our own house, then the reactionaries will clean it for us. They won't use a broom, they'll use an axe, and they'll try to destroy the labor movement in the process. . .

Father challenged the Committee to rout the crooks from the labor movement. "But," he demanded, "Go after the crooks on management's side, too!"

Republican Senators Barry Goldwater, Carl T. Curtis, and Karl Mundt all served on the McClellan Committee. Goldwater had stated at a Republican fund-raising dinner in Detroit that "Walter Reuther and the UAW-CIO are a more dangerous menace than the Sputnik or anything Soviet Russia might do to America."

Father responded by writing the Senator a 12-page letter: "The seriousness of your charge is obvious when one considers the fact that the Soviet Union represents the greatest threat to human freedom in our world and is a world symbol of immorality, brutality, atheism and every vicious act against the standards of human decency and human freedom."

He then suggested to Goldwater that each of them choose three nationally prominent religious leaders to serve as a panel to weigh the charges leveled by Goldwater and "to hear my refutation of same." If the panel determined that father was indeed more dangerous than Russia, "I will voluntarily resign from the presidency of the UAW, the vice-presidency of the AFL-CIO and from the labor movement entirely.

"But if they decide you have not substantiated your charge, I would leave it up to your conscience as to whether you would consider yourself fit to continue to play a role in American public life."

The Senator refused the proposal.

An air of "get Walter Reuther" lingered about the McClellan Committee. One of its complaints concerned a long and bitter strike by the UAW against the Kohler Company, maker of bathroom fixtures. John McClellan named as his chief counsel Robert Kennedy, who went to company facilities in Wisconsin to study the strike firsthand. One of the problems he found was a disagreement over a lunch break. The men working in the enameling furnace room, where the heat was about 100 degrees farenheit, were seeking a 20-minute period for lunch. The company insisted that they had enough time to eat during the two-to-five minute baking spans.

Returning to Washington, Kennedy conferred with his brother John, the inquest's second-ranking Democrat. Both agreed that the Kohler strike was a labor-management dispute and should not be brought into the Committee's investigation.

But Republican senators would not relinquish the chance to smear father. Robert Kennedy said to his aide Kenneth O'Donnell:

"Mundt and Goldwater think that if you investigate any labor union, the union leader will come out looking as dirty as Beck and Hoffa, but that won't work with Reuther. If the public gets the idea that I won't investigate Reuther just because he's a big

162

force in the Democratic Party, that will ruin the McClellan Committee. It could ruin Jack Kennedy, too, so let's go ahead with the investigation of Reuther and see what happens."

Because Robert Kennedy was so hard-nosed in his attacks on the Teamsters, many labor people thought he would approach every union that way. He seemed very impressed with father's records, however, and shared the information with his older brother, Jack, their confidence in father's integrity deepening every day. (Later as president, Kennedy would say: "Once Bobby might have been intolerant of liberals as such, because his early experience was with that high-minded, high-speaking kind who never got anything done. That all changed the moment he met a liberal like Walter Reuther.")

Robert Kennedy's book, *The Enemy Within*, devotes a chapter to the "Get Reuther" movement. Time and again newspaper stories appeared, quoting "reliable sources," charging Kennedy was ignoring continued demands for an investigation of Walter Reuther. The criticism reached such a pitch that Kennedy confronted members of the McClellan Committee, who then publicly professed their pleasure with the progress of the investigation.

The Committee's procedure was to bring the leaders of the organization under inquest to the stand first. But the Republican senators declined to call father. Senator Barry Goldwater astonished McClellan by saying he didn't think they should call my father at all, that he didn't have anything to contribute. Senator McClellan reminded the senators that a good overview of the problem required each side to present its best spokesman first.

"The Republicans said that if Reuther testified first he would steal the show and the rest of the hearings would be an anticlimax," Kennedy wrote. In fact, they threatened to walk off the Committee if they didn't get their way.

Finally father convinced John Kennedy to arrange for him to appear in person before the committee. He told Kennedy he would never take the Fifth Amendment because he had nothing to hide. He also read a letter he had written to Robert Kennedy several months earlier, stating, "Since as president of the UAW I will undoubtedly be involved in the Kohler hearings, I would feel much more comfortable if in advance of the hearings you would find it possible to assign a member of your staff to check into my personal financial affairs."

The FBI Auditor General arrived in Detroit to examine the UAW's books and father's personal expense account. His report showed the UAW spotless. In fact, the auditor said, he had examined many corporate books and had never found a set so carefully and accurately kept. He elaborated by telling how father had his expense account blue-penciled by the secretary-treasurer's office. On one hotel bill there was a $2.50 laundry charge and it was marked off—father had paid this expense from his own pocket, as was his custom.

When father was testifying before the committee, Senator Mundt, a staunch conservative, arrived with a stack of papers. Mundt's opening questions betrayed an air of overconfidence.

"Now, Mr. Reuther, I have before me a payroll of the UAW. I see the name here of Mr. Roy Reuther. Is he related to you?" Father confirmed that he was his brother.

"And I see the name of Victor Reuther on the payroll. Would he be related to you?" Father acknowledged that Victor also was his brother.

Mundt sat back with a grin. "Nepotism," he purred.

But, father retorted, his brothers were on the payroll before he himself was.

The grin plunged to a frown.

Father gave long, detailed answers to their questions. Kennedy wrote: "He knew his subject — unionism — and was smart enough to admit at the beginning the mistakes that the union made. He was a smart, confident, articulate witness and the Republican Senators were no match for him." At the end of the hearings, Kennedy concluded, Goldwater looked "like a man who had taken a terrible beating."

The McClellan inquest placed added strains on our family. Mother got to work digging up the old financial records. She would sit in the living room for hours surrounded by boxes. It was a tedious task, but she was deeply committed to helping father in any way she could.

Rochester was known for its right-wing politics. Linda and I became targets for unkind remarks from schoolmates. Because of the widespread anti-union sentiment, my parents decided it would be better to enroll Linda in a private school. Soon she was off to the

Putney School in Vermont.

I was young and not as politically sensitive as Linda. Once, two boys came up to me at recess. After disrupting our dodge-ball game, they started calling me "Red" and "Communist." I was confused. I knew the names were meant to be bad, but I did not understand their meaning. That evening I asked my father about the incident. "Why were they so mean to me, daddy?"

"Lisa, darling, were the boys mean to you? I'm sorry. You see, Rochester is very set in its ways, so much of my work is not really understood here. I have always fought against communism. I have tried to strengthen the American way of life. Please forgive your schoolmates; they do not understand. They're just saying what their parents say. Ignore them and they'll go away."

The next afternoon I was confronted by the same two older boys. They sought me out and shouted "anti-American, Red, Communist." I wanted to yell back, to argue, to defend my father. Then I remembered his suggestion, and I started to feel strong and unaffected by their words. I knew how much my father loved his country. I stood for a moment, staring back at the boys. Then I turned and walked away. They never bothered me again.

"Why are they investigating daddy?" I asked mother. I had watched her sorting through boxes for many days. It was always difficult for her to answer personal questions. After a moment's pause, she explained how some of the trade unions had become corrupt and were used for the personal gain of a few. Father, she said, wanted to show through the investigation that he and the UAW were honest, sincere and doing good work.

When mother finished working on father's personal financial statements—his income tax returns, canceled checks, savings account records, real estate transactions, bank statements, U.S. Savings Bonds—she turned everything over to Carmine Bellino, the Committee's accountant. Bellino found that father had purchased $1,000 in Nash-Kelvinator stock in 1948 and sold it in 1956. Over the eight-year period he had made $1.26, 16 cents a year, which when revealed in court prompted labor writer Jack Herling to send a note up to father on the witness stand: "Reuther — the fox of Wall Street."

His personal records showed that his salary ranged from $1,730 in 1936 to $20,920 in 1957. Speeches and writings had netted him $11,290, which he turned over to a scholarship fund for the children of union members. (He always donated his honoraria, saying he should live on his union salary, not the spotlight given his position in the labor movement.)

Accountant Bellino testified that father "would submit expense accounts to his union within the per diem . . . It ranged from $7.50 a day to $12.00 a day. I found in instances where he was . . . on business for the AFL-CIO; during that period of time if he did accept the check from the AFL, he would not submit a bill to the UAW. He would elect to receive the smaller amounts and turn in to the union the $40 or $50 per diem from the AFL."

During the inquest, father quoted Senator Goldwater from a television appearance in which he stated, "Kohler had a right not to have a union if he can win a strike." Father commented: "This is a fundamental question. Only the employees—under the law of these United States—can make the decision whether they want a union and which union. An employer cannot make that decision without violating the law. I would like to know if you think under the Taft-Hartley Act, that a company can decide not to have a union and destroy that union? I maintain they can't."

GOLDWATER: I will tell you what: someday you and I are going to get together and lock horns.

FATHER: We are together now and I would like to ask you right now . . .

GOLDWATER: You save that.

FATHER: I am asking a fundamental question.

GOLDWATER: Wait a minute, Mr. Reuther. You are not asking the questions. I am asking the questions. If you want to save that someday . . .

FATHER: I am seeking advice.

GOLDWATER: You come out to Arizona and enjoy the bright sunshine and clean air and save it for then . . . I just want to advise Mr. Reuther of one thing: that he is going to be attacked by me.

FATHER: Attack me on the issues.

GOLDWATER: I would suggest, Mr. Reuther, that you do the same and quit calling me a moral coward and a political hypocrite, a man that ought to see a psychiatrist and Lord knows what else you told the boys in the back room...

McCLELLAN: Can you folks not get off somewhere and talk this out?

CURTIS: Was it alleged . . . that some of the United Electrical Workers leadership was communistic?

FATHER: Oh yes, it was alleged . . . Senator Curtis, I happen to be . . .

CURTIS: Wait a minute, you have answered the question and I have not yielded to you for a speech.

FATHER: Mr. Chairman, I am a very patient man; but I am still an American citizen with certain rights, and I am going to exercise them whether the Senator wants me to or not . . . You take isolated newspaper clippings, pick up this, pick up that, then you try to fabricate a conclusion. . . And if you think it will get you political votes, you go ahead, because you are fooling yourself. The people of this country are going to look at you and say: "What are you doing about unemployment, what are you doing about the farmers, what are you doing about schools?" And these are the things that will determine the election issues in 1958 and 1960.

CURTIS: All right, Mr. Reuther. This isn't the first time you have cluttered up our records here with attacks on members of the Committee. I repeat there is no other citizen in the United States that shows so much disrespect for the Senate of the United States as you.

FATHER: I might say that I have never been treated so disrespectfully as I have been treated by certain members of the Republican minority that sit here. . .

On the last day of the hearings, Senator Mundt told father, "Certainly there is no evidence on the records we have before us of corruption in so far as your activities are concerned." And Goldwater told Bobby Kennedy, "You were right. We never should have gotten into this thing."

With the investigation completed, the McClellan Committee prepared to disband. Goldwater made a statement to the press that Bobby Kennedy was running out on his investigation. When Kennedy got Goldwater on the phone, he asked him, "Why did you say a thing like that?"

"Oh, that's politics," Goldwater whimpered.

The right-wingers kept up the dirty politics. They enlisted the aid of an ex-convict named Joe Kamp, who was an expert at slander and character assassination. According to the *Washington Post*, Kamp had the good wishes and financial assistance of Senator Goldwater.

Pamphlets appeared, smearing father with outrageous lies. One was titled, "Meet the Man Who Plans to Rule America." Another read:

> He is a smart, smug, arrogant labor boss. He is a bold, shrewd, foul-mouthed agitator. He is a vile purveyor of vicious slander. He is a ruthless, reckless, lawless labor goon. He is a persistent prevaricator. He is a cunning conspirator. He is a rabid anti-anti-communist . . . a slick, sordid, conniving politician . . . rabble-rousing opportunist . . . Walter Reuther is an evil genius.

Sometimes father would receive hate letters. One batch came from Vivian Vance, the actress who played Ethel Mertz in the popular TV show *I Love Lucy*. Her letters vehemently condemned father's ideas and activities.

A woman from Seattle wrote a letter that arrived one Valentine's Day: "It has been a source of much irritation to me over the years to observe your Commissar intelligence at work . . . I will appreciate your dropping dead and going to hell as soon as you can arrange it. Why didn't you and Victor stay in Russia?" Signed, "Your Valentine."

Senator Joe McCarthy had sent a telegram criticizing father's criticism of Teamsters President Dave Beck for taking the Fifth Amendment during recent hearings. McCarthy wired that he had never heard father complain about Communists taking the Fifth. "This double standard of morality is something you must have picked up during your school days in Moscow . . . you have long been a disgrace to the workingmen you claim to represent."

In his reply, father pointed out that McCarthy's own 1946 campaign for a Wisconsin Senate seat had been supported by avowed Communists, including one Harold Christoffel, "the notorious and ruthless Communist leader of UAW local 248 in the Allis-Chalmers plant in West Allis, Wisconsin . . . To refresh your memory, may I remind you that your Communist supporter, Christoffel, was expelled from the UAW and later was convicted and sent to federal prison?

In a letter to Senator Jack Kennedy, father talked about his appreciation for his critics:

> In my rare moments of philosophical reflection, I sometimes think that the measure of the attack against the UAW and its leadership is in a sense a compliment. I always feel more comfortable and reassured when professional hate mongers, like Joe Kamp and Edward Rumely, attack us as stooges of the Kremlin and simultaneously the Communists attack us as agents of Wall Street imperialism. With both fanatic extremes attacking us for opposite reasons, we feel assured that we are going down the democratic middle...

Occasionally father was home in time to watch the evening news. Then he and I would watch *Perry Mason*. Once in a while we would stumble across the *I Love Lucy* show, and father would laugh and hiss whenever Vivian Vance came on the screen. These casual times together were precious. We would sit on the couch in the den, munching red grapes or whatever was in season. (We kept a small bowl between us for the seeds.) I felt I was his close friend. That made me proud. I identified with his goals and his personality. He was so decent and forthright—rather like Raymond Burr's Perry Mason. But father's life was *real*, and I was his lucky daughter.

CHAPTER TWENTY-FOUR

OUR
LADY
OF
HYDE PARK

"Lisa is a little fish who likes to swim upstream,
If she keeps on swimming, she will someday find her dream."
— Eleanor Roosevelt's couplet for me

Our family never drove long distances alone. One of father's personal bodyguards would accompany us. I remember seeing guns bulging from their waists. It frightened me, but so did the thought of someone attacking my father.

One of the bodyguards told a story about a trip he'd made with father through New Jersey. The governor had called for a limousine and a police escort for father, thinking that would please him. Instead, it made him very uncomfortable. Whenever they would come to a town, the sirens blared and the citizens stared, trying to see who the big shot was in the back seat. Finally, father asked the driver to pull over and switched places with his bodyguard. They resumed their travels, the guard in back, smiling and waving to onlookers, father up front chatting with the driver.

On one trip east, we were driving Linda to Putney, with a two-day stop at Hyde Park to visit Mrs. Eleanor Roosevelt. Father smiled while describing how "Mrs. R" had complained to him about the infrequency of our visits. Since FDR's death, my parents had managed a visit every summer. Mrs. R knew how hectic father's schedule was. Now that Linda was studying in the Northeast, it would be easier for us to see her at Hyde Park.

170

As a traveler, father was frugal and efficient. We left early in the morning so we could complete the 13-hour drive in one day. This meant long periods of stillness for Linda and me. And father was a bit of an autocrat about the windows and radio — only he could adjust them.

How boring those long trips were. "Are we almost there?" I asked, barely an hour out of Detroit. I liked to feel the wind blow against my face as the car rushed forward. It helped break the monotony. I longed to be out with the trees, wind and sky instead of being cooped up in a car. Linda and I would jockey for a place by a back-seat window. The car, an Oldsmobile 98, had electric windows. I would try to sneak the window down gradually. If father didn't notice, I would consider it a small victory. Inevitably his fine hair would begin to dance across his face. "Shut the window."

"Please father, let me keep it open a little." He knew I would keep trying to suit myself. "Only a quarter of an inch and no more," he replied, driving his usual hard bargain.

Mother shared the front seat with the bodyguard-driver. She had trouble with her spine. It was often painful for her to travel. She sat on a small rubber inner tube that cushioned her back against the car's vibrations.

Father sat with us in the back, behind mother, reading the *New York Times* or some work-related papers. His concentration made the car seem like a library.

My parents' friendship with Mrs. R dated from FDR's wartime administration, when father had been instrumental in planning matériel production for America and her allies.

The practical intelligence of the "young green apple" from West Virginia had impressed the President, who valued him as a friend and advisor. Their relationship extended to work on anti-trust laws and social legislation and continued until the President's death. Father described Mrs. R as his "ear to the President."

"She saw great promise in Walter Reuther, with whom she had developed a close friendship in the war years," wrote author Tamara K. Hareven. "She idealized him as an intelligent, broad-minded, idealistic labor leader. She especially admired his lack of dogmatism.

His experience, world travel, and work in different countries gave him an international outlook that other labor leaders, as well as management, missed. She saw in him a hope for a 'sane and wise leadership' for labor and the whole nation."

Like father, Mrs. R was not afraid to express her own opinions. They shared a spontaneous enthusiasm to create workable solutions to human suffering. As Anna Roosevelt Halsted wrote: "Walter and mother, despite a generation gap, had mutual concerns about humanity throughout the world. When they met, no time was wasted in reminiscence as they laid plans for further action."

In 1945, father had been in a taxi on his way to a White House meeting with Mrs. R when the radio announcer stopped to announce that President Franklin Roosevelt had died at his home in Warm Springs, Georgia. Father was shocked. "I was to meet with Mrs. R to discuss plans for assisting the poor," he later told me. "The news shattered my concentration. I had been listing different proposals to present to her. But destiny had its own plans."

I was 11 years old on this visit to see Mrs. R. Hyde Park was like an ancient fairytale. Mrs. R's house was the old Van Kill furniture factory that farmers had worked in many winters ago. She lived very simply, considering her aristocratic background. I sensed the richness of her life as I explored the house, filled with gifts from friends around the world. Some of her most treasured were from unknown friends, and she would point them out as we toured.

The library was my favorite room—shelf after shelf of books, many inscribed by their authors. After dinner, our family would retire to the library for tea. And tea was the cue for father and Mrs. R to start their lively discussions. She was one of the few people who could outdebate my father. Both had strong opinions and a passion for expressing them. As mother, Linda and I sat listening to them exchange ideas, I sensed that my father was restraining himself in the presence of Mrs. R. Generally assertive, now he was mild-mannered and deferential. Their relationship touched my heart.

One evening, our group was joined by Lorena Hickok, a sensitive writer and close friend of Mrs. R's. Our hostess was calling father's attention to different issues, like the Cold War. Mrs. R was insisting that father meet with Nikita Khrushchev — an historic meeting that would soon come to pass. Then she turned to Lorena Hickok: "You should write a biography about Walter." Father was embarrassed. There had been other books about father's contribution to the labor movement and the world. His modest nature compelled him to shun the idea of any more. Once again, Mrs. R had the last word: "Don't be silly, Walter; yours is a marvelous story to tell."

During the days, we all gathered at the outdoor pool. As I dived into the water, father and Mrs. R would dive back into the issues of the day. I was more comfortable in the water, but their conversations were fascinating. Sometimes Mrs. R would address me. Shy around her, I would choke up a reply, then disappear beneath the water.

Mrs. R swam with steadiness and grace. On this warm September day, she dove into the pool and swam to the shallow end where I was standing.Putting her arm in mine, she challenged me to a race to the other side: "Let's see who can swim to the other side first, Lisa." I balked. "You can do it, Lisa," father called. "After all, you are my little fish."

Swimming was second nature to me. Mrs. R and I glided across the pool, our arms and legs moving in time. I think she was restraining herself just to put me at ease. We swam the crawl on the first lap. When Mrs. R touched the end, she changed to the side stroke. The pace was relaxed. I followed her lead. As we gently returned to the shallow end, Mrs. R gave me a hug. "Good swim, Lisa. Let's do it again tomorrow." I blushed as usual. I wanted to reach out to this noble woman who had that rare ability to share life with almost anyone. "Y-yes, I'd love it," I stammered.

Waking up in Hyde Park was magical. Linda and I shared a small bedroom upstairs. If it was early, we would go downstairs in our pajamas and cuddle up with mother and father in bed. The sheets were golden silk with lace borders. I had never seen such wealth. Mrs. R was unpretentious, but she had many possessions that reflected her aristocratic background. Her house brimmed with exotic details.

After showering, we would all gather on the sun porch for breakfast. Several small square tables stood at intervals throughout the room. Each was meticulously set with fine linens and silver. It was all rather intimidating, especially with Mrs. R sitting across from me.

Breakfast was toast with butter, marmelade and honeycomb. "You can chew the wax with the honey," Mrs. R explained. I tried some; it had a horrible texture and the wax stuck to my teeth. A complicated way to sweeten toast, I thought.

When everyone had finished, the butler would bring in a tray lined with finger bowls, each filled with warm water with a slice of lemon on the edge. Embroidered linen towels waited by for drying. This ritual was my favorite part of the meal.

Our visit coincided with the birthday of Mrs. R's son, Franklin Jr. It was his 45th birthday, but by the excitement in the air, it could have been a big party for a small child. The sun porch sparkled with decorations. As guests filled the room, father noticed that Mrs. R was nowhere to be seen. She had not been at breakfast, either. "I think Mrs. R is up to something," he whispered to me. "She's been hiding all morning."

When our hostess finally appeared, everyone rose to welcome her. She apologized for not being present when her guests had arrived and began to move from table to table as the meal progressed. She conversed with each person as if he or she were her best friend and only guest. Just before the cake was served, Mrs. R stood up and directed our attention to small porcelain candy dishes, one at every place setting. Inside each was a handwritten poem (she'd been up past midnight composing them), depicting some characteristic of the individual. She then requested everyone to stand up and read their verses.

As my turn to read approached, I started to sweat. Mother sensed my embarrassment and held my hand as I stood up. Inside my bright blue dish was a slip of paper with these lines:

"Lisa is a little fish who likes to swim upstream,
"If she keeps on swimming, she will someday find her dream."

I was puzzled. What did it mean? Maybe Mrs. R was writing about my love of the water. Or was she referring to my struggles growing up? She too had been torn, coming up in high society with the world

174

suffering around her. The poem made me feel special. Maybe Mrs. R was clairvoyant. I kept this paper tucked away inside its beautiful dish for years.

While I was growing up, mother would often speak of Mrs. R. I had met her at testimonial dinners and UAW conventions. But it wasn't until our family began visiting her at Hyde Park that I knew her as a friend. She had great compassion and a powerful inner radiance. She seemed to share father's realization of the interdependence of all human beings. Of a wealthy New York family, she had transcended the limits of her own class to embrace the whole of humanity.

It had not been easy for Mrs. R to follow this inner call. Her beautiful mother had mocked her plain features as a girl. She was shy and self-conscious. During one of her parents' soirees, young Eleanor had hidden in the attic and cried. She felt different and could not bear the shallowness of these affairs. Yet from these fragile beginnings, Mrs. R grew to become the world's First Lady, loved by millions.

Her story touched my soul. My parents had always encouraged me to serve others. As I grew up, Mrs. R's example of overcoming inner obstacles to benefit humanity quickened my purpose.

Our last day Mrs. R gave us a guided tour of the historic family estate where, as a young girl, she had met Franklin. He was her fifth cousin once removed. After dancing at one of their family gatherings, Franklin told his mother, "Cousin Eleanor has a very good mind." Mrs. R was alive with stories about Franklin and their children. She described the family feud between herself and Franklin's mother—a strong-willed, domineering woman, who often browbeat Eleanor. But much time had passed and Mrs. R spoke about these difficulties with a wisdom and detachment.

I listened closely as she spoke, a strange new world of family experiences opening up before me. As she showed us the children's bedrooms, she talked about the senior Mrs. Roosevelt's opinions on how she had wanted them raised. It was only when Franklin contracted infantile paralysis at Campobello that Eleanor saw she had to assert herself and abandon her role of submissive daughter-in-law.

"You see," Mrs. R continued, "Franklin's mother wanted him to retire from public life and lead the life of a country gentleman. But I knew this would destroy him." With Mrs. R's support, Franklin resumed his law practice and his political career. Time would tell who best knew Franklin's needs and abilities.

Moving into the hallway, Mrs. R took mother by the hand, myself close behind. A large wooden display case enclosed the delicate christening gowns Eleanor and Franklin had worn as infants. Made of delicate white lace and finely woven cloth, the dresses symbolized a world unknown to me. I had never been christened or baptized. My parents were absorbed in the trade-union movement, with no time for organized religion. Grossvater had told his sons, "The way to demonstrate you love God is to love your fellow man." The golden rule was my parents' religion.

But I could not take my eyes off the beautiful dresses. Seeing my infatuation, Mrs. R stood next to me, pointing out the small buttons and handwork on the clothes. "We were raised in a very proper manner," she said. "Religion was not practiced only one day a week." I remembered a passage father had read me about Mrs. R's morning prayers as a child: "You grew up with the feeling that you had a share in some great spiritual existence beyond the everyday round of happenings." Seeing the Christening gowns stirred something inside me. I longed to experience this world of devotions and deep traditions.

"Come, Lisa," someone called. I blinked away my daydream to find that the others had gone downstairs. Following two steps at a time, I rejoined the group by the front door. "Now we will see the gardens," said Mrs. R.

The grounds were spacious, with many old trees and hedges. The wind made evergreen branches reach out as if to grab any passers-by. The gardens tossed against the blue sky. I imagined being on an enormous ship in the middle of an ocean. The undulating trees were the waves caressing the vessel as it swayed back and forth. Suddenly, Mrs. R directed us to Franklin's grave. We paused silently. The stillness held within it a sense of eternity. I beheld a depth in Mrs. R's face, absorbed in the past yet alive with the present.

"My life is over," she had told reporters when Franklin died. Yet she rose from her sorrow to become a citizen of the world. The end had been just a beginning.

This sense of history, the passage of energy through changing forms, had saturated our tour of Hyde Park. Mrs. R's personal account reflected her enduring affection and sense of humor. Her spirit had gone to her husband's grave, and beyond.

My father had worked closely with FDR. I saw his strong emotions as we stood by the graveside. I didn't realize much. Yet barely a dozen years later, I would wander his own gardens, the ones he had lovingly planted with mother, and realize much more. And remember Mrs. R.

Our family with Mrs. Roosevelt on my first visit to Hyde Park. Linda is at the far right. I am in front.

CHAPTER TWENTY-FIVE

"THE MEANEST GIRL IN THE WORLD"

"The workers, the workers — is that all you think about, father?"

— Me, exploding at father

While I was in junior high school, mother would arrange for me to stay with the family of one of my teachers whenever she and father were traveling. Because my parents were very loving, I was able to cope with long periods of separation from them. Sometimes they would be gone for a month or six weeks. Mother was the best letter writer, so I would receive a day-by-day description of their activities. Also, father had always included me in his projects. He would explain the issues of an upcoming negotiation or the nature of a speech he would be making before Congress. So I felt that he was doing something important and that I was part of it.

When he was home, I was getting up for school as he was getting up for work. Sometimes I would go into my parents' bedroom to chat with him. His routine was to shave after he showered, dressed in his suit pants and a sleeveless cotton undershirt. His body appeared well balanced, despite the shattering injury to his right arm. He showed me the bullet holes in his arm and midsection. Although they had mended, the damage was obvious from all the scars. "Look at this muscle, Lisa," he boasted, flexing his right arm. "I worked like hell to keep this arm moving."

I hadn't realized how extraordinary father's recovery had been. Through his determination, spirit, and positive thinking, he did, matter-of-factly, what others had considered impossible.

Father had strong convictions about worker benefits. Whether medical coverage, guaranteed annual wage, protection for the elderly—all were part of every worker's inalienable rights as a human being. The UAW was pioneering those benefits, and father would discuss them with childlike enthusiasm.

Despite the hectic schedule and grueling negotiations, father's appreciation for his life's work never flagged. "What a wonderful opportunity we have, Lisa. For the first time in history, mankind can conquer the crippling enemies of hunger, disease, and ignorance. We hold within our hands the great responsibility of rising to this challenge."

My lengthy stays with other families only increased my appreciation for my mother and father. Their lives moved to fulfill their altruistic goals. I wondered why out of billions of people I had been born into this special family whose ideals transcended my childish interests.

I understood and obeyed most of my parents' security restrictions for Linda and me, but one rule that seemed unreasonable was that I was never to ride my horse Charlie on the paved roads. I had to limit my jaunts to the pastures and dirt roads near our house. After years of riding in the same area, I grew rebellious.

Once Linda was away at private school, there was no competitor to ride Charlie. Several of my friends had horses, so every afternoon was an escapade. My dog, Soapy, followed us everywhere. Linda had adopted him as a young puppy, sneaking him onto the property before asking our parents. The Williams family, from whom Linda received the pup, lived atop a huge hill near our house. Since Soapy had a bow-tie pattern on the fur of his chest, we decided to name him after Michigan's Governor G. Mennen ("Soapy") Williams, whose trademark was a green and white polka-dot bow tie.

Linda built a fenced-in area in one of the small sheds for Soapy. I came out with her every day when she fed him. A month went by before she broke the news to our parents of the newest family member.

At last Soapy was free to run around the property with our other animals.

Soapy spent much of his time sitting next to Charlie as the horse grazed in the open pasture. When it was time to put on Charlie's bridle, Soapy would walk around with anticipation. Then he positioned himself at Charlie's back heels, where he stayed as we rode, even during a gallop.

One day, I was overcome by the temptation to meet one of my friends at her house. She lived on a dirt road that paralleled the one we usually rode. To reach her, I had to travel a short distance on a paved road. It was minimal, I told myself; I'm not really breaking a rule. We had no sooner set off down the pavement when Soapy was struck by an oncoming car. I was horrified. The driver stopped as Soapy reeled in pain—then died. Sobbing, I rode Charlie back home. The car followed with the body of our faithful dog in the trunk. My disobedience had cost Soapy his life.

My parents were upset with my rebellious behavior. At the same time, they knew what a bitter lesson I had learned. The following morning father helped me bury Soapy. After digging a large hole in a sandy area next to the dog pen, he struggled to carry Soapy's body to the burial site. I was amazed to see how difficult it was for him to lift his dead body. Dead weight, he puffed, is much heavier than live.

The tears began to pour down my cheeks. I felt horrible. I looked at father and suddenly became angry. "Why aren't you crying, father? Didn't you love Soapy?"

Touched by my affection for my canine friend, father's eyes began to water. He tried to show me his devotion to the dog. I was sensitive and this had been a painful lesson. Pacified by this tardy display of grief, I helped him cover the body with sand. Then we tied together two sticks and placed a primitive cross at Soapy's head. I finished the burial by encircling the area with stones. Arm in arm, we walked back to the house.

Father always made an extra effort for his daughters. Especially when it came to our homework, he found pleasure in guiding our attempts to learn, but sometimes he contributed more than his fair share.

When I was 12, my science teacher asked the class to write a short essay on "The Balance of Nature." We had been studying the interdependence of all living things.

When I returned home from school, I was worried about the assignment. I had only a vague idea of what to write. But I knew father could help me. His travels throughout the world had given him a special insight into the delicate balances within nature. Especially instructive was his trip to India, where the problems of hunger and population growth were so critical. When he returned home at six, I explained the assignment, and he kindly agreed to help me. As he spoke, I took notes.

"Today we are witnessing the destruction of nature's balance, Lisa, because man is interfering. We have to use our superior reasoning abilities to protect the natural resources instead of exploiting them. Our industrial revolution poses an extreme example of this disruption of nature, like the problems of pollution and disposal of nuclear waste."

Man's lust for profit, he explained, was destroying his respect for life and the principles of conservation. "It is our responsibility as humans to preserve nature's balance for future generations."

The next day I organized my notes. Father had been a great teacher. The essay flowed easily from my pen. A week later the paper came back with an "A" and the compliment, "excellent analysis." I showed father and we both laughed. "You are the one who deserves the 'A,' daddy."

Alongside my adoration of father ran an ongoing battle of wills. I saw that he thought he was right most of the time. Unaware of the wisdom that age offers, I developed the obnoxious habit of never admitting I was wrong. How often I was expected to embrace my parents' ideals as my own. I recognized them, but they didn't always fit in with my child's world. My early childhood had been frightening. My parents were my only shelter from fear; yet their very lives had brought on that fear. It took a lot of courage to say what I was feeling. Sometimes I exploded.

I recall one evening vividly. It was a tense time for father. He had returned home late from Solidarity House. "The demands are historic," he told mother as we sat down to dinner. "I'm not sure how far to go concerning the contract." He listened attentively as she made some suggestions.

My own thoughts were elsewhere. Father had been gone for several weeks with contract negotiations. Why does he spend so little time with mother and me? I fumed. This is his first evening home and still he talks about his work. For ten minutes, I sat quietly. But my mind was becoming more and more agitated by my parents' conversation. Father made a remark about a particular part of the proposed contract. Suddenly I heard myself mocking his words: "The workers, the workers — is that all you think about, father? Can't you think about Linda, mother and me?"

My outburst struck a nerve. Emotionally he recoiled, then asked me to apologize. I refused. I was stubborn like him, but his age had tempered this characteristic with experience and fairness. My childish needs had made my irrational outburst cruel. And I refused to admit that I might have been wrong.

Father took me by the hand into the hallway. "Bring me a belt from my closet," he commanded. In spite of my protests he used the belt, spanking my bottom six times — not very hard. The humiliation was far more crushing. Still I would not acknowledge my rudeness. "Why can't you say you are sorry, Lisa? You are the meanest girl in the world. Go to your room until I tell you to come out."

I felt I had been condemned for life. A half-hour passed before father came to my bedroom. It seemed like forever. In tears, I apologized. He hugged me and together we went into the living room.

"You see, Lisa, it isn't easy for me, either. I am challenging the most powerful corporations in the world. The pressures are enormous."

Here we go again, thought the "meanest girl in the world." Yet father saw in me a kindred spirit. The bond between us was deep, even mystical. In later years, I would call him my "soul mate."

CHAPTER TWENTY-SIX

CIVIL
RIGHTS
BEGIN
AT HOME

"Just sit down with a peasant in a village of Northern India
and take on the task of trying to explain to him why Amer-
ica, conceived in freedom and dedicated to the proposition
that all people are created equal, a nation that can split the
atom, that can make a pursuit ship go three times as fast as
sound and yet, in this 20th Century, we can't live together
in brotherhood and we continue to discriminate against the
Negroes. It will tax your ingenuity, and you will give them
no answers. You can only give them excuses. And excuses
are not good enough, if we are going to win the struggle of
freedom in the world."
— Walter Reuther, on racial inequality in America.

Family trips, like the ones to Hyde Park, broke the tension of our public life. Often, we would travel west—to places like the Grand Tetons, Yellowstone, and Mesa Verde—to explore our country's natural wonders. Usually, we would meet a UAW member from the region who could show us the sights.

I loved these trips. We were with father constantly, more than any other time. Of course, we weren't really alone; the bodyguard shadowed us everywhere. And there were the normal sibling tensions, Linda and I at each other over trifles. But the public pressures were gone.

Mother's fragile spine often kept her away from the rugged activities. Father, Linda, and I would leave her reading at the lodge while we went hiking with knapsacks and a picnic lunch. While riding the ski lift at Aspen or walking a narrow log across a mountain stream,

I also felt somewhat spineless. Why was I always so frightened? Other kids seemed to be able to do these things without fear. Linda, of course, would tease me. Our age difference made it easy for her to do many things I couldn't. Aware of this, father would give me some special attention.

Another reason for our travels: Father was an avid fisherman. Nothing pleased him more than a chance to angle. One time at Jackson Hole, father was up and out by 5 a.m., armed with bait, a box lunch, and his favorite fly rod. It rained most of that morning. Mother, Linda and I stayed inside the lodge and watched the water fall from the sky. We knew father was out there somewhere, braving the elements in boots and a waterproof suit.

The sun had set that evening and still no father. Mother soothed our fears: "Your father is a young boy at heart when it comes to fishing. You can expect him to be late."

Linda and I were just going to bed when the door opened around dusk. There stood father, fairly bursting with bliss and carrying his catch as evidence.

On another occasion father had been in Mississippi on business and was staying near a place known for its good fishing. He always carried a portable fly rod with him in his briefcase, just in case. This time it paid off. He went fishing and caught such an enormous fish that he had it stuffed and sent back to Detroit.

But father arrived before the fish. Overcome with pride and enthusiasm, he boasted to everyone at Solidarity House about the size of his catch. Every day he phoned the airlines inquiring about a special box. Difficulty had arisen with the baggage and freight. For several days, the fish could not be located, sparking a flood of fish jokes at Solidarity House. When it finally did arrive, the airlines phoned father with the good news. "What was so important in that box anyway?" asked the curious clerk. "My reputation," he replied.

Father shared his love of fishing with my two cousins, Peter and Tommy Wolf. Sometimes I would tag along, but then I had to help put worms on the hooks and keep them ready. As I grew up, my increasing sensitivity to living things compelled me to stop this. I actually felt horrible when father would catch a fish. So I secretly prayed that he would return empty-handed.

Father understood my romantic ideas about nature and mountain climbing. I longed for these private experiences, for the chance to be alone with him, undisturbed.

In a letter to Ceil Schwartz, a friend from Rockport, Maine, father wrote:

> May said that she would talk to you about my hiking boots that she purchased in Rockport. I am having them sent to your house and I hope it will not be too much bother for you to exchange them for a half-size larger and a little wider if they have them. These boots are very important to me in my relationship with Lisa, for I have promised her that as soon as I get my hiking boots we will do some hiking together. Being a good mother, you will understand my problem. I hope this is not too much trouble.

Once in Colorado, we decided to climb to the top of a nearby mountain. It appeared to be about a mile to the summit. No one will be up there, I thought. But when we arrived at the top, we heard voices, and shortly a middle-aged man walked up to my father.

"You're Walter Reuther, aren't you?" he exclaimed, stretching out his hand. My father was wearing his dark glasses, we were in the middle of nowhere and still there was no privacy. My mind was growling. Sensing his intrusion, the man graciously departed. I suppose I should learn to accept this, I told myself. But I knew the lack of privacy bothered my parents, too.

Once on another hike in Colorado, we met Arizona Congressman Stuart Udall on a ridge overlooking a beautiful valley. Father was quite surprised to find his conservation colleague in the midst of complete wilderness. (Udall was later appointed Secretary of the Interior by President Kennedy.) As they walked, father couldn't get over their coincidental meeting. "Isn't it amazing?" he mused. "Maybe someone is making these arrangements for us."

For several summers running, Linda attended the National Music Camp in Interlochen, Michigan. During her summer in the university division, I joined her as an intermediate.

Despite Interlochen's competitive mood, I preferred to lose myself in the natural setting of the Northern Michigan woods. I could always hear hundreds of students practicing their scales or concertos in the tiny practice rooms or outside in the woods and surrounding fields. It was a disciplined atmosphere, where talent was appreciated and nurtured. I majored in dance and choir, and took private cello lessons as well. An accomplished potter at Putney, Linda studied ceramics, sang in the choir, and played the flute.

Mother and father's visits to Interlochen highlighted our summer. Father's schedule did not permit him to make the five-hour drive very often. During my first two seasons, however, Van Cliburn gave concerts, and my parents made it a point to attend.

A few years earlier, the pianist had performed Tchaikovsky's "First Piano Concerto" in Moscow and won international fame. The evening he was to perform the same piece at Interlochen, I was delayed by my nature-lore class on the far side of campus. I ran the entire distance to the Kresge Pavillion, walked quickly down the long steps of the covered area, and found my family in the third row. Breathless, I gave each of them a hug and took a seat. The audience grew still. At that instant a man with pen and paper leaned forward behind father. "Excuse me, Mr. Reuther, could I have your autograph?"

I was furious. I hadn't seen my parents for weeks. Turning abruptly, I retorted: "Excuse me, but father came here to visit his children, not to give out autographs." The man was taken aback, but I felt satisfied. Glancing at father, I saw him blush with embarrassment. The moment passed as Van Cliburn walked on stage.

After the concert, father gave me a short lecture on social etiquette. Nevertheless, I remained upset by the man's intrusion. Many times my parents had explained that now and then we would have to sacrifice our privacy. But I was determined to protect those precious times our family had together. The autograph hunter was my nemesis.

Father's boundless energy was mystifying. "What makes Reuther tick?" was a frequent question among reporters and corporation executives alike. He became a curiousity simply because he wasn't motivated by money. He refused a salary increase; he shunned the social limelight; he subscribed to social issues long before they were in vogue.

He had witnessed the suffering of the miners in West Virginia. He had seen his peers throw stones at the black workers as they were hauled in open freightcars through his neighborhood in Wheeling. He could not shut his eyes to the plight of his fellow men and women, especially when they happened to be people in his own union.

Father's leadership was a delicate balance of thinking and feeling. He had to be in touch with the rank and file. He was their spokesman. But he also felt he had to lead them to a broader understanding of the great responsibility we have in making the democratic system work for the betterment of all society.

The structure of the UAW's constitution contained safeguards against bureaucracy. It was founded on the democratic principles embodied in the Constitution of the United States. So it was not surprising when its designer took an early stand against the violation of people's civil rights. Long before the rank-and-file workers appreciated the importance of this issue, father was forming his opinions and developing policy. As the economic rights of the workers were intrinsically tied to the health of the whole nation, so the civil rights of every individual citizen could not be separated from the overall strength of the democracy. And the union, he reasoned, could not isolate itself from these important issues, even if it contradicted the prejudice of individual members.

And there was plenty of prejudice — especially in the South — but father never budged from his civil rights convictions. Doug Fraser remembered several confrontations between UAW leadership and Southern locals. One time, father sent him to Memphis:

I did not realize how close it was to Mississippi. We had loaned them money to buy a new building on the condition that they would not have segregated toilets and water fountains. And the building goes up and they have "white" and "colored" washrooms. So Pat Greathouse and I were sent down there by your father. We got a court order and took the hall. We changed the locks and painted out the "colored" and "white" signs. Then they got a court order and took the hall back. Then instead of painting "white" and "colored," they painted "white" and "nigger." It was really terrible. I remember a meeting when I did not know if I was going to get out alive. They were furious with us.

There was this one fellow by the name of George Holloway. He got up from the black section and walked through the white section up to where I was at the stage. There was a cluster of tough guys waiting for me at the door and there wasn't any back exit. Well, George Holloway came up to me and said, "Come over here, I want to show you something." He took me over to the side window. I looked out and saw a lot of cars parked out there. He said, "Those are our fellows. Just let me tell you something. We know it took a lot of guts for you to come down here. And we're going to see that you get back to Detroit safely." And we won that battle. It was your father's initiative. They knew we were firm in our commitment.

Irving Bluestone described another confrontation in Birmingham, Alabama:

One of the problems we had was that the blacks were given only the most menial jobs. The shop committee took the position that they weren't going to permit blacks to be promoted into any other kind of work. In line with union principles I simply said to that shop committee, 'You can have your paychecks or you can have your prejudice, but you can't have both.' We made the breakthrough. Now, how does a union and its leadership get away with that during the period of such deep-set feelings of bias that existed in the South? Only because there was such a marvelous job done at the bargaining table. And, of course, Walter was a master at collective bargaining.

Bigoted locals were not the only ones upset by the union's stand on civil rights. In 1957, the radical right printed a pamphlet called "Behind the Plot to Sovietize the South." The pamphlet began: "This booklet tells about the activities of Walter Reuther and his collaborating White and Negro Communist, Socialist, and Marxist kind of labor agitators, who are mobilizing a massive offensive to impose an insidious civil rights program on the South."

Father saw racial injustice as the Achilles' heel of American democracy. Whenever he traveled outside the U.S. people would ask him about America's fight against prejudice.

I went to the foothills of the Himalaya Mountains, in a little village of three hundred people, and we had a meeting and I talked about America — what we were going through trying to bring to fulfillment the great promise of America. They didn't want to know how many Chevrolets General Motors made last year, or whether Chrysler fins had a bigger sweep than the Cadillac fins. They asked me about Montgomery, Alabama. Just sit down with a peasant in a village of Northern India and take on the task of trying to explain to him why America, conceived in freedom and dedicated to the proposition that all men are created equal, a nation that can split the atom, that can make a pursuit ship go three times as fast as sound and yet, in this 20th century, we can't live together in brotherhood and we continue to discriminate against the Negroes. It will tax your ingenuity, and you will give them no answers. You can only give them excuses. And excuses are not good enough, if we are going to win the struggle of freedom in the world.

As he took up the cause of civil rights, father had the opportunity to meet the movement's eloquent spokesman, the Reverend Dr. Martin Luther King, Jr. In 1959, father and Dr. King were together in Miami for a civil rights rally. As the sirens screamed and the patrol cars came skidding up to their hotel, father turned to King and chuckled, "What a couple of characters we turned out to be. We're really starting something!"

King admired father's labor leadership, especially his success in achieving benefits and dignity for working people. In one speech, he quoted father's example about power. "Real power is when you can have the world's largest, most powerful corporation say 'yes' when they want to say 'no.'"

In the coming years, father and King would correspond frequently. In a January 1959 letter, father wrote:

It is a great personal privilege to be associated with you in the struggle to advance the cause of human freedom and dignity and to do the practical job in the vineyards of American democracy, so that America's noble promise will be matched by practical performance.

The courage, devotion and dedication which you have given this cause are a source of inspiration for all of us who are joined with you.

And in a letter dated May 17, 1961, Dr. King wrote my father:

> More than anyone else in America, you stand out as the shining symbol of democratic trade unionism. Through your trials, efforts and your unswerving devotion to humanitarian causes, you have made life more meaningful for millions of working people. Through moments of difficulty and strong obstacles, you have stood firm for what you believe, knowing that in the long run "Truth crushed to earth will rise again." As I have heard you say, the true measure of a man is where he stands in moments of challenge and controversy, when the only consolation he gains is the quiet whisper of an inner voice saying there are things so eternally true and significant that they are worth dying for, if necessary. You have demonstrated over the years that you can stand up in moments of challenge and controversy. One day all of America will be proud of your achievements, and will record your work as one of the glowing epics of our heritage.

Martin Luther King Jr.

Martin Luther King Jr. and father forged ahead in the battle for civil rights.

CHAPTER TWENTY-SEVEN

MRS. R
AT
PAINT CREEK

"The real test of friendship and solidarity is not where one stands when the weather is fair and the sun is shining, but rather where he stands at a time of storm and stress. We will stand with you in Berlin no matter how strong and cold the Soviet winds blow from the East..."
— Walter Reuther, addressing
East and West Berliners , 1959

In 1959, as spring approached, father started an ambitious project. He had been invited to speak at the May Day Freedom Celebration in West Berlin. Twice the world had seen Germany torn by war. Finally, the Yalta conference had bisected Berlin. Now the Soviets controlled half the city and half of the country as well.

Father's German heritage inspired him in this assignment. As he arrived home from Solidarity House one evening, he was carrying an old-fashioned tape player and a German grammar book. For six weeks, he practiced German in speech and on paper. After a week of reciting phrases from the grammar, he began copying down key phrases he might use.

"Lisa, if I speak in German, then thousands of people behind the Iron Curtain will hear an affirmation of their hope for freedom."

I would sit with him for hours, intrigued by his patient practice. German grammar compelled a beginner like father to compose short, concise sentences, unlike the flowing phrases of his English speeches.

Father sat in a straight-backed chair, his brow knit in concentration. He spent hours studying in the den he'd built, its redwood panels blending with the wood hues of his desk. Whatever he did, he did well — whether making home improvements or meeting world leaders. And now he was drilling himself, practicing the language of his parents. He had complete confidence in his mission.

In the aftermath of World War II, the Allies had begun dismantling what remained of Germany's industrial base. Father was against this program. In 1949, he wrote to President Truman: "A major goal of your foreign policy is to prevent the spread of Communist totalitarianism and to preserve and strengthen democracy throughout the world. Establishment of a vital democracy in Western Germany is crucial to that goal. Needless dismantlement of German plants will deprive German workers of employment and will drive them, out of desperation, into the arms of the Communists."

Truman heeded father's warning and the counsel of others and called a halt to the demolition. West German Chancellor Konrad Adenauer later bestowed the country's highest civilian award on father for his fight to keep Germany's industry from disappearing.

At the May Day rally of 600,000, father was the principal speaker. He stood on a large platform, erected at the East-West border, so East Berliners could also hear.

"Berlin is once again the testing ground for freedom," father began in German:

It is not your freedom alone that is being challenged by Soviet tyranny. It is our freedom as well, for freedom is an indivisible value and when the freedom of one is threatened, the freedom of all is in jeopardy.

The real test of friendship and solidarity is not where one stands when the weather is fair and the sun is shining, but rather where he stands at a time of storm and stress. We will stand with you in Berlin no matter how strong and cold the Soviet winds blow from the East.... I can say in truthfulness that the only war in which the American people wish to engage is a war against poverty and hunger, against ignorance and disease. In such a war all will be victors. Stand fast, for you do not stand alone. The people of America — the people of the free world — stand firmly with you in friendship and solidarity.

The people's response was tremendous. Father departed Germany with renewed enthusiasm.

When father returned, he stayed home for several days, resting and answering his mail. I asked about his German speech and his face lit up with excitement. I teased him about his hoarse voice: "Did your German words wear down your throat, daddy?"

Excitement was a frequent guest in our household. One evening, father came home from the office and casually announced that in one week Eleanor Roosevelt was coming to visit. As it would be Mrs. R's first time at Paint Creek, my 11-year-old child's mind started spinning with plans. Maybe I could show her our horse, Charlie, or the hundreds of trees we had planted with our own hands; or father's beautiful handmade cabinets or the waterfall with the fish ladder. Our house itself was full of hidden curiosities. Built in stages, every room had a unique personality. I had been thrilled by Mrs. R's tour of Hyde Park; now it was my turn to reveal Paint Creek.

At its 1957 convention, the UAW had honored the former First Lady by making her a lifetime union member. Father's tribute to Mrs. Roosevelt read:

> In the early days of the New Deal, when a coal miner deep in the bowels of the earth looked up, there was Eleanor Roosevelt finding out how miners dug coal in the West Virginia coal mines.
>
> When a worker and his family living in the slums looked up, there was Eleanor Roosevelt finding out more about the problems of people who needed decent housing. When the sharecroppers were struggling to keep body and soul together ... Eleanor Roosevelt was out there in the fields with them.
>
> All over the world there are hundreds of millions of people who look at Eleanor Roosevelt as the outstanding symbol of human freedom and human decency, as a person of great sensitivity and understanding....

The news of Mrs. R's visit inspired mother, who found a pencil and paper and composed a list of things to do. She was highly organized, but very anxious. Making a list calmed her down.

At the top of the list was a thorough house-cleaning, with special attention to the master bedroom where Mrs. R would sleep. The rugs needed shampooing; the house needed fresh fruit and flowers; we'd prepare food in advance to minimize our time later in the kitchen; we'd ask Mrs. R's social secretary what she normally had for breakfast, plus her likes and dislikes in general and make sure to pen the Paint Creek animals during her stay. Mother never planned so carefully for a guest.

After school I would help mother clean. Just three days before Mrs. R's arrival, however, we encountered a serious problem. Serious to mother, anyway. I found it amusing. We had two large German shepherds who used to live by the guardhouse but had gradually earned the status of family pets. We also had a cocker spaniel, Trixie, as well as two cats, Pepper and Paprika. This colony of domestic animals had raised an enormous number of fleas and then dropped them into our woolen rugs.

Mother and I had been resting from cleaning, when we noticed the fleas. "Look, mummy, the rug is jumping up and down. *What* are those bugs?" After calling hardware stores and even a grain elevator, mother and I drove into town to buy some spray. Mother didn't want to use harsh chemicals. She was fearful of a clinging odor, or worse, an allergic reaction from Mrs. R. So we spent the evening spraying the downstairs and slept upstairs for the night.

The next morning, we descended for a flea body count. "They're still alive," mother moaned. "I'll bet they're immune to that spray."

We returned to the store for a stronger formula. The second application was more successful. Mother, however, still worried: What if a flea bit Mrs. R while she was sleeping? Mother would never forgive herself.

It was fun to see her. She was like a newlywed about to entertain her in-laws for the first time. Despite years of practice receiving diplomats and world leaders, there was a girlish shyness that increased her womanly beauty. "You're just like a little girl, mummy," I said, laughing at her nervousness to cover my own.

It was an autumn day, a perfect time for her visit. The burning bushes were bright red; the golden needles of the larch made it droop delicately to the ground. The more conventional maples, locusts and poplar, were all beautiful in their fall garb.

The intercom system rang. Picking up the phone, I heard the guard announce our guest's arrival. Out the window we could see father walking arm in arm with Mrs. R across the two wooden bridges and the long, winding path. He carefully protected her from slipping.

As they slowly crossed the second bridge, I made a beeline for an obscure corner. "Come on, Lisa," mother chuckled. "Who's a little girl now?" All of my big plans had suddenly disappeared.

As the front door opened, I carefully stayed in the background. After mother's greeting, father brought our guest over to me. "Here is our Lisa," he said, squeezing my shoulder. "She has been counting the days until your arrival" (But count on my red face to disclose my shyness!)

We adjourned to the living room for tea and coffee cake. Mother and I were quite reserved in the presence of our guest. Not father. With his usual exuberance, he showed his friend the table he was building. It was solid walnut, a corner-style table, that he had been unable to complete before Mrs. R's arrival. The top was finished, he explained between bits of cake, but the legs were not. In fact, he divulged, six A&P cans of peaches were now holding up the top. He pointed to the table and grinned: "We took the labels off in your honor."

Mother and I gasped. Had he really said that to our former First Lady? Mrs. R just laughed and laughed.

Then father launched into one of his favorite stories — the saga of the sheep. About a year after our coming to Paint Creek, father had decided to yield to our constant requests for more pets. So one spring day, we piled into the car and he took us out for a surprise. After a suspenseful drive, we arrived at on old farmhouse.

An elderly man approached and father explained that we were there to look at his sheep. I squealed with delight. Father let Linda and me pick out our own animals. We chose a mother and her two lambs, (both purportedly female) and named them Jezebel, Cleopatra and Clementine.

Their first summer with us, the sheep grazed peacefully, sharing the pasture with our horse. As the lambs grew, so did their desire to explore. By fall, mother sheep and her offspring had learned to squeeze under the rail fence where the grass was always greener. Father tried to contain the animals, but without much success. They were masters at breaking and entering.

The winter consigned the sheep to the barn. By the following spring, Jezebel, Cleopatra and Clementine were at it again. The delicate new growth on my mother's magnolias became their first victim. As their roaming increased, the plant fatalities multiplied.

Our pets were becoming a nuisance. What's more, Clementine was not a "she" after all. Our would-be ewe was growing horns which made their mark on people as well as animals. One evening, "she" turned on father and chased him across the two bridges over the creek. Darling Clementine's days with us were numbered.

Father's mind was made up. He knew Linda wouldn't care if he found a new home for the sheep. She had thrown her wooly pals over for Ricky Nelson and the heady life at school. But I was shocked. "They're my friends, daddy, members of our family. You can't just disown them."

Father squirmed, surprised by my deep feelings for the sheep. "They're just animals, Lisa. They'll be happy anywhere." Eddie (one of the guards) had offered to take care of them, he explained. His relatives had a farm in Northern Michigan, so the sheep would have room to roam. But ... I smelled mutton cooking.

The next day, when Eddie arrived to pick up father, I interrogated him about the sheep. Father hadn't briefed him and my suspicions were confirmed. As father walked briskly to the car, briefcase in hand, I blocked his way. "Daddy, you can't give the sheep to Eddie. He'll just eat them or sell them to slaughter." Trapped, father agreed to find a home for the sheep, then left for work.

After several weeks, father found an elderly couple who agreed to keep the sheep as pets. Father grinned at Mrs. R as he described the final farewell. "It was not enough that the couple had promised not to kill the sheep. Lisa even brought out a formal letter for them to sign: 'I hereby promise that these three sheep, Jezebel, Cleopatra and Clementine, will be allowed to live until they die naturally and will not be killed.'"

The document had astonished the new owners. Father explained to them how important it was for me to have their word of honor concerning the fate of the sheep. The old man signed with an "X," and his wife inscribed her name carefully underneath. Then she gave me a hug, saying, "Don't worry, honey, we'll look after them for you." I sensed her sincerity and felt satisfied I had spared my wooly friends from the slaughterhouse.

Mrs. R enjoyed the rambling folksy story. "You're a real fighter, Lisa, just like your father."

It was about this time that I stopped eating lamb and veal. Mother would prepare lamb chops on occasion, but I refused to eat them. It did not make sense, not since I had come to know those sheep. To eat their flesh seemed savage.

The second morning of Mrs. R's stay I awoke very early. My parents were still in bed upstairs in Linda's room. The house was quiet with a certain presence which I ascribed to Mrs. R.

By 6:30, my parents were stirring and shortly mother needed me to help prepare breakfast while father took his shower. We were having waffles and syrup, fruit salad and a favorite of Mrs. R's, herbal tea. The bright autumn sun filled the room that morning. Mrs. R entered the kitchen, looking equally effulgent. "Good morning, everyone." Her face glowed with energy. I was struck by her grace, her appreciation for small things, and her admiration for father's union work.

Mrs. R was a union member herself. She had joined the Newspaper Guild, although as a syndicated writer she wasn't required to. She was proud of her affiliation and was quoted as saying, "I would encourage every woman who works to join the union in her industry."

At eight o'clock father drove off with Mrs. R. My school bus wasn't due for another half-hour, and as mother and I cleaned up the kitchen, I thought about my classmates and myself—how vastly different our lives were. My teacher knew full well the reason for my absence and would be asking me to tell the class about Mrs. R's visit.

Waiting for that school bus, I was floating with anticipation. For once, I wasn't anxious about standing up to speak. My inhibitions flew away. Mrs. R had touched me deeply with her message: "You're a real fighter, Lisa, just like your father."

Father speaks in German to over 600,000 at the Berlin Wall.

The Roosevelt-Reuther team pioneered many causes for human dignity.

CHAPTER TWENTY-EIGHT

NIKITA
ON
NOB HILL

"We hung the likes of Reuther in Russia in 1917."
— Khrushchev to Kennedy at the Vienna summit, 1961

Father had certain sacred cows he would automatically defend with dogged devotion. His speeches were filled with optimistic phrases like "human freedom" and "brotherhood of mankind." I would embrace many of these ideas, but like most young adolescents, I did not fully appreciate the depth and significance of our democratic traditions.

Studying the American Constitution in Civics class was one thing; appreciating firsthand the fruits of this carefully constructed and noble form of government would take personal involvement.

In the post-war generation, we took a lot for granted. We did not have to defend democracy in Europe. And the Viet Nam tragedy tinged our perceptions about our own country. So when father would continually stress the differences between America and the Communist states, I did not grasp the real distinctions. I had studied Marx, Lenin and the Communist Manifesto in school. I saw their obsession with the state and their denial of individual freedom. But it was all theoretical.

Despite father's condemnation of Soviet oppression, he realized it was essential to have open communication with Communist leaders (contrary to his labor counterparts like George Meany, who seemed to think he could "wish" the Communists out of existence.) He emphasized the importance of dialogue among all the world's peoples. So in 1959, ignoring the official foreign policy of George Meany and the AFL-CIO, he arranged to meet with Soviet Deputy Premier Anastas I. Mikoyan, and later with Premier Nikita S. Khrushchev.

During his U.S. visit, Mikoyan expressed an interest in actually seeing AFL-CIO headquarters in Washington, just a block from the White House. Meany rejected Mikoyan's request. Father considered this narrow-minded. Along with three other vice presidents of the AFL-CIO, he invited the Soviet leader to lunch at a union building nearby where he could view the union's headquarters out the windows. Father invited Meany to join the luncheon party; and, of course, the labor boss was furious.

Father valued the chance to meet with the Soviet official and discuss face to face issues of mutual concern. He confronted Mikoyan about the Soviet's harsh suppression of Hungarians. He also brought up their unwillingness to work towards reunification of Berlin. When questioned by reporters about this unprecedented meeting between the Soviet government and American labor, father remarked: "I am told that there is ever present a danger that totalitarian leaders, unaccustomed to soliciting or heeding the views of others, may underestimate the mood and determination of free people to resist encroachment on their rights. I thought it wise to tell Deputy Mikoyan to his face ... that on the question of safeguarding the rights of free Berlin ... the American people are united."

Father felt the meeting had cleared the air. "The American trade union leaders understand the Communists better than the capitalists do," he had told Mikoyan. One who favored the exchange was Republican Senator John Sherman Cooper of Kentucky. "Walter Reuther did a major service for peace by his blunt exchange with the Kremlin's number-two man," he remarked.

Premier Nikita Khrushchev's visit to the U.S. was widely publicized. His public outbursts commanded everyone's attention: pouting because he was unable to go to Disneyland; removing his shoe at the UN and banging it on a desk.

As Khrushchev traveled in the U.S., he often asked, "Where are your workers? I want to meet with their spokesmen." He stated that U.S. workers were afraid that the Communist system would prove ours to be inferior!

George Meany remained steadfastly opposed to meeting with Khrushchev, and no leaders of the AFL-CIO were encouraged to meet with leaders of the Soviet government. Embarrassed that American labor had not responded to Khrushchev's challenge, the State Department phoned father's brother, Victor, at the UAW International Affairs Department in Washington, seeking his help. Victor and father got in touch with seven other union presidents who — disregarding Meany's wishes — met with the Soviet premier. A dinner was arranged for September 20, 1959, at San Francisco's Mark Hopkins Hotel on posh Nob Hill.

The Russian delegation arrived at the Golden Empire Room at exactly 8 o'clock. Uncle Victor greeted Khrushchev in Russian, to which the amazed Soviet Premier responded, "You speak Russian?" Victor replied in Khrushchev's own tongue, "Mr. Chairman, have you forgotten that I spent several years in your country?"

Skeptical of Victor's knowledge of Russian and the Soviet Union, Khrushchev wondered when that was. "In 1933 and 1934, in the Gorky Automobile Plant, named in honor of Molotov." Only recently had the former leader been exiled to Siberia. "Tell me, Mr. Chairman, is the Gorky Plant still named in honor of Molotov?" Khrushchev, his face turning white with rage, hissed, "Nyet. Today we call it Gorky Auto Works."

Father ushered Khrushchev to his seat at the head of the table. Before the arrival of the Premier, he had noticed that the large table legs stood exactly at the place where the honored guest was to sit. Fearing this would cause some discomfort he moved his chair slightly to the right. "Even though I have shifted you to the right, Mr. Chairman," father explained, "I assure you there is no political significance to it."

Laughing, Khrushchev responded: "No matter how much you move me I will still hold to a basic Communist position. Everything is fluid and everything progresses towards communism."

Thus began the fiery exchange between the Soviet Premier and the leader of America's auto workers. The simple adjustment of Khrushchev's dinner chair set a mood that would continue throughout the evening.

At one point father remarked: "I want to ask the Chairman: Is the Soviet Union prepared to contribute to the ending of the cold war by joining the United States and other countries through the United Nations ... in abolishing poverty and ignorance?"

A subdued Khrushchev answered into his napkin: "In our proposal, which I submitted on behalf of the U.S.S.R., it is made clear that the outlays on armaments would be greatly reduced and a certain percentage of the reduction switched to help underprivileged countries."

Father reminded Khrushchev of a proposal he submitted to President Truman in 1950. Father provided him with a copy then and there, suggesting they not wait for disarmament to begin. "Our proposal would create a better climate in which disarmament could be carried forward faster and more effectively."

They talked about Russian industrial designs and equipment in India and Soviet aid to Indonesia and Ethiopia. They discussed arms control and mutual inspections. Father kept asking, "Why can't we work together?" Khrushchev cited the presence of U.S. military bases around the edge of the U.S.S.R.

"The U.S. exploits the wealth of other countries—underdeveloped countries," the Premier observed. "So do England and France. We only engage in trade."

"You exploit the workers of East Germany," father countered. "If you didn't, why would three million of them cross the border into West Germany?"

"You are feverish!" the Premier answered.

"Do you have credentials to speak for the workers of the world?" father asked.

"Do you have credentials to poke your nose into East Germany?" came the riposte.

At one point in the evening, Khrushchev stood, turned his back to the table, bent downward, flipped his coat up and then gave an imitation of the can-can, which he had seen danced at a Hollywood movie studio.

"This is a dance in which girls pull up their skirts," he snorted. "You're going to see that in a movie; we're not. This is what you call freedom—freedom for girls to show their backsides. To us it is pornography. The culture of people who want pornography. It's capitalism that makes the girls that way."

During the discussions members of both sides were being served whiskey and cognac. Toasts, a Russian tradition, were made by each side and there were friendly feelings. During one of these toasts, Khrushchev noticed that father was only touching his glass to his lips—a way of acknowledging toasts he had been using for years. The Premier glared across the table at him: "*Gospodin Valtger*, (a term meaning Walter is Mr., not Comrade) what is this giving only lip service to the toast?"

"Mr. Chairman, I think you should know that when the revolution comes to America, there will be at least one sober trade unionist."

The meeting ended amicably, with the Soviets inviting the American labor leaders to Russia to see for themselves the conditions of the workers. Eventually a delegation from the UAW traveled to the Lake Baikal region in Siberia to visit the enormous hydroelectric plants at Bratsk. They were housed in a villa built especially for President Eisenhower, whose meeting with Khruschev had been cancelled following the U-2 spy plane incident.

The dinner at the Mark Hopkins was front-page news around the world. Many papers printed a transcript of the evening's conversations. Upon Khruschev's return to Russia, the Soviet press ran a story with the headline, "Get Acquainted with Mr. Reuther, Lackey of the Monopolists." The article stated that father had married a Russian girl while working at the Gorky plant 25 years before and deserted her when he and Victor returned to the States. The article quoted father's " wife" as stating:

He vowed his love at first sight. He said that he had dedicated his life to the workers and needed a true girlfriend. He spoke about the chains of capitalist labor which must be broken, about bloodthirsty exploiters—my God, what he didn't speak about!

Anyone's head would have been turned, let alone an inexperienced girl. Soon after we got married he stopped talking about politics, and I no longer heard beautiful speeches about the class struggle. He reiterated without end that one must be careful with money."

"Walter's Russian was certainly too limited for such an extended conversation." Uncle Victor wryly observed. "Official propagandists often overplay their hands."

Even the *Detroit News* , which had been staunchly anti-Reuther, stated:

> The Russians, who have a talent for abuse that approaches genius, have surpassed themselves in their vilification of Walter P. Reuther. The UAW President has been assaulted with a variety of nouns and adjectives in his own country, but it took Moscow to decide that he is a bigamist.

Long after the press hoopla, the dinner with Khrushchev would draw warm response from America's allies. "Later, when Walter and I traveled to lands whose problems we had discussed during the well-publicized dinner," said Uncle Victor, "we received thanks for our firm support of their national interests."

In 1961, when President Kennedy met with Premier Khrushchev at a summit in Vienna, the Communist leader recalled his encounter with my father. "We hung the likes of Reuther in Russia in 1917," he told Kennedy. And in his memoirs he wrote, "The capitalists have bought him off; they paid him enough to represent their interests instead of those of the workers." Khrushchev went on to say that father was making as much money as Henry Ford, a multimillionaire. My father's salary in 1959: $22,000.

Shortly after the Khrushchev dinner, cartoonist Bill Mauldin penned a perceptive portrait of Khrushchev and Barry Goldwater that father had framed for his office. Both men have their arms outstretched for an embrace, and both are saying, "I hate Walter Reuther."

CHAPTER TWENTY-NINE

KENNEDY
FOR
PRESIDENT

*"I can think of nothing more detrimental to this nation than
for any president to owe his election to, and therefore be a
captive of, a political boss like Walter Reuther."*
— Richard Nixon, Republican
presidential nominee, 1960

Summertime, 1960. Our family was off to Los Angeles for the Democratic National Convention. My thoughts turned to the hot sun and the powerful waves of the Pacific Ocean. I was hoping there would be some time for family walks — sand in our shoes, the sun beating on our red heads. We wouldn't tan, of course, but our freckles would have a population explosion. Father, the fairest among us, was the most vulnerable. But he would have so little free time he wouldn't have to worry about too much sun. He had thrust himself into convention issues and would be getting plenty of heat in discussions and meetings.

We landed in LA at the end of July. Mother thought it would be an educational experience for Linda and me to witness a national political convention. She knew father would be inaccessible most of the time. Although he never accepted an offer to run for public office himself, he was constantly involved in helping candidates he felt were socially conscious get elected. He knew most of them personally. And he could recite from memory their voting records on such issues as medical care for the aged, civil rights, conservation and nuclear energy. He was close to four of the five candidates seeking the

Democratic presidential nomination: John Kennedy, Adlai Stevenson, Stuart Symington, and Hubert Humphrey. The other, Lyndon Johnson, had a poor record on civil rights and wasn't trusted by labor.

It was hard for father to have four good friends vying for the same nomination and for his personal support. Well before the convention, he had decided to back Kennedy. Kennedy had shown concern for the problems of labor, he was young and vital, and he had tremendous personal appeal.

After his loss to Kennedy in the West Virginia primary, Hubert Humphrey withdrew from the race. Father advised Kennedy to choose Humphrey for his running mate. Late in the convention, however, Humphrey threw his support to Stevenson, prompting Kennedy to choose Lyndon Johnson instead. Although Humphrey lost on two counts, father did not forget his close friend from Minnesota. He painstakingly helped Humphrey raise money to pay off his campaign debt.

Adlai Stevenson was acknowledged by many to be a brilliant statesman. But because he had lost the two previous elections to Eisenhower, father did not think he would be a good choice for 1960. The party needed a fresh, new candidate. When Stevenson had

Father huddles with Senator John F. Kennedy three weeks after daddy's historic meeting with Khrushchev.

ignored father's exhortations not to run, father was asked by the Democratic National Committee to meet with Mrs. Roosevelt, a long-time Stevenson supporter. In 1952 and 1956, Mrs. R had traveled around the country campaigning for Stevenson, earning her the epithet "jet propulsion with a fringe on top." She was at it again in 1960 when father tried to dissuade her at breakfast one morning. As he saw it, Stevenson's entry into the race weakened Kennedy and helped Johnson. Mrs. R would not budge.

Four days before the first convention session, father met with several labor leaders. He pushed hard to convince them that Kennedy would be the best candidate against the Republican nominee. Most of them agreed and a labor coalition was formed.

Meeting in Kennedy's suite in the Biltmore Hotel, father told the young Senator that organized labor found Henry Jackson, Hubert Humphrey, and Stuart Symington satisfactory running mates. When Kennedy hinted that he had been considering Johnson for his vice president, everyone was shocked. With the assurance of Robert Kennedy, labor had promised their delegates that Johnson would definitely not be on the ticket.

Kennedy said Johnson had wide support and would help the ticket, especially in the South where Kennedy was weak. He also explained to father that if he didn't offer Johnson the post, Johnson could cause trouble for his programs as the Senate majority leader. Kennedy said he had sent out feelers, and was quite sure that Johnson would be pleased with the offer, but would respectfully decline.

Johnson's position in the Senate was actually much more powerful than the office of vice president. And the tall Texan had made statements to the effect that he would never leave his position for that of second fiddle in the White House. So when LBJ actually accepted the nomination, Kennedy was dumfounded.

Bobby Kennedy arrived at father's hotel suite with the news. I was sitting on the twin bed in the next room when all bedlam broke loose. Father, visibly angry, chastised Bobby for this "betrayal." Bobby replied that he also was disenchanted, but that he had had nothing to do with the decision. Mildred Jeffrey, who had been working with the UAW voter registration campaign, fell into a stunned silence. Mother and Joseph Rauh were crying, while Leonard Woodcock and Doug

Fraser seemed to be in a state of shock.

Calls flooded the hotel switchboard. To a person, the union caucus felt betrayed. The delegates from Minnesota, Michigan and California were ready to start an open fight on the convention floor. Party faithfuls condemned Kennedy's choice on national television.

To prevent a party split, father assumed the role of peacemaker. Once everyone had settled down in the hotel room, mother came in to see Linda and me. We were extremely curious. Why was everyone so upset? It was a rare moment when father had lost his composure. I was amazed to see and hear him scolding Robert Kennedy. Why was Johnson so bad?

Michigan Governor G. Mennen Williams pushed for a roll call on the floor. It was thought this might force Kennedy to drop Johnson. Father sent Leonard Woodcock, his able lieutenant, to the Michigan caucus. Speaking with father's authority, Woodcock was able to re-establish the state delegation's commitment to the Kennedy-Johnson ticket, thus avoiding a split. Said Doug Fraser:

> The Michigan caucus met in a boiler room right off the stage of the convention. People were crying, and it was a terrible mess. Leonard Woodcock and I were both trying to settle things down. Woodcock told them that this was a decision Kennedy had made. I don't like it either, he said, but that is the way it is, and we might as well put our best face on. The name of the game is to defeat Nixon.
>
> Then Soapy Williams said he wanted to introduce a speaker. I figured it was John McCormack, the House majority leader in those days, or maybe Robert Kennedy or his younger brother, Edward ("Teddy"). Up on the stage came Ann Landers. I could not believe my eyes. And she said that it was so touching that people feel so strongly about an issue that they were actually in tears. That was all she said. But I will never forget it.

Meanwhile, father confronted George Meany, who also wanted to raise a fuss about the Kennedy-Johnson ticket. Meany called a meeting of the AFL-CIO Executive Council. He wanted to draft a public denouncement of Kennedy's choice of Johnson. Jack Conway, who witnessed the meeting, recalled: "Reuther did the job. Walter prevailed in blocking the Council from issuing a statement of condemnation."

Once the Kennedy-Johnson ticket was official, Kennedy asked my father to visit him at Hyannisport. He asked him to write down the programs he thought most important for the betterment of America. Father stayed home for a few days before going to Massachusetts, working diligently on the assignment. I would sit with him for hours in the den. "This is my favorite pastime," he beamed. "I'm an idea man."

He compiled ten pages of notes to present to Kennedy. They included programs for civil rights, health care, unemployment, and a special proposal for what was to become the Peace Corps.

Four years earlier, father had made a speech before the National Education Association in which he first outlined his Peace Corps idea. "I happen to believe that the more young Americans we send throughout the world as technical missionaries with slide rules, with medical kits, with textbooks, to fight communism on a technical basis, the fewer young Americans we will need to send with guns and flame throwers."

Their first morning together Kennedy and father had a long private talk followed by time on the phone discussing strategy with Johnson, who was on his ranch in Texas. In the afternoon Kennedy had some other appointments. He suggested father accompany his wife, Jackie, for a swim.

"After we went swimming," father recalled, "we sunned ourselves on the beach and she asked me about 'this whole business of security and privacy.' I told her it was the area in which she would pay the biggest price. 'You are making the decision as an adult,' I said. 'But your children aren't able to. You have to work, and work hard, to have your children lead as nearly normal a life as possible. Everywhere you turn, you are going to be a prisoner. You may take over the White House — if Jack wins the election — but the security people will take over your lives.' How true these things we discussed turned out to be."

Father returned from Hyannisport invigorated. He marshaled the UAW forces for an enthusiastic campaign to elect Kennedy. At Bobby Kennedy's request, Uncle Roy became the national director of a voter registration drive. He would travel constantly with Bobby, and sometimes John. When father traveled with John, he would often share the podium with the nominee.

"These two public figures of such different backgrounds had the same inherent qualities that made for leadership," observed writer Jean Gould. "More significantly, in Walter's eyes, only in a democracy could the two stand side by side on equal footing. Wealthy Kennedy had used his money to help him obtain his position; but Walter, without money, had to depend on his personal attributes alone."

Republican Presidential nominee Richard Nixon was not happy with the Reuther-Kennedy team. "I can think of nothing more detrimental to this nation than for any President to owe his election to, and therefore be a captive of, a political boss like Walter Reuther."

After Kennedy narrowly defeated Nixon in the election, my parents were invited to attend the President-elect's Inaugural Ball in January. After several visits to a dressmaker, mother brought home her ball gown. A strapless brocade bodice with a pale silk skirt flowing gracefully to the floor. A fitted brocade jacket covered her shoulders. She modeled it for father upon his return from work that evening. Her elegance and beauty shone from her face. "What a lady I married," smiled her husband.

As for his own Inaugural garb, father was rather uncooperative. He had always refused to shop for clothes on his own. So mother would have to negotiate with him to take time out for occasional wardrobe overhauls.

"Walter, you'll need a new dark dress suit for January," mother suggested. (Father always shunned wearing a tuxedo.) When would he find the time for this? Mother made arrangements with Hiller's Men's Shop in Rochester. They agreed to let father come in for a fitting after closing time.

It was evening when father, mother and I drove with the bodyguard into town. The store manager unlocked the door for us. After the proper dress suit was selected, it was time for the tedious process of fitting. At only five feet, eight inches, father was not tall but his barrel chest, which he carried so proudly, required a size 40 or 42 coat. His shape caused the tailor much trouble; it took him over an hour to pin the jacket. During the fitting, mother and I picked out a new shirt, tie, and pair of socks. Mother guessed this would be the last time for years she'd have father along for such shopping.

210

The night of the Inauguration my parents called from Washington. "It's a real blizzard here," father told us. "I wish Mother Nature would cooperate. The whole city is paralyzed." They had to walk several icy blocks to reach the ball, mother lifting her fragile silk gown above her ankles and holding tightly to father's arm. Some people never arrived, they said. My parents were thrilled. Kennedy's inauguration filled us with hope for the future.

A happy moment at President Kennedy's Inaugural Ball.

211

CHAPTER THIRTY

FACING
THE
FIRING
LINE

"I have nothing against Goldwater. I think he has the finest 18th-century mind in the U.S. Senate."
— Walter Reuther, in an interview with Mike Wallace

Shortly before the 1960 elections, father appeared on national television in an interview with Mike Wallace. Many times he had been on network shows like *Face the Nation* and *Meet the Press*. But interviewer Mike Wallace was famous for his sledge-hammer tactics, which he used to create lively discussions with his guests. He might attack, or simply provoke, slipping into the role of devil's advocate. As brewer Joseph Coors declared in an advertisement, "The most feared four words in the English language: 'Mike Wallace is here.'" A part of the interview follows:

> FATHER: When we get to the place in the development of our society where the tools of abundance can take care of the material needs of the outer man ... the real emphasis then has to be shifted to enabling the inner man to grow. In other words, we've got to develop new appetites, new interest in nonmaterial things. And this really, I think, means the first opportunity for the great mass of human beings to participate in culture.
> WALLACE: Fulton Lewis has written that you are bent on winning control of the Democratic Party and then, conceivably, control of the federal government. He says the government you

212

would produce would make the Nazi dictatorship of Hitler look namby-pamby.

FATHER: It sounds like some of the things that Barry Goldwater would be saying. The point is that if America followed the political and economic philosophy of the ultra-right, the Fulton Lewises and the Barry Goldwaters, America would default in doing those things which essentially are the responsibilities of the whole community. I share the philosophy of Abraham Lincoln when he said that the purpose of government is to enable the people to do together through the instruments of government what they are unable to do without the aid of government.

WALLACE: Who opened up this country industrially, the government or free private enterprise? Are you not grateful to the capitalists, the businessmen of the United States for anything, Walter?

FATHER: I'm grateful for the contribution they made, but even in the early days of capitalism, the government helped a great deal. The railroads got tremendous land grants, the steamship companies got subsidies—they still get subsidies—the airlines got subsidies; none of the great industries developed without some assistance from the government.

WALLACE: How do you get along with —ah — don't you and Goldwater talk at all, you two?

FATHER: I have nothing against Goldwater. I think he has the finest 18th-century mind in the U.S. Senate. I just think Barry Goldwater doesn't understand the forces at work in the world. If you took his book, *The Conscience of a Conservative,* and translated it into governmental action, the Communists would take over the world in the next five years because we would make the free world impotent to meet the basic economic and social forces that are changing the world in revolution.

When the show had concluded, mother and I were waiting for father's call. An hour later the phone rang. Father apologized for being late. "Wallace and I discussed different global problems in the hallway of the studio for an hour after the show." Wallace had asked father how he liked the show. "It was fine except the questions were too long," he answered, at which they both laughed.

"Daddy, Mike Wallace seemed so nasty," I said. "Didn't you feel uncomfortable with his interruptions and his rude questions?"

"That's just his style, Lisa. He wasn't attacking me personally. He's an expert at bringing out controversial issues."

I laughed. "You know what I think, daddy? I think you just like a good fight."

In April 1961, Uncle Victor accompanied father to a World Conference of Automobile Workers in Rome. Also, the mayor of Florence invited them to visit him during their tour. One morning, while viewing Florence's cathedrals and art treasures, the brothers stopped at an outdoor café for refreshment. Waiting for their appointment with the mayor, they sipped cool drinks and admired the statues and fountains in the area.

Suddenly, out of nowhere, there was pandemonium. Small cars, buses, and motorbikes jammed the streets, honking and emitting exhaust fumes. A special processional was underway. Father was disgusted. "C'mon," he said to Victor, and they proceeded directly to the mayor's office, ahead of schedule. Walking in, father announced, "Mr. Mayor, you ought to ban automobiles from your city!"

"But Mr. Reuther," replied the confounded mayor, "you're president of the auto workers," to which my father answered: "Automobiles are made to meet man's needs, not to destroy the environment."

Father meant it. He could not tolerate the ruination of such a jewel as Florence, despite inconvenience and economics. Ten years later automobiles were indeed banned from that part of the city.

Back in the U.S. the next month, President Kennedy asked father to head a committee of private citizens, to be known as Tractors for Freedom. The group was seeking release of 1,200 prisoners captured by Fidel Castro's Cuba while attempting to invade during the disastrous Bay of Pigs affair. The U.S. government could not become officially involved.

Castro had offered to release the prisoners for 500 huge D-8 tractors. He claimed they were to help with agricultural development. But these Super D-8s were for building highways, clearing land for airstrips, or missile sites. Eleanor Roosevelt, Johns Hopkins University President Dr. Milton Eisenhower, and my father formed the committee that Kennedy had asked to negotiate with Castro.

On May 20, the President publicly announced his intentions:

"When Fidel Castro first made his offer to 'exchange' the lives and liberty of 1,200 prisoners for 500 agricultural tractors, the American people responded with characteristic compassion. A number of private committees were organized to raise the necessary funds....The United States government has not been and cannot be a party to these negotiations....I hope that all citizens will contribute what they can."

There were no more than 60 Super D-8 tractors in inventory in the U.S. And tiny Cuba obviously wanted to share these tractors with her close friend the Soviet Union. The committee met and decided to send $28 million in agricultural tractors and equipment in exchange for the prisoners. Castro had specifically said that $28 million was the value of the tractors initially requested.

The Republicans decided to make political hay of the situation, saying lives were being bartered by the Democrats. Kennedy responded by naming another Republican to the committee — former Budget Bureau Chief John M. Dodge — as treasurer.

Capitalizing on the political dissension, Castro demanded $28 million cash instead, as reparations for damage to Cuba during the attempted invasion. Richard Nixon ridiculed the committee for "submission to blackmail." The Republicans then pressured Eisenhower and Dodge to quit the committee. Some even threatened Eisenhower, saying they would stop their contributions to Johns Hopkins if he did not withdraw. To avoid further embarrassment to the Administration, the committee decided to disband.

Castro raised the stakes and many months later Robert Kennedy negotiated an agreement to give the Cubans $62 million in food and medical supplies for the release of the prisoners.

By 1961, the ranks of the radical right were growing in America. The Minutemen were training in guerilla warfare techniques. The Ku Klux Klan and John Birch Society were thriving. Such groups assailed many social programs and spoke against any communication with the Soviet Union. President Kennedy was receiving death threats, many from the radical right.

On a 1961 tour of the West Coast, JFK spoke out against this fanatical fringe, whose affinity for violence had a long history. "They find treason in our churches and our highest courts," he declared.

By the end of the year, the President was receiving many threats against his life, especially from the far right. He asked his brother Robert to get in touch with father, who had lived most of his adult life under similar threats. The President wanted practical ideas for tighter security. Father sat down with Uncle Victor and Joe Rauh, and together they composed a 24-page list of suggestions to help prevent an assassination. A number of suggestions were implemented. Unfortunately, it wasn't enough.

Reflecting on my own heavily-guarded upbringing, I have come to realize that if I am not afraid to die, then perhaps I am free to live. Father must have felt this way, too. Having faced the firing line more than once, he embraced life with greater wisdom and set about living it to the fullest.

CHAPTER THIRTY-ONE

THE
PRESIDENT'S
CHOICE

*"A lot has happened. We have shared a strenuous and
meaningful life together. We've had our hours of adversity
and our hours of achievement. I would choose to do it all over
again if we could do it together."*
— Father's letter to mother on
their 26th wedding anniversary

Father's work often forced him to be out of town on special occasions,
such as a wedding anniversary. Mother had come to expect it. Perhaps
their marriage on Friday the 13th had been an omen of the sacrifices
that would mark their lives together.

Father never neglected mother. He held her close to his heart
despite the distance between them. And on Valentine's Day, he would
always remember to buy her a box of chocolates (he knew her passion
for them!). On March 13, 1962, at 11 p.m., father penned the following
anniversary letter from Brussels:

My dear Mayichka:

I have just come from dinner with Arnie and Victor where we
talked of you, our families — and I told of our beginning 26
years ago.

A lot has happened. We have shared a strenuous and meaningful life together. We've had our hours of adversity and our
hours of achievement. I would choose to do it all over again if
we could do it together. We have loved each other much, or we
could not have made it together in the face of all the difficulties

and the strains and stresses of a hectic 26 years.

I love you very, very much and I am glad you are mine — and I want always to be yours. We have two nice girls and I think we are both very fortunate. Do you remember 26 years ago we were both off to a union meeting in Algonac, Michigan? I didn't know then — and I have learned little since — that one should not be at meetings on one's wedding night . . . the years have only made it more difficult with responsibilities in other parts of the world. . ..

Give both Linda and Lisa a big hug and kiss for me and tell them I love their mommy very very much —

All my love — Walter

P.S. The next 26 years won't be so hard!

Father underlined the last word with bold strokes, emphasizing the stress that so often beset their lives.

Despite his hectic schedule, father did make speeches often. When asked why, he responded with a single word: "Education." He was intent on raising people's awareness of the problems facing a free society. Indeed, the very future of civilization, he maintained, lay in America's trying to provide leadership in the solution of the great issues.

Uncle Victor: "Because Walter himself had such a deep sense of mission, he regarded the opportunity to speak as a challenge to him to persuade his listeners of the rightness of his views."

I don't believe father ever used prepared texts. He would have a few key words scribbled on a half-sheet of typing paper. His speeches often resembled each another because he had a tendency to hammer away at the same important issues. He also believed in the virtue of repetition. But not brevity. A story has it that he once received a six-page memo draft that he declared "too long." Pencil in hand, he set about shortening it. The final product ran to 13 pages.

At the UAW conventions, labor writers would set up pools, betting on the lengths of father's addresses. He knew of it and at one such national gathering said, "Now I have taken a lot of abuse and ribbing and a lot of good fun over the years about the length of my speeches, and I want to tell some of the newer delegates, who are perhaps unfamiliar with my bad habits, that I am capable of making a short speech. But I find it so painful, I do it only in extreme emergencies. I do not consider today such an emergency. So relax."

In April of '62, father held a dinner at Washington's Mayflower Hotel. Top legislators were invited, and among those who showed up were two Cabinet members, 35 senators, and some 167 members of the House. Fifty five of those present were Republicans. Although George Meany was invited, he chose not to attend. While dessert was served, father delivered a 45-minute speech on unemployment and related problems facing the country. "Walter had a joint session of Congress," one of his associates joked afterward. "I knew that he couldn't resist a State of the Union message."

Mother used to say that whenever she heard father give a speech, she wondered how in the world she had the nerve to argue freely with him. But she did, and she held her own.

Atlantic City was home to salt-water taffy, the boardwalk, and conventions. At the UAW's 1960 convention, Linda had come down from boarding school at Putney, with a group of her schoolmates. It was a field trip for studying parliamentary procedure and the workings of a democratic union. I joined the students for many of the seminars and the actual sessions on the convention floor. Father reserved several hours for a personal dialogue with the students. He showed the students the common denominators linking young and old, challenging them to channel their energies into constructive programs by working within the democratic system.

In 1962, the UAW convention in Atlantic City was especially electric. President Kennedy had travelled to Atlantic City to address the delegates. When Kennedy stepped to the podium to speak, the applause was thunderous.

"Last week, after speaking to the Chamber of Commerce and the presidents of the American Medical Association, I began to wonder how I got elected," Kennedy began. "And now I remember."

Later that year, the President looked with concern at the country's latest unemployment figure: 6 percent and rising. He called father for his thoughts.

"When you put it in that framework, 6 percent unemployed, your opposition says instantly, 'but 94 percent are employed.' You must argue the case in terms of people."

So when Kennedy addressed Congress, he revealed that five million Americans who wanted to work couldn't find a job. The situation was becoming tragic. Kennedy made his point.

President Kennedy wanted to name father to the U.S. delegation to the United Nations. Both Adlai Stevenson (then serving as UN ambassador) and Eleanor Roosevelt had urged Kennedy to make father a member of our UN team. It was JFK's policy to clear any appointment from labor, for a national or international position, with AFL-CIO President George Meany. Meany was upset that father was being considered ahead of himself for such a prominent position. So when Kennedy asked him to spare father for the appointment, he flatly refused.

"Meany vetoed it on very personal political grounds," said Uncle Victor. "Jack Kennedy was furious about it. He said to Walter, 'It's a hell of a situation when the President of the United States can't have the people he wants on his UN delegation. But I'm too busy to get into a fight with George Meany over this.'"

Another time, when father submitted the name of his able colleague Jack Conway for the position of Undersecretary of Labor, Meany again blocked it, with the feeble excuse that he had not been notified first. And when Kennedy told the labor leader he wanted the names of a couple of people who might qualify for Secretary of Labor, Meany gave him only one name (as if to say, you take my guy or you're not my friend). Kennedy laughed at the name and then called my father: "What the hell do I do with this old man down there who wants to pawn this kind of person off on me?"

Meany notwithstanding, the President kept father in mind for the UN delegation. Father would spend long hours with Stevenson and Mrs. Roosevelt discussing global problems and their possible solutions. His travels throughout the world had brought him in touch with the leaders of many countries; some counted among his personal

220

friends. He was the right man for the job.

In 1963, Kennedy told father that in his second term he would appoint him to the UN regardless of George Meany. Meany, the President complained, had often rejected good ideas to protect his powerful position; his support was no longer worth the price. Kennedy needed a first-class negotiator and coalition builder working on America's behalf. But fate had other plans.

President Kennedy told the 1962 UAW convention: "Last week, after speaking to the Chamber of Commerce and the presidents of the American Medical Association, I began to wonder how I got elected. Now I remember."

CHAPTER THIRTY-TWO

"THE PUTNEY EXPERIENCE"

"And the cow crunching with depress'd head surpasses any statue...."
— From Walt Whitman's *Song of Myself*

The Putney School — a coed boarding academy high in Vermont's Green Mountains — embraced a vigorous lifestyle, including music and the arts; a cooperative dairy-farm work program; and academic excellence in small classes dedicated to the joy of learning, rather than simply making the grade and getting into college. As the brochure proclaimed, this was "the Putney experience."

Putney was isolated both by geography and by policy. TVs, radios, and stereos were prohibited. The school encouraged the students to participate in the local community as well as cultivate a keen awareness of current events. From this progressive microcosm, it was hoped, a student would graduate and help better the world.

I had always loved to visit Linda at Putney, with its freewheeling atmosphere. The students wore blue jeans to classes, and the girls typically wore long hair and hoops through pierced ears; there was even a hair style called "the Putney braid."

Linda excelled at school, especially in music and ceramics. Rochester's provincialism had stifled her talents and narrowed her interests to dating and rock 'n roll. I saw her blossom in Vermont, surrounded by creative, energetic young people from diverse backgrounds. Being the daughter of a controversial labor leader no longer dominated her sense of self.

Aware of the freedom Putney had afforded Linda, I begged my parents to send me there, too. Maybe I just wanted to do whatever Linda did; but I think there was a deeper motivation. I wanted to break away from the padlocks, fences, and bodyguards. After several admission tests, I was accepted as a student my sophomore year.

In the fall of 1962, father, mother and I made the familiar drive to Putney. Eddie Torlone, father's long-time bodyguard, was at the wheel. He had become accustomed to these 13- to14-hour drives. As we left the interstate in Vermont, my anticipation jumped. A new chapter in my life lay only a few miles ahead.

At last we were climbing Putney mountain, past the headmaster's house, and on to the campus. A brief stop told us my residence assignment, a room with three other sophomores in the White cottage, the same dorm where Linda had lived.

I chose a top bunk. Mother had brought curtains, bedspreads, and a bedside table for me. The room was yellow, perfect for the pretty blue cloth. My parents stayed about an hour. In the morning they planned to come from their motel to say good-bye. Then they'd drive on for their visit with Mrs. R. Classes were about to begin. I was sorry to miss seeing Eleanor Roosevelt, my well-wishing friend. I had heard she was very ill.

"Look at these horrible news photos of Mrs. Roosevelt," mother cried the next morning. "Why can't they give Mrs. R some privacy in her old age?"

Although they were 26 years apart in age, mother and Mrs. R shared a close relationship. Mother and father were protective toward her, especially in her later years. They would phone her often to say hello and remind her to slow down and rest more. Mrs. R's sense of social obligation impaired her hearing that sort of advice. She had long referred to herself as "my husband's legs," and even though he had been dead over 15 years, she continued her own missions.

My parents found Mrs. R bedridden and weak. Extensive tests at the hospital had produced distressing results. But in the course of my parents' visit, she seemed to regain some of her strength, and even her spirit for debate with father.

They shared their hate letters and bad-press clippings. At this last reunion, father had received more and was the "winner," which Mrs. R acknowledged with a chuckle. After all, she had been ill for some time and not active enough to provoke her old antagonists.

Father told her of his invitation to speak in Japan in November. He was expecting a confrontation with the Communists, who had entrenched themselves in the Japanese labor movement. Mrs. R encouraged him to go, saying he could help the trade unionists in Japan as he had in India. She also asked him to get in touch with her grandson Franklin, who was based on a Navy ship there.

Finally, with weak flesh but willing spirit, she asked father if she could present to America's U.N. delegation his idea about winning peace through economic and humanitarian aid. Father, of course, agreed.

On Sunday morning, Mrs. R insisted that father take her and FDR's nonagenerian uncle, David Delano, to church. As the Episcopal service commenced, both Mrs. R and Uncle David dropped off to sleep. Sitting in the front of the chapel in the Roosevelt family pew, father then realized there was no one sitting near them. Mrs. R traditionally had nudged father when it was time to stand, kneel or sit. Unable to interpret the rustling noises behind him, my father resigned himself to sitting quietly until the service was over.

Mrs. R had always been so vigorous, so active and ever busy, that Franklin was said to have prayed, "Dear God, please make Eleanor just a little tired." On leaving the church that last Sunday together, she whispered to father, "I must really be getting a bit tired — Franklin's prayer has been answered!"

"It was the damndest experience," father later recalled. "Finally, the service was over and I got Mrs. R home ... and the next time she was in church it was her funeral. We were the last house guests she had before she died."

My parents called me at Putney to relate the sad news. Father's voice was small and choked with grief. "She was a remarkable woman," he sobbed. Mother took the phone and told me Mrs. R would be buried beside FDR in a simple ceremony at Hyde Park. John Kennedy, Harry Truman and Dwight Eisenhower would stand with heads bowed, while Adlai Stevenson spoke of her greatness.

I was stunned by this very personal loss. When classes were over I went for a long walk in the woods. The sky was gray, the bare trees appeared lifeless, as if mourning this great woman's death. The solemn landscape reminded me of our visits to Hyde Park and conversations with Mrs. R. Her selfless smile passed before me, encouraging me to continue: "And if she keeps on swimming, she will someday find her dream."

My first month at Putney passed quickly. I immersed myself in *Animal Farm*, Bach cantatas and the American Revolution. I was also a member of the work crew responsible for harvesting the vast vegetable garden behind the KDU — the kitchen-dining unit. It was tedious work, but philosophical discussions with my best friend Lydia helped pass the time.

After the news of Mrs. R's death, I became a bit disturbed. I started to long for the familiarity of my parents' company. One morning, I awoke with a severe case of homesickness. For 15 years I had been devoted to my parents, and they to me. The separation now seemed more than I could bear. I could not study or concentrate. Everything reminded me of my parents. While listening to Debussy's *La Mer* in French class one day, my eyes filled with tears. I imagined that the music was describing *la mere*, my mother.

After a week of emotional outbursts, I called home, certain my parents would welcome my intended return with open arms. "Please, mummy and daddy," I sobbed, "let me come home. I miss you so much. I can't stop crying."

The intensity was too much for mother. She handed the phone to father. "Listen, Lisa, you made the decision to go to Putney, and you should stay there at least one semester. Then at that time you can decide."

I was crushed.

Realizing my parents' resolve, I resigned myself to remain the rest of the term. My parents were teaching me an important lesson: responsibility for my own decisions.

In the past, my overbearing emotions had often led me into anger, frustration, and disappointment. It was very hard for me to remain at Putney that first semester. For once in my life, I had to let my intelligence rule my heart. Otherwise I would have stowed away on the next train to Detroit. As the semester passed, though, I awoke to the enriching life Putney had to offer and was ready to return for another term.

Little did I realize that mother was going through a similar crisis back at Paint Creek. My tearful telephone call had only increased her unrest. I was her baby. She had grown accustomed to my companionship, as I had to hers. So my first Putney semester she devoted to producing soup. She made huge kettlefulls and stored it in the freezer. May Reuther was expert at sublimating her feelings. She had years of practice.

Meanwhile I was learning to stand on my own. I took up weaving, playing the cello and writing poetry. Every spring and fall, small groups took a long weekend to go mountain climbing, bicycling and canoeing. The whole school participated, leaving books and pencils behind to explore nature's bounty. The closeness of this tiny society — only 125 students with a high ratio of teachers — found special expression during these weekends camping out under the stars, singing madrigals and playing recorders, eating "gorp" (a trail mix forerunner), and mystery soups made from the ingredients tucked in our knapsacks.

Then there were always the adolescent crushes. I transferred my devotion from my father to a male teacher, whom I idolized for the next three years. Although outwardly it was a platonic student-teacher relationship, my own fantasies carried it a bit further. On the night of my graduation, I quietly entered my teacher's home and covered him with a greenish-heather blanket I had woven for him — the culmination of my love affair. Oh, Putney! Where else could we indulge in such sweet innocence? Such are the pastimes of youth.

Harvest Festival was the highlight of autumn, when hundreds of alumni searched out their Putney roots. Parents joined the homecomers to celebrate the earth's abundance. Bach's *Brandenburg Concertos* and Vivaldi's *Four Seasons* filled the air. From booths one could purchase hot borscht, freshly baked bread and vegetables grown around the famous Putney Elm Tree.

The Harvest Parade found students and farm animals marching side by side, a sight that left spectators holding their stomachs with laughter. When mother and father came for the festival, I took them to the cow barn to show them who was marching with me in the parade: Emily, my five-month-old Holstein calf.

Though only a young heifer, Emily turned out to be as stubborn as an old mule. As the parade entered the main arena, Emily sat down, refused to budge and started munching on the wildflower garland I'd braided for her! Frantically, I tugged at her rope, but the rest of the parade passed us by, leaving us alone on the lawn. When finally she rose to her feet, I grabbed her collar and led her back to the barn. How humiliating. I returned to my parents, and father couldn't resist: "Could Emily have developed her stubborn streak from you, Lisa?"

Near the end of my sophomore year, father came to spend a day on his way to New York for meetings. As usual, it was dinner for three. Never a moment's privacy, but I was thrilled to see my father.

The next morning father arrived at six o'clock sharp to help with chores. "Let's go to the cow barn, father. We still have an hour before breakfast."

Most days, I had barn duty in the afternoons, which meant milking the cows with another student, feeding the calves their special formula and cleaning the milk house. I loved it; I could spend all day with the cows. Poet Walt Whitman said it best in *Song of Myself*:

> ...And the cow crunching with depress'd head surpasses any statue,
> ...I think I could turn and live with animals, they're so placid and self-contain'd,
> I stand and look at them long and long.
> They do not sweat and whine about their condition,
> They do not lie awake in the dark and weep for their sins...
> Not one is dissatisfied, not one is demented with the mania of owning things,
> Not one kneels to another, nor to his kind that lived thousands of years ago,
> Not one is respectable or unhappy over the whole earth.

Father and I moved slowly through the old barn lined from end to end with scores of cows. Some were sitting; others stood peacefully chewing their cuds. He squeezed my hand as we headed for my dorm. "Mother and I were very worried about you, Lisa. You were so unhappy last fall. Now I see that Putney has become your home away from home." I told him how much I loved it, especially the animals and writing in-depth term papers.

Father's bodyguard had been waiting in the car. What a relief to be alone for a few moments! The three of us walked to the dining hall for breakfast. The room's handsome wooden beams arched toward the ceiling, a Calder mobile hanging motionless in the middle. The sculptor's children had attended Putney. So also psychologist B.F. Skinner's daughter, who, the story went, had trouble relating in group situations, herself a victim of the "Skinner box."

After stuffing ourselves with buckwheat pancakes swimming in Putney's own maple syrup, father prepared to leave. It would be a long drive to New York City. I hugged him and thanked him for coming. "*Auf Wiedersehen,*" he waved. "*Auf Wiedersehen,*" I returned as his car descended the mountain.

During Christmas vacation, my parents announced that early in the new year they would be attending a White House dinner followed by one of Jacqueline Kennedy's concert productions. Mother needed an elegant shawl to wear with her gown, so I agreed to weave her one on my return to Putney.

Weaving was fulfilling my artistic aspirations. After mastering the technical skills, I opened my eyes and fingers to combining the natural fibers in unusual ways. The wool's scent reminded me of my childhood sheep friends — Jezebel, Cleopatra and Clementine. I found I could make heavy fabrics or delicate fishnet shawls just by controlling the heaviness of the beater. My eyes reveled in the blending of colors. The rhythm of the process was entrancing. I felt as though I'd been weaving forever.

For mother's shawl, I explored the many combinations of patterns and yarn types available before deciding on an intricate lace design. I would use linen for the warp and soft mohair for the weft, in a blending of white and off-white. I was not alone in my preoccupation with the White House party. On the loom beside mine, Judy Serkin was weaving a shawl for the new wife of cellist Pablo Casals. Judy's father, the pianist Rudolph Serkin, was a a friend of Casals, who was planning several concerts at the White House. Judy secretly hoped his wife would wear the shawl she was weaving.

Putney was full of the children of well-known people. And every Sunday night a prominent guest speaker would address the student body. Once, naturalist Scott Nearing lectured on channels to world peace. His message paralleled father's, though they had their ideological differences. I remembered father telling me about the debate he had attended between Nearing and Norman Thomas— communism versus socialism. Father had come a long way since those early days at City College in Detroit. His enrolling me at Putney was part of his dream that I go further still.

CHAPTER THIRTY-THREE

JAPAN
AND THE
COMMON
GOOD

"Walter Reuther Go Home!"
— Communist placard in Japan, 1962

The 1962 UAW convention established a Free World Labor Defense Fund to protect unions worldwide. With this in mind, father traveled in November to Japan, where he hoped to help unify that country's fragmented labor movement. Twice before, he and his brother Victor had visited this industrial island nation — first on their world bicycle tour, then again after World War II.

On their second trip, he and Victor had been picked up at the airport by a Japanese union car. This was postwar Japan. My father was branded a Yankee trade unionist. On their way to Osaka, a pickup truck tried to run them off the road.

Uncle Victor: "We were driving down the highway, a very narrow road. It reminded me of Alligator Alley in Florida, a highly elevated road with an enormous drop-off on both sides. And this pickup truck starts bearing down on us. My God, these guys must have been kamikaze pilots the way they were driving. They were behind us and they would come up and try to force us over the embankment. They tried three or four times and then our driver found a place to pull over and call the police. We arrived in Osaka and there was a real "commie" demonstration underway against us. In Japan at that time, the Communist Party was mighty powerful in the trade union movement. The crowd surrounded us carrying signs with heavy sticks. And with those sticks they started beating on the car and trying to smash the windows. They started rocking the car with the two of us in it. They damn near turned it over."

The police had arrived and cleared the way for father to enter the hall. Although chalk-white from his experience, he went on to speak before the workers. Among other things, he talked about nuclear weapons and radiation. He had recently filed a report on atomic dangers and concluded that nuclear weapons were so horrendous they should be outlawed.

Now it was 1962 and father was returning to Japan to strengthen the trade union movement by showing his solidarity with the workers. He had been invited by the four largest Japanese unions — all bitter rivals. Father had told them he would come on the condition that those unions meet jointly with him. American and Japanese officials alike viewed father's visit as crucial for Japanese trade unionism's fight against communism.

Met by heavy Communist opposition at Tokyo's Kayo University, father listened and conveyed America's position. Later, he recalled another violent reception to reporter Ralph McGill:

> The 'commies' picked Kyoto, the historic old capital and temple city, as the place where they hoped to create a demonstration. When our group got off the train, we were met by about 80 Communists. They had signs saying 'Go Home,' and so on. Some of them gathered close around me on the pretext of asking questions. Others crowded in and pretty soon I was getting some hard jabs in my ribs and back from their elbows. They were hoping I would lose my temper and strike back so that a fight could start and spread.
>
> We moved on through with them following, still crowding and jostling us. When I got into the cab, two big fellows tried to slam the door on my legs, but the Japanese with us prevented this. The Communists began to beat on the cab and rock it as they cursed and shouted 'Yankee imperialist, go home!' and similar slogans. But they were never able to bring others in with them, and they did not provoke us to angry reactions.

One of my friends at Putney showed me an article in the *New York Times* describing father's hostile reception in Japan. I called mother, who reassured me that he was all right. "What can you expect, Lisa? Your daddy is always sticking his neck out."

The third week in November, father wrote mother a letter from Tokyo:

Tokyo - Nov 19 - 62
11:45 PM
Dear Mayichka:
I hope your UN conference was interesting and you got on to Lisa and Putney OK. I arrived in Tokyo late after 14-1/4 hours of flight and I have been on the go continuously from 8 AM until midnight every night. I just finished my third press interview a few minutes ago.
My schedule today —
8 AM breakfast Trade Union Committee
9 AM Parliamentary Leaders Social Democratic Party
10:30 AM Parliamentary Leaders Socialist Party (left)
12 Noon lunch speech Japanese Labor Institute
3-5 PM speech and discussion - students at university
6 PM dinner meeting largest trade union group (Soyho)
9 PM conference labor leaders
11 PM press interview labor magazine
Two hours with Japanese university students was an experience. The party boys were all set. They had big signs on the walks — "Workers of the World Unite," "Cuba si-Yankee no," etc. At the end of 2 hours I had 80 percent with me, with the commies beat but still trying. Considering that Bobby Kennedy never was permitted to get started in his speech — I came off in good shape. You would have enjoyed it — from nuclear testing — Cuba — Berlin — segregation — John Birch — ICFTU vs WFTU. Japan is built as an imitation of the West, with tremendous energy and drive. The people are bright and the leadership young, which is hopeful. More when I get back. No time for shopping to date and the prospects not promising for they keep

adding to my schedule since I haven't collapsed as of yet.

Give Lisa a big hug and kiss for me and tell her I love her and her Mommy very much.

Love, Walter.

This was typical of the letters mother would receive from father, penned at midnight before he went to bed.

In Japan father managed to steal some of the the Communists' thunder. The Japanese auto makers claimed that it was necessary to export large numbers of cars because their own market was so small. Noticing that their employee parking lots were filled with bicycles, father commented: "Workers find it difficult to buy automobiles on bicycle wages. Your best market is in your own back yard." Years earlier, father had used this logic with Henry Ford. Increase the workers' wages and they will have greater purchasing power to buy automobiles. The greater demand increases production, and so on.

One of father's listeners, Japanese trade union leader Ichiro Shioji, had met him a year earlier at Harvard. As father gave a rousing speech to a standing-room-only crowd in Harvard's gym, Shioji thrilled to hear the American labor leader. Even in this citadel of capitalism, he commanded great power and respect. They met at a reception afterward. Aware of the old injury to father's right arm, Shioji offered his left hand to shake. Father insisted on using his right hand. "Let's see which of us is stronger," he challenged. To Shioji, the firm handshake signaled a firm friendship.

Back in Japan, Shioji boasted of his relationship with father based on his anti-Communist stand. He became powerful in the Japanese trade union movement, but the reason behind his new power was tragic, indeed. He tried to serve two masters.

Nissan Corporation, wanting a cooperative and pliable union, bought Shioji as its point man. Shioji became a vice president at Nissan even while he was simultaneously leading the Japanese auto workers. He threatened, pressured and bribed opposing unions to merge with his organization, which was nothing more than a company union. He used his influence and his muscle to break legitimate trade unions in Japan.

Since 1949, father had been urging the Big Three to produce small, fuel-efficient cars. In an article titled "A Small Car Named Desire," father stated that in 1948 some 20 percent of American families in the higher income brackets purchased 47 percent of the new cars available — mostly big gas-guzzlers. Middle America had to buy the used guzzlers since there weren't any small domestic cars at reasonable prices. And the auto makers liked it this way, as there was more profit in these "luxury liners". A GM statement concluded, "Folks in the U.S. are inclined to like class and dash. Because of that the popular American cars are big, fast, high-powered, advanced in styling, and asparkle with chrome."

Father called their vision near-sighted and dangerous. If the Big Three didn't fill the small-car vacuum, he warned, then the overseas competition would. Only after the small European cars — Volkswagen, Fiat, Renault — began to make a mark on the domestic market did the American corporations wake up and start to build the smaller cars affordable to more Americans. But now it was the 1960s. The European models were riding high, and Toyota and Nissan had begun to test America's waters.

Time and time again, Shioji had assured the UAW that if Nissan came to America it would honor the union.

Uncle Victor: "Doug Fraser [second UAW president after father] was shocked when Nissan opened operations in the U.S. and refused to recognize the UAW. The UAW was at the forefront of pressuring our government to encourage Nissan to open factories here, because we knew we would continue to lose jobs to Japan and other nations if they were encouraged to believe they could continue to ship completed vehicles to the United States, rather than at least beginning with the assembly work here.

"There was an awful lot of sweet talk, but behind it was the strategy of Shioji. He betrayed the Japanese labor movement and double-talked the American labor movement. If he claimed that Walter was his hero, then that is phony hero worship. He was not doing what Walter would have wanted him to do. He sold out his own workers."

Today, Japan has become the world financial center. It dominates the small-car market. On CBS' *Face the Nation* not long ago, GM

Chairman Roger Smith said the Big Three still hope to compete with the Japanese in the small-car market. "It's going to be tough," Smith said. "Right now, we don't know."

Despite Japan's self-imposed quota on car exports to the U.S. (2.3 million), her American subsidiaries have raised another specter — Japanese domination of the mid-size car market, the heart of the American auto industry. Will GM decide it can't compete there, either?

Every other industrialized country producing vehicles has legislation governing trade, as father would point out, to a degree that the United States has never had. "We're a sucker's market," he used to say. "The only market in the whole world where anybody can come and dump anything they manufacture."

Father believed America should use her economic strength to spread freedom. If a country does not respect the basic human rights of her citizens, we should not trade with her. Before she delivers her goods to our shores, let her government act for the common good at home. Hitting the "pocketbook nerve," as father would say, is the surest way to spread freedom.

We can also learn from European countries of the Common Market, whose healthy trade unions have influenced their governments' policies. Those nations have drawn up a code of ethics governing their companies' ventures into the Third World. If a company wants to take its capital and use it in a developing country, then it must turn a certain percentage of its earnings back into that country's health, education, and welfare. The code also prohibits racial discrimination. Humanity is the best policy. If we don't require a decent human rights record from our trading partners, we are encouraging exploitation.

At present, we have no legislation against trading with a ruthless military regime. A corporation works out deals with dictatorships where working people are exploited, puts its labels on the products, and sells them here, where their former employees are out of work. And we wonder, what's happened to America?

The pioneers of the American auto industry — the Dodges, the Chryslers, the Durants, the Fords, the Fishers — were certainly motivated by profit, but they also had a committment to America, a committment the money manipulators who are shipping our economic base overseas do not.

The foreign plant pays no taxes to the municipality of Flint, Michigan, dying home of GM. American labor must stop these plant closings at home and the export of our workers' jobs. The trade imbalance and our shrinking industrial sector point to a crumbling economy. We must pressure our trading partners to lower their exports to America or open their economies to more American goods.

For several years now, Japan has exported increasing volumes of government-subsidized, under-priced goods to the ever-hungry U.S. market, in an attempt to destroy *our* industries. The Japanese are now collecting as much of the world's wealth as the British Empire did at its height and the U.S. did in the industrial boom after World War II.

But the Japanese are not stimulating the economies of other countries by spending that capital throughout the world. "The numbers mean the United States has lost its position as the prime mover in the world economy," declares Richard Hu, Singapore's finance minister. "Now Japan has the tools of capital, and it will be better for everyone if they spread it around as the U.S. did in its heyday."

Before leaving Japan, father met with the four large trade union federations to establish the International Labor Wage Research Center, where economic data would be available to help unions worldwide in their contract negotiations.

When father returned to Paint Creek, he and mother called me at Putney. Father joked about the signs saying "Walter Reuther Go Home."

Mother interrupted on the other phone: "My sign would read, 'Walter Reuther Stay Home!'"

CHAPTER THIRTY-FOUR

"I HAVE
A DREAM"

*"In Detroit, King and labor friend Walter Reuther led
125,000 on a Freedom Walk down Woodward Avenue, and
he thrilled a packed auditorium when he spoke of a dream of
his, a dream rooted in the American dream, a dream of a day
when all of God's children could sit together at the table of
brotherhood."*
— From Stephen B. Oates' *Let the Trumpets Sound*

The Freedom Walk late in the spring of 1963 was the largest civil
rights march to date. Two weeks earlier, U.S Attorney General Bobby
Kennedy had called father for bail money when a large number of civil
rights marchers were arrested in Birmingham, Alabama. Father
arranged for the UAW to send $160,000.

"Employers in the South printed leaflets saying don't vote for these
nigger lovers who gave $160,000 to help the NAACP and Martin
Luther King," recalled Uncle Victor. "In the middle of an election,
they would print those leaflets. Well, we'd lose some Southern elections over that issue — but it never changed Walter's thinking about
it."

At the end of the Freedom Walk, father and Dr. King were to be the
keynote speakers at Detroit's Cobo Hall. I begged to go to the rally.
Father knew the situation would be tense. Racial violence had been on
the rise everywhere, especially in Detroit. The rally was an attempt to
unify the black community behind a peaceful approach to their
grievances. To allow them to "lift up their voices and sing together."
It also gave the white community an opportunity to help smooth racial
tensions, which affected both black and white.

Mother and father decided that the advantages of my going to the rally far outweighed the risks. When the evening arrived, I rode in the back seat of the car with father. He was going over some last-minute notes for his speech. Just fragments, really; there was no formal script.

The car pulled up to the back entrance of Cobo Hall. The body-guard stopped and got out first. Placing his hand on his gun, he moved to father's door. There were policemen everywhere. I had not antici-pated such an army. "Wait here, May," father instructed. "Eddie will come back for you and Lisa." Tumultous energy in a swirl of faces and a crush of confusion surrounded us outside. I appreciated the steel shelter of the automobile.

A minute later the guard returned and guided Mother and me into a conference room reserved for the guests of honor. Seeing us enter, father came to escort us to the others. Several men rose to acknowl-edge mother's presence. She had been close to A. Philip Randolph, a civil rights veteran. Randolph joined King as we approached. Both men radiated an inner strength, a quality I also recognized in my father. I was humbled and grateful to be among these dedicated men and women. I offered my hand in solidarity. "We shall overcome."

Looking at King and Randolph, father placed his arm around my shoulder: "My daughter Lisa is going to carry on the struggle for human dignity. She shares our quest."

I was embarrassed, but honored. Throughout history, great people had struggled to help their fellow human beings. Driven by the dream of brotherhood, leaders had emerged who worked for the common good. My father's words weighed heavily on me. How could I fulfill his expectations? As a young girl, I had felt the burden of love. I wanted to care for my younger friends, to protect my animals. As I grew up, the burden increased. I tried to run from this inner voice. But it stalked me.

The master of ceremonies moved to the microphone. Mother and I sat in the first row. I surveyed the crowd, mostly black. Whatever had brought us to the rally was greater than any individual, black or white.

My father spoke second. His message was simple: "We have learned the lesson that only in the solidarity of human brotherhood, only as you stand together with your fellow man, can you solve your basic problems. I've often thought, why is it that you can get a great nation like America marching, fighting, sacrificing and dying in the struggle to destroy the master race theory in Berlin, and people haven't got an ounce of courage to fight the master race theory in America?"

When Dr. King stepped up to speak, the crowd fell silent. For the first time, he delivered his now-famous "I Have A Dream" speech. Listening to his voice, the audience became like children. Tears in an old man's eyes showed he was hearing a message he had held within his own heart for years. "Free at last, free at last," King was saying. " I say to you today, my friends, that even though we face the difficulties of today and tomorrow, I still have a dream ... It is a dream deeply rooted in the American Dream. I have a dream that one day this nation will rise up and live out the true meaning of its creed: 'We hold these truths to be self-evident, that *all* men are created equal.'"

As King's speech ended, the crowd rose in one spontaneous movement. The thunderous clapping of thousands of hands seemed the very sound of freedom itself.

Mother and I returned to the conference room to wait for father. The applause continued for a long time. Father was beaming as he entered with King. The turnout had been enormous, with no incidents of violence.

A police escort guided our car back to the freeway. "What a glorious moment," father began, and then he was off again, speaking of dreams, equality, opportunity, education, God. "All right, daddy," I teased, "we already heard your speech at Cobo Hall." We laughed. We knew what a preacher he was, his enthusiasm boundless.

It had been a long day. I slipped my arm through his and rested my head on his shoulder. Happily I fell asleep.

That same year, the Institute for Humanistic Studies in Aspen, Colorado, sponsored a panel of distinguished people to discuss moral, ethical, social and cultural questions facing society. Father was invited to participate, so that summer our family traveled there.

Aspen summers were rich in culture. Besides the Institute, there was a school of music and the performing arts. The crisp air and mountain views invited us to explore life deeply.

Every morning, mother, Linda and I swam for an hour, followed by 20 minutes in a sauna and a quick dip in an icy pool. The balance of the morning we devoted to horseback riding or hiking trails that led to magical places.

At Aspen our family became very close to Dr. Jonas Salk and his son, Peter. Like father, Dr. Salk was a panel member and he shared father's conviction that scientific advancement must be tempered by moral astuteness. His polio vaccine had been a scientific break-through. But where, he asked, was the vaccine to prevent mankind's misuse of scientific discovery?

After lunch, mother, Linda and I would listen to discussions at the Institute. Several books formed the basis for the talks, and mother kept up with the suggested readings. Often the dialogues became too complex or esoteric for me. But I was awakening to the world of ideas.

One day father invited me to go climbing with him on the gentle slopes surrounding the Institute, a rare treat for both of us. Trails to the mountaintop could be climbed in a couple of hours. After our ascent we gazed over the vast range with deep green valleys.

"We had a fascinating discussion today," father began. "One of the books we're reading is by Plato. He presents detailed accounts of reincarnation." Father and I had discussed this Eastern concept before. The idea that we have lived in many bodies and will continue to do so until we reach perfection. Our talks had begun back when father returned from India.

"Plato held that the pure soul falls from a plane of absolute reality because of sensual desire and then takes on a physical body," he continued.

"You think we have actually lived before, daddy?"

"I don't know, Lisa. Here in the West we think horizontally. What you see is what exists. That's our whole reality." The ancients, by contrast, he said, were vertical thinkers. They saw cosmic forces underlying our temporal reality and guiding us over a continuum of many lifetimes.

"I've always felt a strong sense of destiny, Lisa. I know there are goals I must achieve in this lifetime. Who knows? Maybe these are preparing me for my next."

"How does Plato say reincarnation works?" I pressed.

"Quite simple," he replied. "If a person lives a life according to moral and spiritual laws, then in his next life he is promoted to a better situation. And if he lives his life breaking those laws, his situation and body worsen."

His answer appealed to me because it wasn't all fatalism and predestination. There was room for free will. He quoted the Greek saying that "man is the architect of his own destiny." It made sense. We're not God, but we are responsible for our actions. Nor was life merely a brief flash followed by heaven or hell. We're granted as many lifetimes, as many chances, as we need to perfect ourselves. What a kind and reasonable vision of the absolute! Talking philosophy on the mountain, I felt I had known father for many lifetimes.

Even as he was exploring the mysteries of life, father was helping organize the largest civil rights demonstration yet — the March on Washington.

In a June 28 letter to Attorney General Robert Kennedy, father affirmed his committment: "I am making civil rights the priority item in the period ahead, and if there is anything I can do to be helpful, I hope that you will feel free to call upon me."

Predictably, George Meany lined up the AFL-CIO Executive Council against the proposed march. Only one other member besides father voted in favor of participating. Disregarding the wishes of the elderly labor chief, father gained support of many other unions. For years he had struggled with Meany's narrow vision of labor's responsibility, but this time he would not acquiesce. The march's impact, he realized, would be weak without substantial white participation.

The President was cautious. He was concerned about the possibility of violence. This made father more determined to work with local union leaders and other organizations to ensure a peaceful outcome. His youthful decency and the sparkle in his eyes excited my own idealism. He was a knight of the faith striving for victory.

Eventually, Kennedy met with the organizers of the march. "This is a very serious fight. The Vice President and I know what it will mean if we fail... a good many programs I care about may go down the drain — so we are putting a lot on the line. What is important is that we preserve confidence in the good faith of each other." Kennedy requested the organizers to make every attempt to involve whites. Otherwise, he said, the demonstration might hurt the Civil Rights Bill making its way through Congress.

As the march approached, thunder sounded to the left and right. The Black Muslims condemned the event. The American Nazi Party said it was going to countermarch. Reactionaries were lashing out. The President was counting on father's peacemaking abilities.

On August 28, 1963, nearly a quarter of a million people, black and white, assembled before the Lincoln Memorial to bring pressure on Congress to act on the proposed Civil Rights Bill. The UAW brought in thousands of people from around the country, transporting them by bus, train, automobile and airplane. Theirs was the largest contingent.

Violence was a real possibility. Around Washington, extra police reinforced the regular shifts of officers. Many residents locked themselves indoors. Congressmen were asking for special protection at the Capitol. Across the Potomac, 4,000 troops were ready and alert.

The march's program read:

> The Washington March of August 28th is more than just a demonstration.
>
> It was conceived as an outpouring of the deep feeling of millions of white and colored American citizens that the time has come for the government of the United States . . . to grant and guarantee complete equality in citizenship to the Negro minority of our population.
>
> The march will be orderly, but not subservient. It will be proud, but not arrogant. It will be nonviolent, but not timid. It will be unified in purposes and behavior, not splintered into groups and individual competitors. It will be outspoken, but not raucous.

The march commenced with the *National Anthem*, led by Marian Anderson. The crowd included celebrities such as Charlton Heston, Sidney Poitier, Marlon Brando, and folk singer Joan Baez.

As the speakers made their presentations, anxiety mounted over John Lewis, the chairman of the Student Nonviolent Coordinating Committee (SNCC). Lewis, a Georgia congressman today, was scheduled to speak before father. Many of the organizers were concerned that his speech might incite violence, that he wanted to use the march to make a radical statement against the Civil Rights Bill. Reportedly, his statement read, "We cannot support the

Administration's Civil Rights Bill. There's not one thing in that bill that will protect our people from police brutality . . . I want to know — which side is the federal government on?"

Martin Luther King and A. Philip Randolph had approached Lewis with a request to see his prepared remarks. Lewis had refused. Many of the white religious leaders were disturbed. Archbishop Patrick O'Boyle said he would withdraw from the program if Lewis did not change his address. Assistant Attorney General Burke Marshall asked father to use his influence lest Lewis' speech upset the gathering.

Moments before Lewis' turn to speak, father and NAACP Executive Secretary Roy Wilkins approached Lewis on the steps of the Lincoln Memorial. They demanded he show them his entire speech. Reluctantly producing his script, Lewis watched as father and Wilkins struck provocative phrases they thought might incite a disturbance. "I looked up at Abe," father later recalled, "and I said, 'Abe, I need your blessings and your help.'" The confrontation tempered the speech and kept the peace.

After Lewis, father was introduced to speak. An elderly black lady standing near Irving Bluestone turned to her friend and asked: "Walter Reuther, who is Walter Reuther?" Her friend replied, "Oh, he's the white Martin Luther King."

Father concluded his speech challenging Americans everywhere to seek equality and first-class citizenship for every American, "from Boston to Birmingham, from New York to New Orleans, from Michigan to Mississippi."

At father's suggestion, President Kennedy had invited the march leaders to the White House after their speeches to show his support. Everyone was elated by the peacefulness of the event. Kennedy congratulated the organizers. When he complimented Dr. King on his "I Have A Dream" address, the minister humbly reminded the president that father's speech had also been very well received. "Yes," Kennedy smiled, "I have heard Walter speak before."

Returning to Paint Creek, father exulted over the march's outcome. We had not gone with him to Washington. Shuffling through his briefcase, he brought out a program. At the top was the inscription, "To Lisa and Linda, Best Wishes from Martin Luther King, Jr."

Martin Luther King Jr. and father before their speeches at the Lincoln Memorial; the 1963 March on Washington.

Dr. King, Whitney Young and father, exhilarated at the large turnout for the march.

CHAPTER THIRTY-FIVE

THE
KENNEDY
ASSASSINATION

"A young eagle fallen in full flight, snatched from the heavens by a bitter fate...."
— From Walter Reuther's memorial poem for JFK

Aspen and the March on Washington filled me with a new sense of possibility. When I returned to Putney that fall, I became immersed in the poetry of Walt Whitman.

"He's a poet of the common man, not highly intellectual," a friend told me. As Vermont's leaves turned red and gold, I thrilled to the world Whitman opened before me.

As a boy, father also read Whitman. He sent me a copy of *Leaves of Grass*, inscribed "To my Lisa. May this open your eyes. Love, Dad." My parents' love for the poet gave greater meaning to my readings.

> Swiftly arose and spread around me the peace and knowledge that pass all the argument of the earth,
> And I know that the hand of God is the promise of my own,
> And I know that the spirit of God is the brother of my own,
> And that all the men ever born are also my brothers, and women my sisters and lovers,
> And that a kelson of the creation is love,
> And limitless are leaves stiff or drooping in the fields,
> And brown ants in the little wells beneath them,
> And mossy scabs of the worm fence, headp'd stones, elder, mullein, and poke-weed.

Whitman's words illumined my spirit. Many times I had felt a oneness with nature. But he affirmed a spiritual dimension beyond change and challenged the notion that death is the end.

> And to die is different from what any one supposed, and luckier.

> I pass death with the dying and birth with the new-wash'd babe, and am not contain'd between my hat and boots,
> And peruse manifold objects, no two alike and every one good,
> The earth good and the stars good and their adjuncts all good.

> I am not an earth nor an adjunct of an earth,
> I am the mate and companion of people, all just as important and fathomless as myself,
> (They do not know how immortal, but I know.)

Along with the fear that had stalked me since childhood, I too had sensed the presence of that dearest friend, that smiling witness watching over me. To my amazement, Whitman was expressing my innermost feelings. Like him, I knew intuitively I was "not contained between my hat and boots."

My growing fascination for the wisdom of the East inspired me to do an independent study of Mahatma Gandhi. His spirituality, his fearlessness, his nonviolence and civil disobedience against the British — his wisdom in action.

As I read his autobiography, I was drawn again to India, that ancient and mystical land. I kept a journal, which my teacher reviewed, and vowed to go to India someday. There were no tests, formal grades, or report cards. But each student received personal attention and a critique at term's end. Putney's "enlightened approach" fanned my desire to learn.

There were darker moments, too. At the end of my sophomore year, I heard that three boys had been scheming to kidnap me and demand a ransom. It may have been a joke; I don't know. But I do recall my utter surprise. It sounded so far-fetched.

A sledgehammer would strike an old train rail at Putney to announce the end of classes — or an emergency. On November 22, 1963, the curved antique rang mercilessly. The headmaster herded us into the meeting hall to make the announcement. President Kennedy had been shot dead. Then, after a brief explanation: "Everyone please go to your afternoon work assignment."

Tears poured down my cheeks as I ran back to my dormitory. I felt like screaming. I wanted to go for a long walk in the woods and yell to the trees. But my supervisor was right behind me. "Lisa, everyone must go to the next activity. Everyone must follow these instructions. Go now."

It was a nightmare. I couldn't believe it. I needed space. I had many strong feelings for President Kennedy. I'd met him personally at several UAW conventions and Labor Day celebrations. His youthful aura, his boundless energy, his committment to social improvement and arms control — all had a deep impact on me. I was furious at my supervisor, and more, at fate itself. I think the school was afraid of mass hysteria; so back we went to our work duties.

My head pounding with confusion, I started peeling potatoes for the evening meal. Peeling potatoes! I counted the minutes until my job was over. I wanted to slip away for a quiet walk. And I needed to call my parents.

Their voices cracked with anger and grief. Father and Kennedy had been linked by a common quest, a vision of a better world. Overcome as he was, he talked and helped me regain my hope for the future.

A few days later, father left for Kennedy's burial at Arlington National Cemetery. He, Uncle Victor, and Hubert Humphrey were in the Washington hotel suite of West Germany's Willy Brandt watching TV accounts of the assassination and Lyndon Johnson trying to calm a shocked nation. Sweden's Olaf Palme and Britain's Harold Wilson, also in the room, felt the shooting was a very carefully planned plot, perhaps by the radical right. Father and Victor shared their skepticism, especially after Jack Ruby's gun silenced Lee Harvey Oswald.

Shortly after the burial, father received a phone call from a concerned and weary Lyndon Johnson. "My friend, I need your friendship and support now more than ever before." Johnson asked father to compile a list of the most pressing problems facing the nation.

Topping the list would be civil rights, exposing and prosecuting hate groups, better education, wiping out unemployment, and turning America's energy more toward the pursuit of peace.

Although father had opposed Johnson's vice-presidential nomination a few years earlier, he was inspired by LBJ's desire to pass much-needed domestic legislation. Kennedy's Civil Rights Bill and the crusade against poverty were keys in Johnson's vision of a "Great Society." His mastery of the legislative process enabled him to push Kennedy's policies through Congress.

For months after the assassination, father was a frequent visitor to the White House. The meetings didn't receive much publicity, though an unhappy conservative writer, J. Evetts Haley, wrote: "Now nobody seems to move in and out of the White House with greater ease than the arrogant radical, Walter Reuther."

"President Johnson relied on Walter quite a bit," Hubert Humphrey later observed, "in foreign policy and civil rights — for both advice and support. Johnson's domestic legislative policy was just what Walter had hoped and prayed for. He was consulted [on that program] as often as any man outside government."

As for Johnson's foreign policy, father was skeptical, calling LBJ "an unknown quantity, almost surely ignorant regarding Southeast Asia and Africa." Vietnam bore that out. But despite their split over that tragic war, one UAW official called Johnson and my father "big armpit buddies." A week after he succeeded Kennedy as president, Johnson wrote father.

> Nov. 30, 1963
> Dear Walter,
> I was greatly strengthened by your warm message. I need the support and help of the dedicated, imaginative people like you if the unfinished work is to be carried on, and I find renewed strength in the thought that in the days that lie ahead I can count upon you.
> Warm regards.
> Sincerely,
> Lyndon

As Valentine and Anna Reuther's 60th wedding anniversary

approached, the Reuther clan made plans for a grand reunion at Grossvater and Grossmutter's home in Wheeling. The old farmhouse on the hill had been the site of many nostalgic gatherings. Father told anecdotes about their times of scarcity and hard work.

Grossmutter in particular had earned a special place in her children's hearts. She was six months younger than her lifelong husband. Now that Grossvater was in his 80s, the doctor asked him if he were still shoveling snow in the winter. He was, Grossvater replied. The doctor cautioned him that he was getting old and that perhaps he should give up that chore. At that point, Grossmutter scolded: "See, I told you, you shouldn't shovel the snow at your age. *I* should shovel the snow!"

I admired Grossmutter's nurturing skills; her resourcefulness; her ability as a cook and seamstress — the feminine strengths that balanced Grossvater's disciplinarian personality. And I was attracted to their simple, hard-working life on the slopes of Bethlehem, West Virginia.

"Is Bethlehem related to the place where baby Jesus was born?" I would ask. The name piqued my fascination.

The highlight of the drive to Bethlehem came as we ascended the large hill before their house. Chuckling to himself, father took the car phone and dialed his parents' number. "Hello, *Mutterchen*, this is Walter." Even as the car was turning into the driveway, they would exchange light-hearted words. As Eddie quietly turned off the engine, father would continue to converse from the car while mother, Linda, and I tiptoed into the house. "Surprise!"

The family had grown so large that we gathered in the private dining room of a local restaurant. After many toasts to the guests of honor, the group launched into a round of German folk songs. Everyone would stop to hear Grossvater sing a deep bass chorus to a Schubert lieder or hear Grossmutter repeat her delicate cuckoo refrain. Mother accompanied us on the piano, while father immersed himself in the sing-along spirit. Whether carrying the weight of a pending strike or a critical Congressional vote, when he shared music with the family, he left his responsibilities behind.

The UAW had planned to honor John Kennedy with its Social Justice Award. After the fatal shooting of the President, the award was presented posthumously, Robert Kennedy accepting on his brother's behalf. It was his first public appearance since the assassination.

According to a February, 1964 story in the *New York Times*, Bobby Kennedy told the UAW convention delegates he had wanted very much to address them because there was no other organization with which the President had been more closely identified than the auto workers union.

"You played a major role in putting him in the White House and made it possible for him to achieve at least part of his program," Kennedy said. "He always had a very special place in his heart for the UAW."

To honor the late President, father wrote a poem, which he later sent to Jacqueline Kennedy with notice of a $230,554 gift from the UAW to the John Fitzgerald Kennedy Memorial Library Fund.

In his verse, father referred to JFK as "a young eagle fallen in full flight, snatched from the heavens by a bitter fate. . ."

> He gave new dimension to human dignity
> through his fearless fight for human
> rights, his compassionate concern for
> the aged, his devotion and dedication to
> youth and by his courageous contribution
> in extending the frontiers of social
> justice. . .
>
> No words are strong
> enough to express our determination to
> carry on in the spirit in which he lived.

The 1964 UAW convention also included speeches by President Johnson and Secretary of Labor Willard Wirtz. Already father was working closely with Johnson on his upcoming campaign, so participation in the UAW convention helped LBJ reach more of its growing membership.

At the 1964 Democratic convention, father was pressuring

Johnson to select Hubert Humphrey as his running mate.

UNCLE VICTOR: "It can be fairly said that Walter was the person most responsible for convincing Johnson that Hubert Humphrey should be his Vice-Presidential nominee. And Hubert certainly knew that Walter was the key guy in that."

Dissension plagued the convention that year. Mississippi was represented by the traditional "white lineup," but the Mississippi Black Freedom Democratic Party threatened a floor fight if they were not seated and allowed to vote. The resulting deadlock posed a difficult political situation for President Johnson, who asked father to come to Atlantic City and intervene.

But father, who was in the heat of intense contract negotiations with General Motors, told the President that he couldn't leave Detroit. Then Johnson asked Humphrey to pressure father, who gave in and flew to the convention on a "red-eye" special. Immediately he entered into the intense, all-night negotiations between the Mississippi delegates and the Black Freedom Party. By morning he had helped reach a compromise that provided the Black Freedom Party votes, but not seats, at the convention.

Every Labor Day, father would give a speech at Detroit's Cadillac Square. Mother, Linda, and I would sit with Governor Williams in a roped-off area by the speaker's platform. Up to 150,000 would attend.

In presidential election years, the Democratic nominee would launch his campaign with a speech at the Square. Kennedy had spoken there four years earlier, and now in 1964 destiny had renamed the Square in his memory. The leading speakers were President Johnson and father.

Photographers snapped photos of LBJ with Henry Ford II raising up one of his arms and father raising up the other. Father had committed the UAW's political muscle to the Johnson-Humphrey ticket, as he had to Kennedy-Johnson in '60. And again, Uncle Roy led the voter-registration drive.

With such diverse backing as Ford and Reuther, Johnson's election seemed a shoo-in. Yet less than 5,000 showed up to hear his Labor Day speech. And a truckload of "Welcome LBJ" signs mysteriously failed to arrive at the site.

On his way back to the airport, the President admonished father and Detroit Mayor Jerome Cavanaugh: "There's a lot of legislation still to get through Congress and, Walter, if you could just forget the labor movement in Norway and Russia long enough to help out, that would be fine.

"You fellows better get off your ass and work, because if they elect a Republican House of Representatives, it will do nothing but investigate for two years; and Walter, you'll be in Norway, but Jerry (elbowing Cavanaugh in the ribs), you won't get that trillion dollars for Detroit."

Nevertheless, father felt there was no real contest in this election. The Republicans had chosen as their candidate father's arch-enemy Barry Goldwater, whose opinion of social welfare programs was loud and clear: "I don't believe in federal aid to education, or aid to the aged, or any kind of medical assistance."

Father and President Johnson during the 1964 campaign.

Goldwater also had denounced a minimum wage for workers and was famous for foreign-policy statements that went well beyond the brink: "Do anything that needs to be done to get rid of that cancer [Cuba]; if it means war, let it mean war," and "I'd drop a low-yield atomic bomb on Chinese supply lines in North Vietnam."

The Republican nominee's public attitudes toward war led to a joke among union members: If Goldwater is elected President in November, his first speech will begin: "Ten, nine, eight, seven, six, five. . .." The *Saturday Evening Post*, hardly a liberal mouthpiece, stated: "Goldwater would not make a good president. He has not even made a good senator."

Mother and I took an active part in campaigning that year. She had arranged for me to work as a full-time volunteer at the Democratic Headquarters of Oakland County in nearby Pontiac. Although Pontiac had a strong core of Democratic workers, the surrounding suburbs provided a challenge. Back at Putney in the fall, I joined a group of close friends to do more volunteer work at the local level. The thought of Goldwater as President motivated me to work diligently for Johnson, no matter where I was.

The week after Johnson's election, father went to Brussels for a world meeting of trade union officials. On the way, he stopped in London, where he met Berlin major Willy Brandt and had lunch with Prime Minister Harold Wilson at No. 10 Downing Street. In a letter to me at Putney, he wrote:

> After meeting with Prime Minister Harold Wilson, I had a few minutes to walk through the old section of the British Parliament building and I am always moved deeply, for this is the cradle of the whole governmental structure of the Western democracy. Since Westminster Abbey is next door, I walked through the great church where kings and queens are crowned. Many kings and queens and far too many generals are entombed in Westminster Abbey. However, in one section of the Abbey, England has enshrined her poets and great men of literature — Shelley, Keats, Browning and others. How much better of a world we will have when the world will honor the scholars and poets and not the soldiers.
>
> I am thinking of you and send much love.
>
> — Dad.

253

CHAPTER THIRTY-SIX

THE
HARD
BARGAINER

"I'd like to get in a poker game with you when the stakes aren't a billion dollars."
— Former GM President Charles E. Wilson's
friendly challenge to father

The year 1964 was an historic one at the bargaining tables in Detroit. The first step forward was taken with Chrysler where new pension safeguards for workers were secured. With Doug Fraser at his side, father announced: "I believe the agreement we have reached is the most historic ... with respect to the broad problem of pension security for workers."

In response to this new contract, one retired Chrysler worker, a 39-year veteran, said: "You get to where you can hardly say anything, you feel so much gratitude for what the union did for the retirees. The union said benefits had to be increased and hospitalization paid for, so we all could live like human beings and they kept their word."

Gains included optional early retirement, more medical and insurance benefits, wage increases, supplemental unemployment benefits, survivor benefits, paid vacations and added relief time (from 24 minutes to 36 minutes). As one newspaper editor observed: "Even in the army, 10 minutes rest per hour is allowed. On assembly lines the workers must keep going hour after hour without any letup."

"We're always being driven," a worker reported. "I have to get in and out of each car four times to hook up vent cables on each side — in 90 seconds flat."

On a rainy Friday morning that year, father and chief negotiator, Ken Bannon, emerged from a strenuous 24-hour session with the number two auto maker, Ford. Smiling before the host of reporters, father said: "We have duplicated the precedent-shattering Chrysler package, with a little frosting on the cake." The "frosting" was a Christmas bonus effective in 1965.

Nineteen sixty-four had been a banner year for Ford. At the New York World's Fair, the small, sporty Mustang had been introduced by company executive Lee A. Iacocca. Its success was immediate, breaking sales records and landing Iacocca on the cover of Time and Newsweek. Much later Iacocca was to tangle with Henry and fall on his way up the Ford ladder, then bounce higher to the top of Chrysler, where the first UAW representative ever was elected to the Board of Directors. The representative was UAW President Doug Fraser, who played a key role in Chrysler's comeback and saw some striking similarities between Iacocca and father.

"Iacocca has a great devotion to the privacy of his family as did Walter. Then too, Iacocca is flamboyant and a hip shooter; Walter was a hip shooter, too," Fraser observed. "And Iacocca, I would argue, is shy sometimes." Doug told me of different occasions when he and father would arrive at a meeting in progress. He said that my father would often peer through the door's window and wait until there was a break in the meeting before he would enter. Doug felt that father had a genuine shy streak. I agree. "And Iacocca is very protective of his family," Doug continued. "I would bet if Walter was asked what was the greatest sacrifice he had to make — was it getting into the violence? — he would say no. It was giving up so much time that he denied his family."

Fraser recalled the intensity of the 1964 Chrysler negotiations, which resulted in a UAW victory and set the precedent for Ford and GM settlements that followed. As negotiations reached the crucial phase, the number of negotiators had been reduced to six. For Chrysler were Bill O'Brien, John Leary and Bill Baringer. Representing the workers were father, Irving Bluestone and Doug Fraser.

"There was a strike deadline of 11 a.m.," Fraser recalled. "Walter was pressing for the worker's right to optional early retirement. Sensing Chrysler's indifference, in the middle of making the point he abruptly stopped talking. A nervous silence hung over the bargaining table. No one said a word for nearly two hours. Suddenly, one of the anxious Chrysler spokesmen blurted out, 'For God's sake, somebody say something. We've got to settle this thing by 11 o'clock.'"

Father broke his sober mood with a grin: "OK, let's get down to business."

Father's skill at the bargaining table once prompted former GM President Charles E. Wilson to tell him, "I'd like to get in a poker game with you when the stakes aren't a billion dollars."

At Solidarity House, father's colleagues saw him in other ways. Said Uncle Victor:

> I was living in Washington and shuttling out to Detroit frequently for overnight trips. I learned over the years that it was difficult to accomplish what I needed to with Walter during the regular work day. So I'd get in late in the afternoon and would often go home with him.
>
> Well, one evening we didn't check out of Solidarity House at the normal hour, say 7 o'clock. We stayed right there, talking and talking and, my God, it must have been 10:30 before we finally walked out of Walter's office. We started down the hallway, and here is a security man coming in the opposite direction. He stops dead in his tracks and shouts, "Goddammit, Redhead, what are you doing here still? You didn't tell me you were staying late!"
>
> Here's a security guy, an employee, blowing his top because Walter violated security. Well, Walter was caught dead in his tracks, and his jaw dropped and he looked real serious at first. Then he just burst out laughing and said to me, "I guess we've got a pretty good rank and file when an employee can say to the president, You red-headed sonofabitch, don't you do this to me again!"

Writer William Manchester once described the security around father's office as an "intricate maze of narrow corridors [making] visitors feel like balls in a pinball machine."

Other accounts reveal father's total absorption in his work. Once visiting congressmen noted how many really gorgeous secretaries worked at Solidarity House. Father looked around and blushingly acknowledged that his guests were right. One of the women later remarked, "I honestly think it was the first time he ever saw any of us!" He had taken enough notice, however, to have modesty panels fastened to the desks of women employees so that their legs would not draw unbusinesslike stares.

Manchester also wrote about father's popularity with the female rank and file. "His appeal to women is immense. During the UAW presidential balloting in 1948, the 60 feminine delegates voted for him almost as a bloc. Women of strong liberal bent often swoon over him."

As father saw it, the strength of free enterprise depended largely on the willingness of individuals to take the initiative in solving the problems of the day. In one attempt, he launched the Citizens Crusade Against Poverty and personally convinced the UAW Executive Board to give a million dollars to the cause.

Father was constantly frustrated that the auto industry, one of the largest power bases in the world, did so little to relieve humanity's social problems. The auto barons seemed the most reluctant to share their wealth with those in need. I saw father as a modern-day Robin Hood. He represented the majority poor and took their cause to the bargaining table, where he would preach to the industrial aristocracy about moral responsibility to the community. Corporation negotiators were mostly millionaires. Father was making just over $20,000. But he deftly outfoxed them and never forgot his constituency back in Sherwood Forest.

GM's chief negotiator, Louis Seaton, sat across the bargaining table from father for 24 years. Their battles became legends. They played a sophisticated chess match, with father moving for the common man and Seaton plotting for the corporation's shareholders. "There was never any monkey business there," Seaton remarked. "And away from the table he was another kind of individual — concerned with the problems of everyone in the community, not just the people he represented.

"Between contracts we'd meet for a kind of 'State of the Nation' report that never received much publicity. That's when I realized the grasp Walter had on the broad problems of the day. He was no narrow visionary."

257

Seaton further described father as a man absolutely prepared, who knew how to gamble with a terrific sense of timing. And Seaton appreciated that father knew he, as a professional, was guarding the interests of the corporation's shareholders. GM's chief negotiator said father never attacked personalities, nor did he let recriminations mar negotiations. "He was a terrifically competitive adversary."

If historians were asked who has used the auto industry's energy to do the greatest good for the largest number of people, father's name, I believe, would top a number of their lists.

In December, mother called me at Putney with the news that father was going into Henry Ford Hospital to a have a spot removed from his right lung. Actually, he had known of his illness seven months before he consented to surgery. But there had been other, more pressing priorities for him, namely negotiations and the national political campaigns.

The *Detroit News*, known for its conservative slant, ran an editorial that mother clipped and mailed to me:

> The chronicles of chivalry relate how Saladin, the Saracen, sent his personal physician to minister to a respected foe of the Crusades, Richard the Lion Hearted. In this context, but transplanted to the wars of labor and management, UAW President Walter P. Reuther is resting today in the careful hands of Henry Ford Hospital's staff. The mood is a tribute to the red-headed crusader in UAW colors, who invaded industry's domain, set up catapults before its castles, and offered holy war or peace under duly negotiated contracts.
>
> But Reuther went through the long weeks of negotiating for the Big Three auto contracts without revealing his personal problem. Neither he nor his opponents at the bargaining tables softened their assaults. For this short period, it's nice for Reuther to rest and convalesce in the assurance that all the folks who back him and all who oppose him are united at last. They're united in the hope he'll soon be back on his feet again.

When father left the hospital, he told reporters he was having some pain, but "the spirit is stronger than the flesh, and I can smile."

"Your father is in perfect health, Lisa," mother called to tell me. "We'll see you in a few weeks." I must have been repressing my feelings more than I realized, for as soon as she finished speaking, the tears started to pour from my eyes. "That's wonderful," I sobbed. The rest of the term passed quickly as I anticipated our holiday reunion.

Christmas was a time for the family to relax and be together. Father was home recuperating for two weeks and catching up on paperwork. Linda was home from the University of Michigan in Ann Arbor, and I was back for a month's break from Putney.

Mother poured her energy into creating a spectacular assortment of taste treats. Uncle Roy's family would join us, and close friends would always show up for our Christmas Eve sing-along.

After warming up with *Silent Night* and *O Come All Ye Faithful*, father would distribute place mats with *The Twelve Days of Christmas* in pictures. Then he stepped to the center and conducted the choir, urging us on with his boyish enthusiasm.

As we approached the phrase "five golden rings," father raised his arms into the air, commanding us to slow down and stress every syllable. "Five golden rrrings!" The r's rolled on at his command. As we reached the final phrase "and a partridge in a pear tree," father would be grinning from ear to ear. To see his pleasure was as much fun as singing the songs.

After emptying our stockings on Christmas morning, Linda and I would lead all our animals into the living room and give them homemade gifts. Meantime, father would enter the kitchen in his brown flannel robe, roll up his sleeves, and begin his annual task of preparing Christmas breakfast for the family. First, he squeezed fresh orange juice, which he delivered to mother in bed. Then, he prepared pancakes or waffles, fruit salad, hot chocolate, and a small pot of coffee. He performed this duty as faithfully as he would his life's work, attentive to every detail of feeding the family.

After breakfast father led us in dancing the hora around the living room. We held hands as he circled us, twirling with his hands above his head. "Watch this move, girls." Placing his hand level with his head, he kicked high, gracefully tapping his hand with his foot. Father held up his hand near us. We giggled as we tried to kick it. Then Uncle Roy would go into his "dying swan." Entering the room, mother burst out laughing. "Quite the dance troupe!"

Later in the day, our psychologist friends Helen and Fritz Redl would stop by. Fritz had done valuable work with disturbed children. By using their negative defense mechanisms as a strength, Fritz helped children once considered unreachable. After the Christmas dinner, he would leave and then reappear as jolly St. Nick, with full physique and a "Ho! Ho! Ho!"

Careful lest conspicuous consumption spoil the Christmas spirit, my parents stressed the exchange of love over the exchange of presents. Being together was what counted. We sat by the fire and discussed the birth of Jesus, and the sacrifice he made for humanity.

Then more friends arrived and father would be full of stories about his world travels. He related historic moments with due humility. He was happy serving his fellow human beings. As more friends dropped by to listen, he filled them with hope for the New Year.

After the guests left, father showed us the incision from his operation. Eighteen inches long, it extended from his stomach to the top of his chest. "The doctors had to pull my ribs apart to enter the lung region," he explained.

In later years, he would have sharp pains in this area, prompting him to return to the doctors. Everything had healed fine, they would say, to which father replied: "Just see, Lisa, the doctors take care of one problem and in the process they create another!"

On returning to work, father put his foot down about smoking in his office. The "No Smoking" sign should have been posted years ago. But father was sensitive to his staff and didn't want to impose his own standards on them. The operation changed his mind. "I finally did it, Lisa," he reported one evening. "I told the men that they can't smoke in my office. I've been breathing their dirty cigarettes for years."

Back at Putney, I studied William Sumner and the social Darwinists. Was the individual entirely responsible for his fate in society? Was society itself at all responsible? I shared my parents' conviction that government must be more than a mediator between competing self-interests. It must work hard to reach the thousands the system left without life's basic necessities. Indeed, the percentage of disenfranchised seemed to grow larger every year.

My senior-year idealism soaring, I exchanged many letters with my parents, often written on colored paper with pressed flowers and

260

poems. "Once again, I am with you both in soul and mind," read one closing. "Thank you for sharing your reality — and being so vital."

In another letter, I compared father's love of carpentry to Rousseau's own reflections. "Rousseau speaks of the nobility of working with your hands and doing manual labor, for it brings man close to nature. His favorite profession is cabinetmaking because, 'it is proper, it is useful, one is able to do it in his house, it keeps the body alert, it makes the workman skillful and industrious, and in this useful work, elegance and taste are not excluded.'" Father's skill as a cabinetmaker brought him fulfillment. Our modern age is fragmented and automated. Returning to an elementary skill like carpentry could save the inner person from the emptiness of modern life.

Perhaps no place seemed emptier — or busier — than New York City, where father and I would meet during my spring breaks from Putney. Coming from my pastoral setting in Vermont, I felt wary of this asphalt jungle. Its vast population moved at a pell-mell pace. I walked arm-in-arm with father, a few steps ahead of the bodyguard. Hardly a barefoot romp around Putney.

"What Broadway play are we going to, daddy?" I asked one year. He answered with a wink. *Barefoot in the Park.*

The Civil Rights Act of 1964, the strongest civil rights legislation since the Civil War, established equal rights for all citizens in voting, education, public accomodations, and in federally-assisted programs. President Johnson signed the bill into law, then distributed souvenir pens to those who had helped its design and passage. Father was absent for the signing, but Uncle Roy was there to receive his pen. Both had worked with the Leadership Conference on Civil Rights and had helped break the filibuster that had blocked the Act from passing in the Senate.

When father returned from his trip, he showed me the pen President Johnson had reserved for him. He had a large collection from historic signings, which he kept in his top dresser drawer. "Here, Lisa, this pen is for you. It's from the Civil Rights Act." Knowing how significant the legislation was to him, I was overcome. "Just remember one thing, Lisa. Every human being is the same on the inside. We all have potential far beyond what we can ever imagine."

CHAPTER THIRTY-SEVEN

BATTLING
HATRED

"When there is hatred in the heart, there is no room for reasoning in the head."
— From father's 1965 commencement address
at St. Mary's Dominican College

Signing the Civil Rights Act was one thing; implementing racial equality — particularly in the South — was quite another. On Sunday March 7, 1965, 500 civil rights demonstrators in Selma, Alabama, received brutal beatings at the hands of state troopers. Father immediately sent a telegram to President Johnson:

> I urge you to take immediate and appropriate steps, including the use of federal marshals and troops, so that full exercise of free assembly and free speech may be fully protected. Sunday's spectacle of tear gas, night sticks, whips and electric cattle prods used against defenseless citizens demonstrating to secure their constitutional right to register and vote as American citizens was an outrage against all decency. This shameful brutality by law enforcement agents makes a mockery of America's concept of justice and provides effective ammunition to Communist propagandists and our enemies around the world who would weaken and destroy us.

A hundred years earlier, Selma had been the site of the last battle of the Civil War. The main issue in that conflict had been slavery. The war abolished that — but not the racism behind it. Now once again in Selma, the cancer had become active.

262

Determined to overcome brute force with moral principle, Martin Luther King called for another march on Tuesday, March 9. Civil rights champions from around the nation responded to King's call, my father among them. King had personally requested that he come to show solidarity.

A few years earlier my parents had marched with James Meredith in Jackson, Mississippi, in the conflict that ended with the first black student being admitted to "Ole Miss." The last five miles had been especially tense, with students waving rebel flags and yelling "Nigger go home!"

"The potential for violence was strong," mother had phoned, "but stronger was the sense of hope."

Now again mother called me at Putney, telling of their plan to join King in Selma the following day. Although she made no mention of danger, I had read the reports of Sunday's violence. I could imagine the tension of the upcoming march and the treatment white demonstrators could expect from the bigots.

That night I dreamed the marchers were being chased by hooded men carrying burning crosses. They were beating the demonstrators with the crosses and shouting that the white marchers were traitors to their race. It was a horrifying scene; chaos was everywhere. Father and mother were separated in the melee. I saw mother's face twisted in horror. I screamed out and awoke.

Sitting up in bed I couldn't stop sobbing. Ever since I could remember, I had been afraid for my parents' safety. Tomorrow they would clash with the forces of darkness and terror. But fear never daunted father. "The test of one's convictions is not how you behave when it's convenient and comfortable. The test is, do you stand up for the things that you believe in when it takes courage?" I remembered these words and took heart.

But on Tuesday it was impossible to get the march out of my mind. That evening, father called me from Selma. The troopers had restrained themselves, thanks to the many prominent people marching and the presence of national television coverage. Mother described the gathering after the march. "Everyone squeezed into a tiny church. We sang *We Shall Overcome* and King spoke. It was so hot everyone was perspiring; we were so close together we could feel each other breathe. The feeling was victorious."

Father had given a three-minute speech at the march, perhaps the shortest of his career. "The struggle will be carried on until every American can share in the blessings of human dignity. Let us take heart, our cause is just and human justice will prevail."

Back at Putney, I was working on a term paper about apartheid in South Africa. Famous for her diamonds and gold, infamous for her racism, South Africa was — and still is — a classic case of money interests resisting social change. At a time when few institutions were ready to take a stand against state-sponsored racism, father pushed for action by the labor movement and the U.S. government.

In a letter dated April 22, 1965, father wrote me about the situation in South Africa:

> Unfortunately, the call for an economic boycott of South Africa was never supported by the leading Western nations — England and the U.S. — who could have enacted real economic pressure on South Africa.
>
> The ICFTU [International Confederation of Free Trade Unions] boycott did have some small effect in terms of consumer goods. But the key to making an economic boycott effective is to cut off oil and other basic materiel and supplies. Such action requires a will on the part of the principal nations to challenge the leadership of South Africa. Unfortunately, such will is lacking.

Writing on about apartheid, I recalled that in November 1960 our family had attended the Detroit debut of Miriam Makeba, the black singer in exile from South Africa. She was touring the U.S. as an emissary for her homeland's oppressed. The auditorium fell silent as the large ebony lady entered the stage. Her face radiated enthusiasm and love; her lyrical voice expressed a courage that smashed the oppression of racist rule; and her uncanny clicking sound, produced in the back of her throat, carried a uniquely soulful power. Miriam Makeba was magical.

At home one evening on a break from Putney, I was going over some of mother's clothes that she had given me. The windows were open. A pleasant breeze filled the bedroom as the creek rushed swiftly by. Father was reading in the den.

Suddenly the phone rang. Knowing father was absorbed in his work, I rushed to answer it.

"Is this Lisa?" a deep voice inquired. "Hello, this is Dr. King. I remember meeting you at the freedom rally. We're still struggling in this uphill battle for human dignity, Lisa. I'm happy you're with us."

Dr. King's voice overwhelmed me with excitement, but there was interference on the line. Some clicking and other strange noises. Many times I had suspected that our phone was bugged. As I put down the receiver to fetch father, I felt an eavesdropper's presence. I warned father, who picked up the phone and talked with King at length.

Over the years, J. Edgar Hoover had kept up surveillance on father and our family. FBI memos recently released show the Bureau kept tabs on mother's brothers and parents; father's sister, brothers, and parents; and even Linda and me. And when Linda and I moved away from home, they continued their investigation. They were trying to find something they could use to publicly discredit father.

"If we are a nation conceived in liberty, then it is shameful that Walter Reuther could have ever been subject to such surveillance, absolutely shameful," observed former Attorney General Ramsey Clark. The FBI's reluctant conclusion: besides father, there were no other relatives "up to their neck in communism."

Ever since FDR, any time a President wanted to appoint father to a government post, Hoover would label him a "Communist subversive." Despite volumes of documented evidence of father's long fight *against* communism, Hoover never allowed that information into his dossier.

"The country is the loser," observed author John Barnard, "when we apply irrelevant, off-base, wacky political tests of the kind Hoover was using with Reuther ... on the basis of such flimsy, nonexistent evidence, it seems like a psychological obsession of some kind."

Just before the March on Washington, father was urging Attorney General Robert Kennedy to curb Hoover's belief that every activist fighting for civil rights was a Communist. "[Reuther] was accusing the nation's number one G-man of having exaggerated the Red menace," said one story, "thus contributing to the public frame of mind on which right-wing extremists feed." These news stories only increased the fury of Hoover's attacks on father.

"Our activity in the civil rights movement intensified Hoover's paranoia," said Doug Fraser. "I'm sure in Hoover's distorted mind it proved what he'd been saying all those years."

In the spring of 1965, father was invited to give the commencement address for the graduating class of St. Mary's Dominican College in New Orleans. Hoover received a confidential FBI memo about the invitation and he wrote in the margin: "They must be pretty hard up to have Reuther as a speaker."

Before the commencement, the public was invited to dial a New Orleans phone number to hear "an important message." Callers heard taped Hooveresque warnings about subversives prowling "the nation's campuses to draw young blood for the vampire which is international communism." The message ended: "Are you a Christian? Do you want an atheist to deliver the last message to your graduating child? This man is Walter Reuther, who signs his letters, "Yours for a Soviet America."

"The ways in which Mr. Hoover would destroy the freedom of Walter Reuther were endless," said Ramsey Clark. "It goes way beyond the mere intrusion and violation of Fourth Amendment rights. It was finally an effort to destroy Reuther's voice."

On father's arrival at the Catholic college in New Orleans, he was hissed and booed by members of the White Citizens Council. They carried picket signs reading, "Don't let our youth live under the hammer and sickle." FBI agents snooped around while rednecks shouted "Atheist!" and "Communist!" A racially mixed group was counter picketing the right wingers with signs, "Damn the Klan" and "Black and White Together." Father was escorted between the opposing pickets and into the college.

Standing before the graduating class, father told the students that unless brotherhood is achieved through understanding, there is the possibility of the destruction of the human race. "When there is hatred in the heart," he concluded, "there is no room for reasoning in the head."

Selma, Birmingham, Jackson — father was always there, with mother usually at his side. He compared America's civil rights struggle to a one-game World Series. "No play-offs, no return matches, no next season. That's what we're in." We must use our best players, he stressed, to win this victory for American democracy. After all, how could we convince other nations of the worth of the democratic system if we could not live up to our own vision of equality?

CHAPTER THIRTY-EIGHT

"LAND
OF THE
MIDNIGHT
SUN"

"O my God! Not a socialist summit!"
— President Johnson on the international
leaders gathering at Harpsund, Sweden

My final semester at Putney flew by. Looking ahead to college, many students had set their sights on the big Ivy League schools of the East. But I was determined to find a small college with the same personal and pastoral atmosphere I'd thrived on at Putney. I was leaning toward Earlham College in Indiana.

On graduation day, the madrigal group performed with the baroque ensemble's oboes, recorders and horns. The economist John Kenneth Galbraith gave the commencement address. As he stepped onto the wooden platform, he nodded to father, who was seated in the third row. Both men had been deeply involved in the Kennedy Administration.

As a last memento of our Putney experience, every student received a hand-painted diploma with a small picture of his or her typical activity. Mine showed a red-haired girl sitting atop a mountain reading poetry. "There you are, Lisa," father smiled. "My little transcendentalist."

Back in 1949, father had joined with other world labor leaders to form the International Confederation of Free Trade Unions (ICFTU). The original World Federation of Trade Unions had become Communist-dominated, and many leaders were concerned that Soviet influ-

268

ence would spread unchecked throughout postwar Europe. Father was elected chairman of the ICFTU's committee that drafted a major manifesto calling for "bread, peace and freedom."

In the summer of 1965, the ICFTU convention in Amsterdam brought our family to Europe. While father was absorbed in international labor issues, mother and I would explore the cultural and artistic heritages of Europe. I was excited about visiting my family's roots in Germany as well as the Scandinavian countries, famous for their progressive social programs. This was my Putney graduation present.

Mother had to rest a lot the week before we left. Surgery had fused several vertebrae on her spine, now aggravated by the 13-hour drive back from Putney. The pain showed on her face, as it would for the rest of her life.

The day before we flew out, my sister Linda left for California to teach underprivileged children. That left two ladies still packing. Father's traveling experience and simple tastes had him packed in ten minutes. But mother packed everything from a travel iron to water-purifying pills to an electric adapter for father's shaver. Neither of us could believe her collection of luggage. Even if she wore a different dress each day, she could not possibly have used everything. "Maybe you didn't have many pretty dresses when you were a little girl, May," father joked. "But you certainly have made up for it."

I had lost my fear of flying and was extremely excited about my first trip overseas. The Bluestones met us at the airport gate, along with father's bodyguard, Johnny Bommarito. Irving and father sat together on the plane so they could go over proposals for the ICFTU. Mother and I were behind them, with Mrs. Bluestone and another delegate across the aisle.

Leaving New York City, our ascent took us past the Statue of Liberty. I recalled a Herblock cartoon celebrating Eleanor Roosevelt's 70th birthday. In it, a mother and young child were standing before the famous statue, the child saying, "Of course I know — it's Mrs. Roosevelt." I slept on the plane. Father woke me in time to see the sun rising double-fast over the clouds. I napped again till we arrived in London, where rain and mist blocked the sunshine.

Father filled his time in England with appointments. That left mother and me free to sightsee — Windsor Castle, the Thames,

Regent's Park, Buckingham Palace. London was rich in history, but not as romantic as I imagined Paris would be. As we flew toward the city on the Seine, father was humming the French national anthem, one of his favorite walking tunes. En route to our hotel, he announced he had three days free. "No meetings, no appointments, no responsibilities."

We spent a couple of days at the Louvre. I especially liked the Chagall exhibit. Mother had given me several Chagall reproductions when I was smaller. The floating figures and sense of whimsy appealed to my poetic feelings. After a couple of hours in that enormous museum, father would bid us adieu and go to sit somewhere and open his briefcase. He appreciated art, but his pragmatic mind always came back to his work.

The sky was cloudless the day father and I visited Napoleon's tomb. Rays of sunshine penetrated our bodies with warmth. But as we approached the gray, lifeless monument, suddenly we felt cold. Father stared at the marble marker. "This is the great tragedy in human history," he said, thoughtfully. "Time and time again, the human race pays tribute to these warriors, instead of recognizing the peacemakers."

That evening we drove to the Cathedral de Notre Dame. As our guide pointed out architectural wonders, I was swept into a different world. I left the group to wander the secluded corners. Softly chanting the Latin litany of the Catholic mass, I felt like a nun from an earlier century. *"Kyrie eleison, Christe eleison."*

"Lisa, where are you?"

The guide summarized her presentation: "This majestic cathedral, which was divinely spared from destruction during the two world wars, is a source of inspiration and great spiritual strength even today."

Leaving the massive shelter of the cathedral, we decided to walk. A light sprinkle fell, adding to the charm and mystery of the city. The rain had emptied the sidewalks — my cue to invite father to skip. We would do this in each new European city. Sometime, somewhere, we would find a secluded spot where we could let go and skip along together, arm in arm. Father may have been a bit embarrassed, but I think he really enjoyed it. He motioned to mother, indicating we would meet her at the end of the block. Then away we went, like two big kids, skipping down a narrow Paris street.

Following our three-day spree in Paris, father and Irving Bluestone flew to Amsterdam for the preliminaries of the ICFTU convention. Mother, Zelda Bluestone and I set off by car so we could stop along the way. We visited the Thiems Cathedral and spent the night at a labor center in Agimonte. Then on to Brussels and Bruges and finally, Amsterdam.

Our gaiety turned to sadness the day we arrived. Adlai Stevenson, then America's ambassador to the UN, had died outside the U.S. Embassy in London. Father considered Stevenson the greatest man he had ever met. Deeply aggrieved, he wired his condolences to the statesman's family.

Exploring Amsterdam, we saw the house where Anne Frank had stayed while hiding from the Nazis. I had seen the movie about her and felt rage and grief afterward. I stood with mother in the doorway to the rooms where she and her family had hidden so long, then finally been caught. Anne Frank had known far greater fear than I; yet her courage lived on, even today.

Father took a day off to join us on a bus tour to the Hague, where mother and I sought out paintings by Van Gogh. We had both studied the expressionist painter in art classes. I was attracted by his strong use of color and his overpowering feeling of movement. When mother recalled his tormented life, I wondered if his search for happiness had produced these creative masterpieces. The sunflowers so alive, the fields of grain seemingly swaying right on the canvas.

The highlight of our Netherlands visit was a performance of Beethoven's Ninth Symphony with its stirring *Ode to Joy*, performed exuberantly by the National Orchestra and Chorus. As the chorus rose to sing in the final movement, the entire audience stood with them, celebrating the joy of the soul. The applause lasted 20 minutes, revising my notion of the "reserved Dutch."

Following the ICFTU convention, our family was invited to Stockholm by Arnie Geiger, head of the Swedish labor movement. Father was very close to Geiger. From their very first meeting, the two men had seen eye to eye. And their friendship extended to our family members. Linda had stayed with the Geigers during her European travels. And Arnie's only daughter, Britta, had stayed with our family when she came to America in her teens.

For years I had wanted to visit Scandinavia, with its mystique of social progress. While father met with Arnie Geiger, mother and I toured a modern day-care center, years before day-care facilities would develop in the U.S.

Stockholm's subway system also impressed us. Here was efficient, attractive public transportation through a city where streets were clean and safe. It was all a matter of priorities, mother said. If we wanted our cities this way, surely we had the resources.

The highlight of our visit to Sweden was Harpsund, the official summer residence of Prime Minister Tage Erlander. In 1963, international authorities on economics, East-West relations, arms control and unemployment had gathered at the Harpsund for an "informal summit." The relaxed atmosphere allowed participants to candidly reveal their minds and search for solutions not bound by political considerations.

Said Uncle Victor:

The boys at Harpsund take a break. Father rows, while (from left) Hubert Humphrey, West German Chancellor Willy Brandt and Swedish Prime Minister Tage Erlander enjoy the ride.

Harpsund gatherings were a rare happening in the world. You don't often get heads of state together who meet under such informal circumstances that they can literally say to one another, "hey, that's a damn good idea; I'm going to use that in my next speech."

At that point in Walter's life, I saw him beginning to realize the magnitude of his position because he and Hubert Humphrey were the only two Americans involved in this, another reason he felt so close to HHH. Walter began to think more deeply about relations between nations, about Third World countries, about nuclear and environmental issues.

At Harpsund '63 the list of attendees had been impressive: Harold Wilson, Willy Brandt, Ludwig Rosenberg of the German Trade Union Federation, George Woodcock of the British Trade Union Congress, Arnie Geiger, Tage Erlander, and the prime ministers of Denmark and Norway. From America, father came with Hubert Humphrey.

On June 20, 1963, columnist Victor Reisel noted father's purpose at the gathering:

A group of men from two continents, who may someday have the political power to reshape policies of governments, will meet quietly at an estate called Harpsund....

Though it is not reported much in our country, Reuther has been intensely active in the building and strengthening of international labor organizations on a global industry-wide basis. This he has done by bolstering what is known as the International Metalworkers Federation, whose headquarters are in Geneva.

By linking up with metal workers' unions abroad, Reuther hopes to coordinate collective bargaining across the world. . . Mr. Reuther is at the forefront of the movement. Having prime ministers and presidents as allies won't hurt it at all.

President Kennedy had also kept an eye on Harpsund that year. When father and Humphrey returned to the States, the President requested them to brief him on the meetings.

Humphrey had planned to attend Harpsund '65, as many of the same leaders would be gathering again. Before the '64 elections, however, he mentioned the meetings to President Johnson, who had chosen Humphrey as his running mate. Johnson's political alarm rang: "O my God! Not a socialist summit!" So Humphrey missed Harpsund '65.

While the leaders met, their wives and family members joined our hostess, Mrs. Erlander, for discussions. She was a gracious lady, encouraging mother and me to relax and enjoy the country setting. We all sipped lemon tea on the patio and discussed the issues of the day. Later we would dine with the men and hear reports of their meetings. The atmosphere was informal and friendly. Despite political differences, everyone discussed the problems with candor and a sincere desire to find solutions.

At one luncheon, people from German labor took note of my eating habits. I had been using the summer to cleanse my body and lose weight. Once I had set my mind, it was easy to resist the pastries, starchy entrees and heavy meat dishes. For lunch I was eating fruit and cottage cheese. "Why are you being so extreme?" asked Mrs. Rosenberg, a robust German woman.

I related ideas I had studied regarding fasting and nutrition, and the cleansing of toxins from the body. Mystics attributed much of their power to fasting I said, and Christ himself had fasted. Controlling the demands of the flesh enhanced one's spiritual awareness, advised many holy teachers. And I experienced that fasting helped me achieve more resolve within myself and strengthened my constitution. The women listened attentively. Their conclusion: eat more!

After the Haprsund meetings, Britain's Prime Minister Harold Wilson wrote father that he had used some of his remarks in his own writings. In his book, *A Personal Record: The Labour Government 1964-70*, Wilson noted:

> I had been greatly impressed over the years by my contacts with Walter Reuther, leader of the American Automobile Workers . . . and his sophisticated approach to the challenge of automation. He had been my guest at No. 10, and at my request had given me a brief on modern union organization. His approach was to force the pace in industrial efficiency. This was the basis of my appeal: insist on high wages, but force the pace on productivity so that every organized firm could meet it.

I celebrated my 18th birthday in Sweden. With Putney behind me and college ahead, I was coming of age. We had a small dinner at the hotel with the Geigers, Uncle Victor's son Johnny, and the Bluestones. Father brought me a bouquet of deep red roses and arranged to fulfill my birthday wish: to hear Irving Bluestone sing Schubert lieder.

At a sign from father, Irving stood up and serenaded us with his clear tenor voice. Many of the melodies I recognized as the German folk songs we had sung with Grossvater and Grossmutter, like *Roeslein* and the theme from Schubert's *Trout*. And so I entered womanhood — with family, friends, flowers, and lots of ice cream.

Several members of the Swedish Labor Party accompanied us throughout our Scandinavian tour. As a farewell present, they arranged for us to go to the "Land of the Midnight Sun." This part of Sweden was so far north that in winter it was without sunlight for days. Yet in the summer, the sun was still in the sky at midnight. When we arrived by charter flight, I saw how barren and cold the land was. Imagine the winter!

We stayed in a primitive wooden lodge. Mother and I shared a small room while father stayed with a member of the Swedish Labor Party. A sauna adjoined our quarters. Mother and I were determined to stay up and view the midnight sun.

Late that evening I was sitting in the scorching sauna wrapped in a towel. Suddenly mother opened the door and grabbed my arm. "You won't believe it, Lisa. There's a huge orange ball in the middle of the horizon!"

Peeking out the window like two small children, mother and I could scarcely believe our eyes. To see bright colors fill the ether at this hour was eerie — like a canvas from science fiction. I took a quick shower and put on my pajamas. As I lay my head on the pillow, the sun was shimmering farewells over the surreal Swedish landscape.

The next day, we were enroute to Denmark where we were met by Knud Laurentzen, owner of a large fleet of ice breakers. Knud was a wealthy man, but one with a strong social conscience. A close friend of my parents, he had been active in the underground during World War II, helping people escape Germany in his boats. Since all his children were home for summer break, we would be staying in a nearby hotel.

Knud remembered father's love of fishing. He took us fishing for an entire day in his small boat, his son-in-law, father and me. "Now Lisa, don't start praying that we won't catch any fish. You'll spoil our whole day!" said father before we left. Crossing my fingers, I agreed.

While the men fished, I stretched out, let my fingers hang in the water and enjoyed the warm sun and strong wind. At the end of five hours, father had caught one large fish, the other two none. It seemed a fair compromise with fate.

One night Knud arranged for me to spend time with his children and their friends. I went to his home for a party, complete with music, dancing, sparkling drinks and cheese. I enjoyed being with my peers, away from serious adults for a change. After several hours one of the boys escorted me back to the hotel. It had been an exciting evening and I was feeling quite happy.

When we arrived at the hotel room, I bid the boy a shy goodnight. But he insisted on coming into the room. A little alarm sounded within me, but I didn't want to seem rude so I agreed. Anyway, my parents were sleeping in the next room. But had I been somewhat teasing and suggestive during the evening? What was this new side of me that I felt emerging? As we entered the room, I turned on the bright overhead light. Suddenly, he was on top of me, trying desperately to pull off my clothes. "C'mon! We know you American girls are hot and loose!" He persisted, I resisted and the girdle mother had given me to wear frustrated him. After a few minutes, he gave up and left.

Crying, I turned off the light, preferring to undress in the dark. My body was shaking. Just a few weeks earlier at Putney, the son of a world-famous medical researcher had come for my graduation. I had had a crush on him since our families became close at Aspen. He was a student at Harvard and we had been corresponding. After a long walk in the woods, he cornered me in an empty barn. Nothing as brutal as tonight in Copenhagen, but what would happen to me in college? Was this what men were like? Burying my face in the pillow, I cried myself to sleep.

The final week of our trip we sought out our roots. Father had promised to take me to Germany where my grandparents had spent their childhoods. Our German relatives met us at the airport in Stuttgart. We drove to the old family graveyard where my great-grandparents were buried. Grossmutter had grown up in a plain house with a stable below for the family cow. A family living off the produce of the land and the milk of the cow. This simple life appealed to me.

Our extended family gathered for meals and a sing-along. Again I saw father lose himself in the rhythm of the old German lyrics. Instead of toasting with German beer, we sipped homemade grape juice from Reuther vines. The clan knew and respected father's strict attitude toward wine and liquor.

Our last leg through Germany took us into the Black Forest, where storytellers have described elves living in moss-covered houses amid cotton-candy clouds and trees of broccoli. But the Swiss Alps were the best. As our car climbed through dark green forests toward snowy peaks, I tried not to blink lest I miss a moment of their beauty.

While mother shopped in a small resort town, father and I kept a promise to go hiking together. With our lunch in a small knapsack we set off, passing through tiny villages reachable only by foot. Each family seemed to have a little vegetable garden and a few cows grazing by the path. One home had a symmetrical wood pile outside, whose center supported a small shelf for a potted red geranium.

We came to an area where there was no path, which seemed to please father. How he loved to blaze trails! Several times he had to grab my hand and help me up a steep slope. Or wait patiently while I caught my breath — he who had had lung surgery less than a year before.

After a lengthy climb, we reached the summit. We gazed down upon a beautiful lake. Father pointed to the timber line on the mountains across the way. "Now you know we are high." As it was cold on the unprotected pinnacle, we came down to a sheltered spot where we opened our lunch of dried fruit, nuts, cheese, bread and a canteen full of apple juice. Appetites sharpened by the climb, we savored the meal as the best in memory. It was a victorious moment, and then it passed. I remembered the words of the Swedish writer Strindberg: "The only victory worth winning is victory over self."

I looked up. "Look at the sky, daddy. It looks like rain." The

Father photographed me on our ascent up the Swiss Alps.

summer temperature was dropping rapidly as the sun went behind a big black cloud. We scurried down the slope, seeking refuge. Just as we entered a large cow pasture, the sky opened. Luckily there was a wide tree in the middle of the meadow. We reached it in a moment, letting its broad branches serve as our umbrella. All around us the water poured down in sheets. When the rain stopped, the fields were muddy and slippery. I fell a couple of times as we continued our descent. We sang as we went, father caroling his favorite union song: "Like a tree that's planted by the water, we shall not be moved."

We slipped and slid our way back to the hostel where mother waited. She was delighted at father's strength and lung power, and pronounced his surgery a complete success.

We had intended to return home by steamship, but a workers' strike put us back on a jet. The future awaited us — father's union work, mother's art history classes, and my freshman year at college.

CHAPTER THIRTY-NINE

DROPPING
OUT

"I want to go away. Away from college, away from Paint Creek — and away from you!"

— Me, dropping out

Earlham is a small, respected college developed by the Quakers. Visiting the campus my senior year at Putney, I had been drawn to the small meetinghouse where the Friends sat in silence until the spirit moved them to speak.

Another spirit moved me at freshman orientation. I met Jim. We shared interests in books and classical music. I was quickly in love.

The love affair centered around our studies. I was applying myself to the Bible and writing a paper on the historical Jesus versus the Christ of faith. I wanted to major in philosophy and find the meaning of existence. In freshman humanities, we studied Martin Buber, C.S. Lewis, and Socrates. I delved into existentialism and the idea that man creates his own meaning through commitment.

During Christmas vacation, Jim came to visit me at Paint Creek. He was an intellectual. I envisioned him as a college professor, living in an old Victorian house filled with shelves of books. Our home with its sharp, angular lines was hardly Victorian. Intimidated by father's tough-mindedness and mother's pointed questions, Jim could not relax. Neither could father, who always had trouble relating to his daughters' male friends. When Jim left, mother criticized him: "He doesn't have your depth or your social conscience." "Shut up," I thought.

280

Returning to Earlham in January, I found an estranged boyfriend. He realized the difference in our backgrounds and resented having been on trial at our home.

There was another problem. My disappointing encounters with boys had made me a prude, so his passions were unrequited. He probably thought I would never change. We broke up.

When the absorbing relationship ended, I become emotionally unstable. My intense attachment turned to intense suffering. Then the chemistry major across the hall from me took cyanide and killed herself. For the next year, I was an emotional wreck.

One solace for me was music. I especially loved the works of Bach, the church classics and the Negro spirituals. I sang with the Earlham Concert Choir, which toured the East Coast every winter. When the choir arrived in New York, father met me at the hotel. He took me to a restaurant for cheesecake, and then out for a brisk walk. For a couple of hours we strode arm-in-arm, his bodyguard behind us struggling to keep up.

On the bus back to the Midwest, I wove dozens of "God's eyes," using toothpicks and colored fibers. Once home, I brought a tree branch inside and hung my collection on it. Native American lore says these mystical symbols help one remember God.

My second year at college, I continued to search for answers to life's big questions. A few of my friends were studying determinism and Eastern philosophy. Others were exploring the world of marijuana and LSD. My favorite trip was a good book by Hermann Hesse or Albert Camus. I was looking for an epiphany, as James Joyce would say, a revelation. But a fearful mind was conspiring with an adolescent body to keep me in darkness.

My morale had cracked, but my manner was still intact. I continued to busy myself with extracurricular activities and score good grades as well.

At the end of the fall term, mother and father came to Earlham for Parents' Day. The Concert Choir performed and the Dean asked me to do a reading at the Friends meetinghouse. I was scared and excited. He had chosen a simple and beautiful passage describing Christ's affirmation of renunciation. After the meeting, father came up to me. "Whoever chose that reading, Lisa, must know your heart." If he does,

I thought, then he must know how confused I am.

Confusion, of course, was par for the '60s. The chaos on the campuses mirrored the chaos at large. Many of my generation were "turning on" and "dropping out." One of my schoolmates dropped into a mental hospital. Drugs couldn't provide answers; only a new consumer good. The truth was inside, not in chemicals. Even my parents knew *that*, though they couldn't tell me definitely what the truth was.

By winter term 1967, I wanted out. Earlham, while personal and protective, was also restrictive. Following a long walk with a friend after hours, the Dean of Women placed me on probation. My inner search had led me to a dead end. I concluded my life had been too sheltered and had no meaning of its own. I wanted to experience the world for myself. I called home.

"Mother, I want to drop out of college and experience real life. I want to be on my own."

I had the idea of moving away and getting a job. Mother said I should come home and talk things over. The next morning father's bodyguard came to pick me up. As the car drove off the Earlham campus, I knew I was doing the right thing. My path was somewhere else, away from this conservative corn belt and the academic game of papers, tests, and grades.

By the time we reached Paint Creek, I was emotionally distraught. Father was involved in important meetings, but he took the night off to have dinner with mother and me (and his bodyguard) at Chung's Chinese restaurant in Detroit. As I sat in the restaurant, a young woman of 19, I faced the same old feelings. I was still my parents' little girl, a bundle of long-simmering frustrations. I remembered when I was nine years old coming home one evening after spending the afternoon with a girlfriend. Mother was grocery shopping in Rochester. I walked to the gate. The padlock was fastened. I rang the bell connected to the guards' apartment. No answer. I walked up to the guardhouse and knocked. Nothing. I returned to the gate and shook the bars, but still it remained locked. "Why is this happening?" I screamed. "Why can't I get into my own house? I hate it. I hate this fence, this place!" I pounded on the gate with my bare fists, tears of rage gushing from my eyes. It was pitch black before mother finally returned from town. I was sitting on the ground in a little ball, trying to stay warm. Mother was deeply sorry. "But why don't you give me a key, mummy?" I had begged them for one, but they refused, afraid it would fall into the wrong hands. I hadn't been able to get in our house then, and now as I sat across from my parents in this restaurant, I wondered if I would ever be able to get *out*.

After ordering, father said in his matter-of-fact voice, "OK, Lisa, what's happening?" Evidently, he wanted a three-minute synopsis of my emotional condition. The presence of the bodyguard piqued my anger. Here I was, going through an emotional crisis, and this outsider had to hear me pour my guts out. After 19 years, I finally said it: "I want to go away. Away from college, away from Paint Creek — and away from you!"

Yes, Lisa Reuther's life had been perfectly wonderful *and* perfectly hellish. When I was 17, I went on my first date. We went to see the film *Night of the Iguana*. On the way home, my escort kissed me on the cheek. I was panic-stricken. Inside the house, I found mother reading in bed. I ran to her as if to a confessor and told her what had happened. She laughed and winced at my sincerity and confusion.

Sex had not been an acceptable topic for discussion. When Linda and I had to start dealing with our sexuality, father was Mr. Goody Uptight. And mother's recent back operation had left her physically rigid. Their puritanical combination created the impression that sex did not really exist. I grew up thinking sex was acceptable for animals but not human beings. It was dirty, sinful — certainly forbidden fruit.

Father and mother were bewildered by my emotional outburst. I was sobbing, trying to explain why I needed to be on my own. It was a painful experience for all three of us. Every time I looked at the bodyguard, I wanted to scream, "Get out of here! Can't you see I want to be alone with my parents? Can't you see the suffering you've caused us all these years?"

Poor man. It wasn't his fault. He was "only a player, too."

CHAPTER FORTY

HELLO
CESAR,
GOOD-BYE
GEORGE

"I haven't felt anything like this since the old days."
— Father, picketing with
California grape strikers

Some dropped out, but more were left out. Perhaps none in America were worse off than migrant farm workers. I didn't have to travel to California to see the plight of these poor people. Michigan's orchards were full of seasonal laborers. Some of them picked apples in Romeo, a town very close to Rochester. The landed gentry there viewed their shabby migratory lives with suspicion. These were outcasts, with absolutely no skills to elevate themselves.

As early as 1961, father had gone to bat for the farm workers at the annual AFL-CIO convention in Miami. At that time 49 migrant workers had been jailed for striking, and George Meany wanted to fire the organizer of the strike, Norman Smith. Father angrily objected, saying the firing would break the workers' spirit for sure. "A grass-roots organization is needed," father said, "if we are going to really help these people."

By 1965, Cesar Chavez had emerged as the voice of the migrant farm workers. Inspired by Chavez, father sent Uncle Roy to visit Delano, California, strike headquarters for the grape pickers. Roy soon learned that field workers picked fruit and vegetables 10-12 hours a day, 7 days a week. Often there was no clean drinking water or toilet facilities. Children usually worked alongside their parents because there were no day-care facilities and only off-and-on, substandard schooling.

After touring migrant labor camps in Southern Texas, four medical doctors reported they had found "an endless parade of illness, deformity, disability and human suffering." The children routinely had parasites, skin disorders, and ear infections resulting in partial deafness. With no medical insurance, pregnant women trying to enter hospitals in places like McAllen, Texas, were told: "Pay the bill, or we keep the baby."

Workers lived in ramshackle, roach-infested shanties or took shelter in abandoned school buses. Those who tried to negotiate with growers or went on strike were roughed up and "accidentally" sprayed with insecticide. Despite all this neglect and abuse, Chavez took a firm nonviolent stance.

Uncle Roy encouraged his brother to visit Delano. Father flew there and immediately found himself walking the picket line, while the sheriff threatened the families of pickets with arrest. Picking up a large red sign, father led the march. That evening at 6:30, he addressed an overflow crowd at Filipino Hall: "This is not your strike," he told them, "it is *our* strike!" The crowd roared with appreciation. "Viva Reuther! Huelga! Viva la causa!"

Father met with the city manager and the mayor of Delano, urging them to help the farm workers win their civil rights. He met with grape growers, stressing the need to recognize the union. "Ford Motor Co. once said it would rather shut its doors than recognize our union," he told them. "But in time they recognized us. And in time that proved to be the best decision for both the company and the workers." He urged the growers to treat their workers likewise.

The press played up father's visit to the migrant workers; and the strike took on national importance. Wherever he went, he was followed by a horde of reporters and cameramen. "I haven't felt anything like this since the old days," he told them. The media's spotlight pressured the growers to curb their violent reaction toward the strikers. People from far and wide were coming to join the picket line.

By 1966, father was seeking national political involvement for the migrant workers, calling on his friend Senator Robert Kennedy in Washington. Father had become close with Bobby, closer even than he had been with John. They shared a similar vision of social justice, and a similar sense of humor. When Bobby's wife, Ethel, wrote father about the radio controls in their station wagon being positioned too far to the right, father replied: "I have written to the Big Three about your problem and asked them either to place the radio closer to the driver or to issue an arm extension with each of their automobiles. But I must warn you that my influence with the automobile companies is exaggerated."

Already Robert Kennedy was part of the Senate's Migratory Labor subcommittee and somewhat aware of the farm workers' suffering. Father wanted him to go to Delano to witness conditions firsthand and talk with all sides in the dispute. Although Kennedy was overburdened and overscheduled, he told his aide Peter Edelman, "If Walter Reuther and Jack Conway want me to do it, I suppose I'll do it!"

Father had a hunch that Delano would fire Kennedy's passion for the underdog. He was right. After Kennedy's first day with the grape pickers, he became an activist. Peacefully picketing strikers were being arrested. The sheriff said the growers had told him, "If you don't get them pickets out of here, we're going to cut their hearts out." So the sheriff had removed them from danger — by *arresting* them.

"This is a most interesting concept," Bobby Kennedy retorted. "How can you arrest somebody if he hasn't violated the law? I suggest that during the luncheon period the Sheriff and the District Attorney read the Constitution of the United States."

When a meeting hall was arranged for Kennedy to address the farm workers, growers filled the hall with their own men so no one else could attend. Facing the crowd, Kennedy dismissed one side of the hall and let the workers in to fill the other side.

Kennedy told the farm workers they had a right to form a union and that he endorsed their right. Chavez recalled, "Not only did he endorse us, he joined us. When reporters asked him if we weren't Communists, he said, 'No, they're not Communists; they're struggling for their rights.'"

President John Kennedy had once told my father, "You fellows are educating Bobby." Father answered, "We're only doing what comes natural." And now father was pressing Bobby to act. In the faces of the farm workers, he saw the poorest of America's poor. Feeling their misfortune was a turning point in Robert Kennedy's life. As UAW official Paul Schrade would later observe, "it convinced him to run for President."

Heartened by Kennedy's commitment to the farm workers, father invited Chavez to come to Detroit in 1967 to raise funds for organizing. Although George Meany warned him not to go, Chavez went anyway. The UAW helped him secure food and clothing as well as money. Then Chavez arranged for father to travel with him to Mexico. He hoped father's influence with Mexico's trade unionists would stem the flow of strikebreakers who were crossing the border and undermining union efforts in the U.S.A.

Chavez's next tactic, borrowed from his hero Mahatma Gandhi, was a hunger strike. Father flew to Delano to help publicize this cause and to deliver a check for $50,000 for a new union headquarters. He found the hunger-striking Chavez weak and lying on a canvas cot at

Father and Cesar Chavez lead the farm workers in their march for basic human rights.

strike headquarters. The men embraced. "You will prevail," father told him, "for your cause is just."

After the fast, Chavez told father how much his visit meant. "Walter you have given me great confidence." $\quad$ 4-8-01

By August 1966, the National Farm Workers Association had joined the AFL-CIO, no thanks to George Meany. Meany had been against the merger, figuring the dues collected from the migrant workers would be insufficient to organize them. Father was outraged, arguing that the issue was moral, not financial.

After the merger, father requested that several members of the AFL-CIO Executive Board raise funds for the farm workers and their strike. Meany opposed the idea. Then, when such a committee was formed, Meany did not even ask father and the UAW to join it — though father was the only Executive Board member to have visited and marched with the farm workers. Meany was still playing a power game.

Eleven years of compromise, heartaches, accusations and empty promises formed the "working relationship" between George Meany and father. "I like to get along with Meany," father would say, "but when there are things to get done, I'm going to do them. Meany's basic problem is that he's too damn comfortable." Meany viewed father as a threat to his job. Shortly after the merger of the AFL-CIO, Meany had shouted across the table to father, "I don't trust you!"

These two leaders of American labor were as different as night and day. Meany, a plumber from the Bronx, loved cigars, cool drinks and poker. Once, having set an Executive Board meeting at a time inconvenient for four of its members, he snapped: "I don't give a damn if no one shows, so long as Dubinsky is there with his deck of cards."

Meany had surrounded himself with faithful cronies who could be counted on to vote as he wished. As time passed, the club of elderly labor leaders grew more and more conservative. And Meany encouraged them to stay in office until death. Meany himself remained president of the powerful AFL-CIO until he was 85 years of age, stepping down just two months before his death.

In 1964, at the age of 56, father had the foresight to incorporate a clause in the UAW's Constitution forbidding anyone to run for office after the age of 65. When he requested the amendment, father said, "We must do this now, because when we get older we won't want to, and it's the best thing for our union. We must make room for younger people with new ideas."

That same year, *New York Times* labor writer A. H. Raskin wrote: "When Meany does leave his post, Reuther is the man most likely to succeed," to which the AFL-CIO boss responded, "I haven't any great interest in that because when that time comes, I won't be around." Obviously he intended to stay in the saddle until he dropped.

Father wasn't alone on the receiving end of Meany's scorn. When the ICFTU would not give Meany a free hand to do as he pleased, he withheld a check for several hundred thousand dollars and demanded repayment of $800,000 which the Federation had already spent for worldwide assistance. He then withdrew from the international labor organization, calling the staff of the ICFTU "a bunch of fairies."

When President Kennedy had come to speak at the AFL-CIO convention in 1961, Meany left father off the escort committee. Father, of course, had worked diligently for Kennedy's election and was closer to the President than anyone else on the committee. He was hurt. Meany only grinned, saying it was an oversight. He enjoyed putting father down — and affirming his own power.

In 1963, President Kennedy created a ten-member committee to carefully research all U.S. foreign aid programs. In March, the group had a series of meetings. After finagling a seat as the labor representative, Meany did not attend a single session. Many progressive labor people could have contributed to this effort; the AFL-CIO president had simply wanted the prestige of the appointment.

Disappointed with Meany, father told one reporter, "Why did I have the big fight with George Meany over the March on Washington? Why did I call this meeting on poverty? Why am I so interested in education? This is part of my job as a labor leader—helping solve the problems of the community. Not just economics. There are new frontiers to be conquered. They are as unlimited as the human imagination." One of father's colleagues characterized the stalemate with Meany this way: "Walter was a crusader and idealist. Meany was a business trade unionist, annoyed when new ideas and proposals for dramatization of issues were advanced. His immediate, automatic response was massive inertia."

At the 1965 AFL-CIO convention, father and Leonard Woodcock drew up a resolution criticizing America's Vietnam policy as too militaristic. The hawkish Executive Board accepted the resolution provided father would not make waves for their own proposals. A year later, when some observers at the AFL-CIO convention voiced dissatisfaction with the Vietnam War, Meany shouted from the podium, "Throw the kooks out!"

Later, Meany admitted his shortsightedness on Vietnam. This error reflected the real problem about his leadership. He simply didn't know how to listen to labor's more enlightened members, especially father, whom he mistrusted.

Father felt the AFL-CIO's support of LBJ's Vietnam policy was simply delaying the time when the U.S. would have to face up to its own domestic problems. "I never wanted Meany's job," he said. "It's got nothing to do with collective bargaining. I don't know if Meany could lead a poverty crusade or the fight for health care. I know I can lead these fights as president of the UAW because our guys respond. I wouldn't want to just hold the hands of reluctant labor politicians. I'm action-oriented and the UAW is where the action is." According to UAW rules, father would have forfeited his leadership of the UAW had he been elected president of the AFL-CIO.

The UAW's days in the AFL-CIO were numbered. It came to the point where father felt there was no longer any hope. At the AFL-CIO convention in 1966, Uncle Victor gave the press information concerning undercover CIA operations involving the AFL-CIO. Father was disturbed about the leak and Meany, of course, was infuriated. He raised quite a fuss and from then on his relations with the UAW went straight down.

In February 1968, the UAW Executive Board unanimously agreed to withdraw from the AFL-CIO, concluding:

> The AFL-CIO is becoming increasingly the comfortable, complacent custodian of the status quo.... Basic provisions of the constitution have been violated. On occasion even a completely unanimous mandate of the AFL-CIO convention itself has been thwarted when it did not meet with the personal pleasure of the president of the AFL-CIO.

Within a month of leaving the AFL-CIO, father formed a new labor federation called the Alliance for Labor Action (ALA). He was joined by the International Chemical Workers, the National Council of Distributive Workers, and the two-million-member Teamsters Union. The shady Teamsters and the squeaky-clean UAW made strange bedfellows indeed, but father saw it as a marriage of convenience that could actually work on important issues like the Vietnam War, the deployment of antiballistic missiles, and social legislation.

In April 1968, a group of 48 American labor editors rated the top labor leaders on their "abilities, innovative ideas, ethical standards, and contributions to labor's and the nation's progress." Reporting the survey's results, the *Wall Street Journal* noted:

> Walter Reuther of the United Auto Workers Union may be fighting a losing battle in the halls of labor. But he was rated the "nation's greatest living labor leader."

Robert Kennedy and Walter Reuther — fighters for the people.

291

CHAPTER FORTY-ONE

HOUSING
FOR
EVERY
FAMILY

"You can make automobiles, refrigerators, and TV sets by automation, but you make consumers in the same old-fashioned way, and that is where the shortage is."
— Father's natural economics

In the first half of the 20th Century, because of the cyclical nature of the economy in general and the auto industry in particular, hundreds of thousands of workers were periodically out of a job. Father felt it was the responsibility of the auto companies to manage their factories in such a way that there was regular and steady work for their employees.

When the economy slowed in 1953 and tens of thousands were idled, father decided it was time to push for the guaranteed annual wage. In 1955, it was accepted in a modified form, allowing an eligible laid-off worker 65 percent of his take-home pay the first four weeks and 60 percent for the next 22.

Guaranteed annual wage became known as SUB, supplemental unemployment benefit. SUB reached full bloom in the 1967 negotiations with Ford, when the laid-off worker was awarded 95 percent of his pay for up to one year. Father's negotiation victory landed him on the cover of *Newsweek*. A syndicated cartoon that week showed President Johnson telling an aide: "I just read the Ford contract — maybe we should send Walter Reuther to negotiate with North Vietnam."

Father was proud that the workers now had some job security, but it bothered him that the program was interpreted by some as an incentive not to work. He stressed that a worker could not get SUB if he quit, only if he were laid off by the company.

Later, when the company bragged of some of the progressive features of the contract, father asked: "If they're so good, why did they fight us when we first proposed them?"

But he said it was to Ford's credit that when the union kept pushing for job security, the company became interested, hired its own experts, studied the situation with an open mind, and came to the conclusion that it made sense.

"Our union and the Ford Motor Company pioneered the guaranteed annual income for the automobile production worker," he told the press. "Even during the periods of cyclical layoffs, he and his family can maintain their standard of living and pay their bills.

"Do you realize what that means to the American economy? It's carrying on the same idea that Henry Ford developed, the idea that makes this great flowering of production possible. You couldn't have had the benefits of mass production and technological advances without purchasing power on the part of the American consumer, and that consumer is nobody but the American worker.

"Working together across the bargaining table, Ford and the union have hammered out a most secure base for the American economy to continue to survive."

SUB became the heart of the workers' safety net. But father recognized that there were other threats to job security. He was worried about what automation would do to our country, replacing thousands of people with machines. His fears have been vindicated. Advances in automation and the exporting of work have killed millions of jobs, and the cutbacks are continuing. Auto companies have announced numerous plant closings, and the ripple effect of related job losses more than triples the total cutback.

Fred Borowski, principal of Holy Redeemer High School in southwest Detroit where General Motors has closed its Cadillac and Fleetwood plants, said that for years there had been an unwritten agreement that the workers and area residents would accept the pollution and the heavy traffic if the plants were kept operating and the workers kept working. "People in this area can't believe that after their loyalty and the loyalty of the workers, GM is just turning its back on them."

Southwest Detroit City Hall Manager Ed King said: "The plant gave us life. Then you wake up one day and they announce the plant's closing. And you think 'Hell, I've been taken for granted all my life.'"

During the last decade, over a million industrial jobs have been lost in the U.S. every year. And better than half the new jobs are below poverty level, minimum wage.

The damage these plant closings have done to America, its communities and citizens are immense. They rape the cities and towns of a major portion of their tax base. Schools, churches and small businesses are shut down as a direct reaction. American men and women who have been making payments on their homes for years wake up one day and suddenly realize that the value of their home has drastically dropped as their town begins dwindling into a ghost town. And if the corporation offers to relocate the workers to a new plant (which doesn't happen often), the real estate sharpies have purchased all the land and the worker has to pay an inflated price for it. This type of economic violence against honest, hard-working Americans is running rampant and must be stopped.

Why an incredibly diverse corporation such as General Motors, with all its high-paid "brainpower" and nearly unlimited resources can't figure out a way to produce some type of marketable item and keep their employees working is beyond me. Certainly, if they can't figure it out themselves, they should go to various departments of the state and the engineering schools and draw on their practical ideas on how to keep the facility operating and America working.

Father felt that the government should have a sound economic plan for employment. He told one audience:

> America must come to the sober realization that in the complex 20th century technological society it is dangerous and unrealistic to believe that the blind forces of the marketplace somehow are going to make everything come out just right so that we can achieve full employment...
>
> We in the labor movement must point out that America must free itself from the paralysis and prejudice which would have us believe that rational democratic planning is somehow sub-

versive or un-American. Every other democratic country in the world has some kind of national planning agency whereby they look at the total needs of a society and come up with a rational and responsible program that relates to the allocation of resources in meeting the national goals of that society.

Father knew that if any of the three factors in the economic equation — capital, labor, consumer — became disproportionate, the whole system would falter. And if the middle class went broke, democracy would be in big trouble.

While touring a Ford automated engine plant in Cleveland, father was asked whether curbs should be placed on development of highly automated manufacturing. "Nothing could be more wicked or foolish," he replied. "You can't stop technological progress, and it would be silly to try it if you could."

To a congressional committee looking into the problems of automation, father said:

We fully realize that the potential benefits of automation are great, if properly handled. Automation can bring freedom from the monotonous drudgery of many jobs in which the worker today is no more than a servant of a machine. It can free workers from routine, repetitive tasks that the new machines can be taught to do, and can give the workers who toil at those tasks the opportunity to develop higher skills.

But we must not overlook or minimize the many problems which will inevitably arise in making the adjustment to the new technology, problems for individual workers and individual companies, problems for entire communities and regions, problems for the economy as a whole.

What should be done to help the worker who will be displaced from his job or the worker who will find that his highly specialized skill has been taken over by a machine? What about the businessman who lacks sufficient capital to automate his plant, yet has to face the competition of firms whose resources enable them to build whole new automated factories? Will automation mean the creation of whole new communities in some areas, while others are turned into ghost towns? How can we increase the market for goods and services sufficiently and quickly enough to match greatly accelerated increases in productivity? Finding the answers to these questions and many others like them will not be an easy process and certainly not an automatic one.

Father called automation the "second industrial revolution" and warned Congress: "When the first industrial revolution took place, no effort was made to curb or control greedy, ruthless employers. Businessmen took advantage of unemployment to force workers to labor 12 and 14 hours a day for a pittance so small that not only wives but children scarcely out of infancy had to enter the factories to contribute their mite to the family earnings. The benefits which we today can so readily recognize as the fruits of the first industrial revolution were achieved only after decades of privation, misery, and ruthless exploitation of millions of working people."

Father recognized that automation would tend to eliminate unskilled and semi-skilled jobs first and create new jobs requiring higher levels of skill. So, he said, a means must be found to train the displaced workers so that they can handle the more highly skilled jobs automation will create. And they will have to be paid while they are being retrained, because "they have to live and support their families." He urged that older workers be allowed to take early retirement.

"You can make automobiles, refrigerators, and TV sets by automation," father wryly observed, "but you make consumers in the same old-fashioned way, and that is where the shortage is."

In the mid-sixties, father turned his social eye toward developing housing for low-income families. "We have the resources and the technological capability to re-house America," he told the media, "and to put high-quality adequate housing within the reach of millions of American families who desperately need housing and who currently find housing beyond their economic reach."

For a long time, father had wanted to see all Americans living in clean, safe, comfortable housing which was also within their means. During World War II, his plan to build planes in the auto factories had helped to win the peace. So why not, he asked at the end of the war, convert the Willow Run bomber plant into a facility for production of low-cost housing components?

According to father's figures, the plant could turn out enough parts for 20 million economical two-bedroom homes. Such homes could be assembled for $6,000 each. He knew mass-produced homes weren't ideal, but they could offer more privacy and dignity to inner-city and rural families to whom nothing else was affordable.

Father's concern for the housing problem surfaced during contract negotiations with General Motors. While both sides sat, waiting to find out if the company had accepted the union offer, father was seen scribbling madly in a notebook. Everyone thought he was writing out a press release in case GM refused the UAW's demands and a strike had to be called.

Unable to contain his curiosity any longer, one of father's colleagues asked him if he were preparing a statement for the press. "Oh, no," he answered. "Don't worry, we won't have to strike. They will give us what we want. I'm drawing up plans to help rebuild the slums of America by using the people who live in them."

In 1966, President Johnson invited father to join his cabinet as head of the new Department of Housing and Urban Development (HUD). Father declined, preferring to stay with the UAW. But many of his ideas soon appeared in HUD's "Operation Breakthrough." His concept of industrial housing called for mass-produced modules, three-dimensional boxlike components built on an assembly line, pre-painted and containing basic plumbing, heating, electrical wiring, carpentry, and plaster. The units would be trucked to sites, utilities would be fastened to city services, and the final assembly accomplished.

In 1969, father met with representatives of the Big Three auto makers to discuss how they could assist in acquiring an urban land bank for low-income housing, with a minimum of four 600-acre parcels in the suburbs and large packages of land in inner-city areas. The Detroit experiments with factory-built housing, the *Philadelphia Evening Bulletin* reported, "roughly cut in half the costs of construction per square foot." That year the government estimated the need for new homes at 27 million.

In the late sixties, father would co-anchor the national-level task force of the Urban Coalition, along with David Rockefeller, president of the Chase Manhattan Bank. In a letter to Rockefeller's wife, Peggy, written after they had met at a dinner in Cambridge, Mass., father outlined a housing plan as it was being implemented in Detroit:

In the six-county area of metropolitan Detroit, we have established the Metropolitan Detroit Citizens Development Authority, which is a non-governmental organization dealing with housing problems in the area. Currently we have $50 million worth of housing in the pipeline which includes both conventional and industrial housing. Our conventional housing is running approximately $18 to $19 a square foot and through our industrialized housing, we have succeeded in reducing housing costs to $9 per square foot. I am enclosing a brochure of the single-dwelling home that is being built under our sponsorship which provides 1,200 square feet of housing at $11,700, including land and basic utilities of electric range, refrigerator and garbage disposal.

In another note to David Rockefeller, father acknowledged "the existing archaic building codes and antiquated attitudes" that would be obstacles on the course to more low-income housing in America.

The same year father declined Johnson's invitation to head HUD, he publicly criticized LBJ for not seeking more anti-poverty appropriations from Congress. "Reason will yield to riots and bitterness will yield to bloodshed," father warned, unless more was done for the disadvantaged, especially in housing. His prophecy was sad but true. Less than a year later, Detroit's blacks exploded in a major race riot.

Early in the morning of July 23, 1967, a plainclothes policeman entered a "blind pig" on Detroit's West Side. It was 3:34 a.m. when the officer ordered a drink. Moments later, another police officer who had been waiting in a squad car outside, smashed in the door with a sledgehammer and began making arrests.

The police had expected to find a handful of drinkers left over from Saturday night. Instead, the club was packed with friends of servicemen who had just returned home, two of them from Vietnam. It took four paddywagons to carry them all to the police station.

By that time, a large crowd of angry blacks had gathered on the hot streets. Youths were yelling "Pigs!" and "Leave my people alone!"

By 6:30 a.m., the youths were looting stores and the crowds were growing. Fires began to blaze, setting off alarms through the area.

That afternoon, baseball fans were attacked as they drove home from nearby Tiger Stadium. Blacks and whites alike were armed and shooting to kill.

Governor George Romney and President Johnson were at odds over sending in federal troops, so Mayor Cavanaugh asked father to intervene. Father called Washington, eventually speaking with Supreme Court Justice Abe Fortas, who was advising Johnson on the best course of action. Father requested that National Guard troops be deployed immediately to Detroit.

Soon tanks, armored cars, and troop carriers were patrolling the city streets. By riot's end, 1,628 buildings lay in smoldering ruins, 5,000 people were left homeless, and property-damage estimates ran as high as $500 million. The death toll was 43, with 347 serious injuries reported and over 7,000 arrests made.

Detroit, a city of fabulous wealth and crushing poverty, a melting pot of ethnic groups that never really melted, a jewel that in the last century had been called the "Paris of the Midwest," saw many of its neighborhoods reduced to rubble. Over the years, many of the blocks of beautiful homes had become overcrowded, crime-ridden ghettos. Black and white leaders sat down together to try to resolve the long-standing problems and begin rebuilding the nation's fifth-largest city. They faced a monumental task.

Father prepared a detailed report, giving his analysis of the problems and ideas for workable solutions. "That's what we all should have done, had some real ideas ready," said Henry Ford II, impressed by father's presentation. "Not just sit there and wring our hands."

Father was asked to sit on the New Detroit Committee and twice shared a plane to the state capital of Lansing with Henry Ford and GM Chairman James Roche to lobby for passage of fair-housing legislation. One participant remarked: "It was the damnedest conglomeration of power you ever saw in your life. It was business power, labor power, money power." In spite of their combined influence, the proposed housing legislation was defeated.

Immediately, some of Detroit's radical black leaders started denouncing father and the New Detroit Committee for the failure. Calling father "paternalistic," they claimed "Walter Reuther has attempted to dictate to the black community ever since the UAW came to power." They called him "a liberal around the country and a despot in Detroit." A little over a year earlier these same firebrands had forced the NAACP to drop father's name from a list of candidates for its national board, on which father had served for many years. So father ran on an independent slate and won easily.

A small group of black militants in the UAW began to sharply criticize father, pressing for more posts of authority within the union. Father met with them and made it clear that he would not give token posts; they would be awarded on the basis of merit. "There are no white answers or black answers," he affirmed.

The UAW faction then linked up with the small Detroit League of Revolutionary Black Workers, which was active in 12 plants. They turned out leaflets criticizing father as racist and called others in the rank and file "white racist pigs."

In Washington, meanwhile, many black leaders attacked the notion that whites could help solve the problems of the black community. Michigan Congressman John Conyers told Vice President Humphrey that "Reuther doesn't understand the black problem any more than you do." Whites who had worked against racism and poverty were hurt.

Early in 1988, the Coalition for the Homeless estimated that there are three to four million homeless in the United States. A half million are children, and the fastest-growing group are families.

Jonathan Kozol, author of *"Rachel and Her Children—Homeless Families in America,"* states: "The majority of homeless families I encountered are no different from any other working people. Most working families in the U.S. are three paychecks and one bad illness away from the shelters."

Why? Lack of low-income housing. Many of the homeless have been driven to the streets because their housing gobbled half to three quarters of their income. Mass-produced homes, of the sort father envisioned, *remain* a feasible solution.

CHAPTER FORTY-TWO

MOVING
OUT

"Why do the kids put beans in their ears?...They do it 'cause we said 'No.'"
— From the Broadway musical *The Fantastiks*

Dropping out of college was my own choice, but it was also a sign of the times. The society that gave us war abroad and riots at home also provided unprecedented opportunity to explore "alternative realities." The counterculture was at its headiest. I embraced its music and speech, its diet and dress, and its peace and love. But it had its dark side, too. Drugs and violence.

Society was — and still is — sick with materialism. The drugs and violence that consumed "the revolution" were the latest symptoms of the disease. Some mistook them for treatments, others simply surrendered to the disease. Yet most of us still have hopes for a sane and healthy world.

My parents wanted me to finish college. "How will you get a good job without a good education?" I lacked motivation but appreciated their concern, so in the fall of 1967 I enrolled as a philosophy major at nearby Oakland University in Rochester. I lived at home for one semester, then moved to campus for the winter-spring term. I still wanted to be on my own, to escape being my parents' daughter. Was I fated to follow in their footsteps, bound to Paint Creek?

I knew I would need financial independence. My first step was to get a job at Pontiac State Hospital as a child-care worker. The job put me in touch with love-starved children who desperately needed friendship. I had always been interested in social work; so to develop my counseling skills, I changed my major to psychology.

I was looking for an apartment to share in Pontiac, an easy commute to the university as well as the hospital. When spring term ended, I told my parents, "I'm moving out." It seemed a natural step. I would be 21 soon and had completed nearly three years of college. But mother burst into tears and father was dogmatic: "You can't move out until you're 21. It's the law."

Nevertheless, the same Reuther spirit that had rebelled against-Prussian oppression also ran in me. I was furious. Their interference only increased my determination. So we negotiated a compromise: I would move to the guest house.

It was a splendid facility and I finally received a key to the gate. But it still wasn't my idea of freedom, so I took the liberty of inviting my boyfriend, Greg, to move in with me. My parents never said a word and I told myself they didn't know, but surely the security guards must have said something. Greg's rock music alone was enough to disturb the peace at Paint Creek.

The day I turned 21, we packed our bags and left for a dilapidated two-room efficiency in Pontiac. It sat over a storefront and cost $35 a week. A real dump.

After a while, father came by to put a deadbolt on the back door, which previously had no lock. You can imagine how my mother felt, just knowing about the general appearance and location of my new "home." Later, I moved to an old green duplex with a spacious yard next to the railroad tracks. The building shook with every passing of the Detroit-to-Chicago express.

Although I had escaped them physically, I was haunted by my parents' sense of mission, of service to others. Though I could barely take care of myself, I wanted to save the world. My heart's desires were beyond my capabilities, but the pride of youth blinded me to my shortcomings. What could I realistically hope to accomplish? A paralyzing anxiety gripped me. I had thought I would gain new freedom by leaving home. But thoughts of my parents followed me wherever I went. At mother's suggestion, I submitted myself to psychotherapy.

I had an instant rapport with my therapist. Within a few months, I was displacing my own feelings onto her. In a dream full of Christian symbolism, I gave the cross to my psychiatrist because I could not carry the burden. When I recalled this dream, my friend said it was unusual for a patient to have this type of dream within such a short period of therapy.

"You must recognize this inherent desire within yourself to help others," she said. "But you do not have to be the same as your parents."

Her words gave me hope that I could live my own life, but mother's overprotectiveness made it difficult. She was calling me every day, asking why I felt I had to live away from home. Mother never learned to relax about her girls.

One Broadway musical, *The Fantastiks,* includes a song with the lyrics "Why do the kids put beans in their ears?... They do it 'cause we said, 'No.'" The psychiatrist wrote my parents, stressing the need for them to "let go." They never mentioned the note. I found it years later.

My parents' love for me and my own honesty ultimately pulled me through. I felt that if I abandoned my friends I would again lose my sense of self, merge with my parents and vainly try to live up to their expectations.

I resented father's tight-strung personality and his obsession to protect his reputation. I did not yet appreciate what a good name could accomplish. In my self-centered young womanhood, I was only aware of the increasing impositions of my father's career.

Occasionally, when my parents were out of town, I would take friends to Paint Creek. We would walk the bridges and commune with nature, or play music inside as we looked out at the lights shining against the trees.

One evening we stayed until midnight. The following Saturday I went home to see my parents. Mother greeted me warmly, but father was gruff. "You kids have no respect for your elders," he began. He became angrier as he talked. "I want you to understand one thing, Lisa. My home is my castle and I make the rules here."

A neighbor had seen me leaving late with my friends last weekend and told mother. "It was an unreasonable hour, Lisa," father carried on. "You can't be here with boys late at night." On another occasion, some of my friends stopped by the house just as my parents were pulling out for a business trip. It was a hot summer day. As we entered the house, one young man (who I later learned was on LSD) was so taken with the pastoral beauty of Paint Creek that he threw off his clothes and jumped naked into the stream. His happy shouts extolling heaven and how wonderful it was to be in it drew the attention of another neighbor. She must have used binoculars to see what was going on. In a moment the phone rang. It was father calling from his car on the way to the airport!

"Just what the hell is going on?" he demanded.

I explained what I could — I hadn't really witnessed the whole disrobing and swimming. I told father it had been done without my knowledge or consent. He wasn't satisfied with the story and told me that we had some talking to do when he returned home.

A confrontation with father was long overdue. Yet I was delighted to see his emotional side overtake his usual logical, controlled self — the negotiator who approached every challenge with a cool intelligence. He was just plain mad, and that reaffirmed the real love that bound us together.

No doubt we were driven by destiny. The dangers impelled my parents to exercise a control that exceeded the normal, healthy balance between parent and child. Time and again they would intervene in areas where most children have a certain degree of freedom. The normal tendency to rebel during adolescence was exaggerated by the years under their extreme veto power. Also, destiny was always destroying our privacy. Growing up as the daughter of a public figure, I began to see life as a series of performances, each one being scrutinized and evaluated. While my parents would usually tolerate my intermittent rages at the loss of privacy, they could never help me cope with these feelings, so I grew up convinced they were perverse.

Of course, my loss of privacy was just a tiny serving of theirs. Once in Venice, my parents were laying back in a gondola enjoying an open-air concert when they heard a voice from another craft: "Hey, Mr. Reuther, could I see you in the morning at your hotel?" Father told mother, "Maybe I should go and tip over his gondola!"

Another time in Copenhagen, my parents arranged for a night off, free from the bodyguards. Mother said they "just walked around the city until the early hours of the morning. It was wonderful to just be alone with your father, without anyone looking over our shoulders." What would have been a normal evening for other people became the highlight of their trip.

In the summer of 1967, mother suggested I get away from it all and attend camp. I landed a counseling job at Tamarack, a Jewish fresh-air camp, where I worked in the Advanced Pioneer Division.

The Pioneers lived primitively in canvas tents pitched on simple wooden platforms. The unit had a canoe trip planned for every two-week session. I loved the excursions, especially when we portaged between lakes in Wawa, Canada.

On one of these adventures, I was canoeing with another camper on very still water. We had set up camp on a small island in the middle of the lake and were out in a canoe to explore. As we moved along the edge of the lake, I saw the reflection of the trees on the placid water. The ancients, I recalled, saw our world as the reflection of a higher reality. Alice's Wonderland? Dorothy's Oz? Where in the world were we?

From the first days of camp, I would discuss questions like this with 17-year-old Steven Rubin. He was a talented artist who worked in the camp's arts and crafts division. We spoke frequently about predestination, yoga, and the Tao. At one point, Steven gave me a small rosewood crucifix. We shared an obsession with Christ's supreme sacrifice.

Besides exchanging books of poetry and philosophy with me, Steven taught me the Hare Krishna mantra. For thousands of years, he said, India's sages had been singing this song to raise their consciousness to a spiritual dimension. Although I didn't understand the meaning of the mantra's 16 Sanskrit words, the sound stirred my spirit. I remember the day we first sat in the woods and chanted. It was as if a deeper part of me started slowly to awaken.

As my enthusiasm for the mantra increased, I proceeded to teach it to my Pioneers. Then, at one of the camp sing-alongs, I stood up and taught it to the whole camp. For maybe ten minutes, all the campers were swaying to the mantra. By season's end, however, Tamarack's staff had made it clear that I was *not* their idea of a good Jewish girl.

The last campfire of the summer, Steven and I sat together like brother and sister. He had been planning a trip to New York City, where he had friends in Greenwich Village. "There is an old swami who lives there now," he told me, "and he can teach you more about mantra meditation."

Considering my parents' plans for me, I was certain they did not include a trip to New York to look for a swami. Nor was I ready for such an encounter. I had many hard lessons to learn. And much personal tragedy to endure.

The same summer I learned to chant Hare Krishna, counterculture poet Allen Ginsberg taught the mantra to Bobby Kennedy in Washington. Ginsberg had learned the chant while touring India. With the musical support of his harmonium, he sang, "Hare Krishna, Hare Krishna, Krishna, Krishna, Hare Hare, Hare Rama, Hare Rama, Rama Rama, Hare Hare."

"Now what's supposed to happen?" Kennedy asked.

"It's a magic spell for the preservation of the planet," the poet answered.

Kennedy grinned, "You ought to sing it to the guy up the street," motioning to the White House and its occupant, LBJ. "He needs it more than I do."

CHAPTER FORTY-THREE

FOUR
FRIENDS
LOST

*"How much inner strength, how much deep commitment,
how much faith does it demonstrate, that when your husband
and the father of your children is lying in state in Atlanta,
you leave and carry on the march for the garbage strikers.
This is the mark of a great and wonderful human being."*
— Father praising Coretta Scott King
after her husband's assassination.

Times were changing. My moving out of Paint Creek turned another page in my life. Even as others' lives were ending.

In November 1967, Grossvater Valentine Reuther died peacefully with Grossmutter and her five children around his bed, singing his favorite German lieder.

Two months later Uncle Roy, who had accepted an extra-heavy workload in the 1968 presidential campaign, suffered a massive heart attack. Instead of calling an ambulance, Roy insisted his wife, Fania, drive him to the hospital. He was dead on arrival.

Roy's death was the first loss in the triumvirate of the Reuther brothers. Roy was the political barometer and advisor, Victor the intellectual, and father the pragmatic leader. (Their older brother, Ted, who never became involved with the union, was known as the "white sheep" of the family.) Before father would bring any new ideas before the public or the rank and file, he would discuss them with Victor and Roy.

UNCLE VICTOR: "After many years of sweating through ideas, beginning with the family circle, it was the gospel truth that when Walter was giving a speech, he could stop in the middle and I could finish it to his satisfaction." They worked well as a team, Victor observed, "because there was incredible frankness. Walter was the president of the union in staff meetings. But when Walter, Roy and I met, it was just Walter, Roy and I. If we thought Walter did something stupid, we told him so. Walter never deluded himself. He didn't listen to sweet talk. This quality of self-criticism is so rare in our society. Roy and I both shared a great satisfaction in Walter's achievements. We never envied him."

At the memorial service for Roy, the same question was written on many friends' faces: "Why this sweet man and why at such an early age?" Robert Kennedy came in and sat in the private room reserved for the family. He was on one side of father, I was on the other. As the eulogy commenced, I glanced at both men, their faces drawn with sorrow. Bobby had traveled far and wide with Roy. From JFK's 1960 campaign to civil rights and voter-registration drives in the South to marching with the farm workers in Delano, destiny had them side by side.

On Lincoln's Birthday, 1968, about 1,300 black sanitation workers went on strike in Memphis. As the weeks went by, father flew down to help Dr. Martin Luther King organize a march for the sanitation workers. He gave the strikers a $50,000 check from the UAW to "demonstrate we mean business." When some auto workers objected, father was quick to remind them that in the early days of their own union it was the clothing workers and coal miners who had come to their assistance.

Addressing some 50,000 workers, father declared: "I serve notice upon the mayor of Memphis and the people who have to make this decision that they will not starve these sanitation workers into submission."

Dr. King had arrived in Memphis amid a barrage of death threats. He was well aware that he had powerful enemies trying to silence his voice. On the evening of April 3, he told an overflow crowd at the Clayborn Temple that "like anybody else, I would like to live a long life. Longevity has its place. But I'm not concerned about that now.

I just want to do God's will...So I'm happy tonight. I'm not worried about anything. I'm not fearing any man."

The next day, as he stood on the balcony of the Lorraine Motel, he was shot dead. Father was crushed by the loss of his friend, this great crusader for human freedom with whom he had developed such a close working relationship. King had been on "a union mission," a fact that deepened father's grief.

The very next day, King's widow, Coretta, led another march on behalf of the striking workers. "I was never so proud to hold the hand of my wife and march behind Mrs. Martin Luther King and her three children leading that march," father later told a UAW convention. "How much inner strength, how much deep commitment, how much faith does it demonstrate that when your husband and the father of your children is lying in state in Georgia, you leave and carry on the march for the garbage strikers. This is the mark of a great and wonderful human being."

Two months after King's death, father flew to Los Angeles with Irving Bluestone and Leonard Woodcock for the California Democratic primary. He had not yet endorsed a candidate, since two long - time friends were vying for the nomination — Hubert Humphrey and Bobby Kennedy.

Father flew with Irving to San Francisco on primary day to have dinner with my sister, Linda. During the day, Kennedy won the primary in South Dakota as well as California. Toward evening, UAW West Coast Director Paul Schrade met with Bobby and convinced him it was a good time to call father for his endorsement. Bobby tried but couldn't reach him. As John had eight years earlier, he felt that father's endorsement was crucial. He resolved to try again the next day.

With Paul Schrade at his side, Bobby descended to the Embassy Room of the Hotel Ambassador. He told the cheering crowd: "What I think is quite clear is that we can work together, in the last analysis, and that, despite what has been going on in the United States over a period of the last three years — the division, the violence, the disenchantment with our society — whether it's between blacks and whites, between the poor and the more affluent, or between age

309

The Reuther brothers (from left): Roy, Walter and Victor.

Mother and father (bottom right) in Dr. Martin Luther King's funeral procession.

groups, or on the war in Vietnam — we can start to work together. We are a great country, an unselfish country, and a compassionate country."

When Bobby left for a press conference, he took a short cut through the kitchen, where he stopped to shake hands with the workers. It was just past midnight when Sirhan Sirhan entered and shot Bobby twice in the head. One bullet ricocheted and grazed Paul Schrade. Both men fell to the ground.

Father and Irving were shocked at the news and immediately flew to Los Angeles, where Bobby lay mortally wounded. They visited Paul Schrade in the hospital, then father flew to New York to stand by Bobby's casket at St. Patrick's Cathedral as a member of the honor guard.

"I'm absolutely certain that as more friends came under the gun — Martin Luther King, Bobby Kennedy — Walter became very aware of the fact that there may not be much time left for him," said Uncle Victor. "I think he was fatalistic in the same sense that Martin Luther King was. King accepted the fact that we live in a very precarious, dangerous world where there are forces unleashed that may cut off our lives at any point. 'But while I'm around,' each was thinking, 'there are a few things I want to do.'"

That same year, father and Victor themselves had a brush with death on a late-night flight to Washington. It was drizzling as they descended toward the runway. Suddenly, the plane struck a 12-foot vertical steel girder. "Some four feet of the girder was rammed into the tail section of our jet," Victor remembered. "Another six feet of the girder projected from the tail to the ground." As the craft touched the landing strip, sparks flew in all directions from the dragging steel. The pilot maneuvered the craft into an open field to minimize the risk of an explosion. The rescue crew hustled the two brothers to a waiting car. As they rode into Washington, father calmly remarked, "I guess this wasn't meant to be our time."

The family education center at Black Lake was my parents' dream project. While the UAW was committed to improving the quality of people's lives, father and mother observed that the new generation of workers often lacked the skills, or even the motivation, to build a happy and healthy family. The Family Education Center would help the union's families to grow with the goals and values of a working democracy, and develop new leaders as well. My parents hoped that the workers would find at Black Lake the same sort of inspiration and growth they had found at Paint Creek.

To design the project, father called on the help of his lifelong architect friend, Oskar Stonorov. A Quaker, Oskar lived with his family on a farm in Pennsylvania. He and father shared interests in personal growth and social reform. Many times father had hosted Oskar at Paint Creek for brainstorming sessions. Oskar's passionate nature complemented father's more self-contained personality. A letter from Oskar reveals their light-hearted relationship:

> Dear Walter:
>
> It has been a HELL OF A LONG TIME since I have seen or talked to you, both of which are among my most favored occupations! I know that you have been immersed in a thousand tasks! However, next to pleasure there are a number of things we ought to review on Solidarity House. Could you set a date? Or better yet: Could I see you before or after you get to Philadelphia on the 15th? Or still better yet: Would you spend a night at Avon Lea? The children ask, Betty asks, Where is WPR? I ASK: Give him to us.
>
> Devotedly, Oskar.

Ironically, father first heard about the beautiful site at Black Lake from Henry Ford's notorious security chief, Harry Bennett. After severe battles between union organizers and Bennett's men, Henry Ford finally recognized the workers' right to collective bargaining. At one of their first bargaining sessions, Bennett told father that the next meeting would have to be postponed. He was going to spend a few days at a resort in Northern Michigan. At the next session, Bennett showed father photos of the lodges and scenic property.

Impressed by the natural beauty, father thought of the workers and remarked, "After the revolution, we'll own that place."

Decades later, father and mother's dream became reality. In 1966, the UAW passed a resolution to develop family educational centers. To help find a suitable first site, Irving Bluestone called his close friend, Stan Michaels, then the president of the Camp Owners Association of America. "I'd like to help you, but on certain conditions," Michaels responded. "First, I don't want to be paid for it. Just cover my expenses. And secondly, I want the opportunity to sit down with Walter Reuther in his office, shake hands with him and talk. I'm such an admirer of his."

After several exploratory visits with Michaels, Irving was shown the property at Black Lake. He loved it and reported his find to father. All the UAW officers flew up to look at the property and unanimously agreed that this was the right place.

Lou Maxon, a wealthy Detroit businessman, had constructed the original buildings at Black Lake. It was the custom for affluent auto executives to travel there for entertainment. The union's purchase of the camp for family education had a sweet poetic justice. The UAW bought 800 acres, including a full mile of sandy beach. In addition to the old buildings, father and Oskar envisioned a Leadership Studies Center, with seven classrooms, an office area, and a library. An expansive gymnasium-auditorium complex arose first. Then came a sound studio, saunas, and a solar-heated pool, followed by accommodations for more than 500.

All of the buildings were connected by long teak passageways with huge windows, permitting easy access even in the snowy winter months. Hallways met to form the "hub," a charming circular room with benches and a fireplace in the middle. This was one of father's favorite spots, where he hoped people would come together for conversation, companionship, and inspiration. The hub houses a zodiac sculpture Oskar made in Italy. The bronze objects are the signs of the zodiac, and the hand-blown glass pieces are the planets. The constellation indicates father's horoscope. Father was both touched and embarrassed by Oskar's artistic gesture.

During the cold months prior to construction, father, mother, and Oskar would frequently go to Black Lake for weekend planning sessions. The two fireplaces would blaze in the main lodge where they stayed. Spreading the vast blueprints near the hearth, they would scrutinize every detail. After many hours of concentration, Oskar would sit down at the piano and play like a virtuoso. At the sound of a Strauss waltz, mother and father would kick off their shoes and dance like two young kids.

Said Uncle Victor: "It was a delight to see this man who was so dead serious 98 percent of the time, always grappling with important domestic and international problems, and personally involved with every detail of Black Lake, yet he could relax. He had a recuperative power that amazed me. This gave him the stamina to tackle the serious nature of his work."

As the construction progressed, father was often personally present to supervise. He marked every tree to be cut down and made certain none were disturbed unnecessarily. Several of the roofs were built to skirt the trees. He insisted on propane gas heat, forbid incinerators, and buried the telephone and utility lines. He wanted the center to be functional yet retain a natural beauty. "We made it this beautiful to bring the best out of everyone who comes here," father would explain on tours wearing his Swiss mountain hat. "I believe no one can leave here without being enriched spiritually."

My parents' personalities still fill the Black Lake compound. Father knew every detail of the center by heart. And it was with great devotion that he gave his tours. "This center is about the most crucial issue of our times," he would say, "the quality of leadership."

Indeed. America had just lost two of her most promising leaders. Father looked forward to the Democratic convention that summer and contemplated what might happen next.

Robert Kennedy and father, less than a month before RFK's tragic assassination.

CHAPTER FORTY-FOUR

THE WHOLE
WORLD
WAS
WATCHING

"Frankly, Hubert, if you don't have the courage to come out now against the Vietnam War, you don't deserve to be elected."

— Uncle Victor, to Hubert Humphrey
during 1968 presidential campaign.

With renewed impetus, father pursued the cause of peace. By the late 1960s, the Vietnam War had become a painful thorn in America's side. My generation — raised in conflict, afraid of the bomb — was questioning the traditional values that shaped modern society. Many of us were disillusioned and searching for alternatives.

Vietnam became the glaring symbol of what was wrong with the status quo. The quicksand conflict promised no tangible gains for democracy. Was America's public commitment to freedom concealing darker imperialistic interests in Southeast Asia? The U.S. was violating the Geneva Accords that required we do everything possible to establish free elections. It seemed deals were being made in the name of anti-communism.

In our family, Vietnam was a hot issue. Father was keenly aware of the domestic gains made under President Johnson's leadership. His vice president, Hubert Humphrey, had been father's choice. The Administration's Great Society programs were largely effective, and father did not want to hinder the momentum by opposing Johnson's foreign policy. Although he considered the war a tragic mistake, he sacrificed his personal feelings and expressed the support of the UAW. He avoided putting the union in direct opposition to the President of the United States.

To me, the whole conflict was absolutely immoral. It was black and white, I thought, and father's inability to see this immorality proved to me he had sold out to capitalism. He was now part of the problem.

Whenever we were together, we debated the war. That several of my friends were being drafted gave me a personal stake in the issue.

One Saturday, I came home from college to ask father questions for a political science paper. I was studying McCarthyism, about which he had a lot of personal insight. After an hour on the McClellan Committee, our conversation inevitably turned to Vietnam.

"You have to understand, Lisa, the Vietcong are without scruples. They will murder thousands of innocent people for their own political end. Human decency is not an issue for the Communists."

"It's a civil war," I countered, "And Ho Chi Minh is a Vietnamese nationalist, not a stooge of the Russians. Why don't we set up elections and let the Vietnamese people decide?"

"It wouldn't be a fair election," he insisted. "The Communists won't allow democratic elections. They would win and then liquidate vast populations who disagree with them."

"But what about our own selfish motives, daddy? Why are we really in Southeast Asia? Why don't we deal with all the unfinished business here at home?"

I was naive as to the delicacy of father's position. As UAW president, he had to use great discretion in expressing himself. Others, like Emil Mazey and Uncle Victor, also disagreed with the union's support of Johnson's policies. And father allowed this as long as no one used the UAW to promote their individual beliefs. Victor later described the difficulties of father's position:

"Walter never really believed this was a war in which we should have entered. But as head of an organization, you really hesitate to break openly with the President of the United States on a foreign policy issue. Whether you like it or not, you don't always have the luxury of a personal opinion. I had talked to Walter enough about the Vietnam War privately to know he thought it was one of our greatest

316

tragedies. And I think that if there were any way he could have manipulated Johnson to pull out, he would have."

Military escalation pushed father further away. In the fall of 1967, he had this to say on *Meet the Press*: "If I were the President, I would, I believe, be willing to cease the bombing of the North in the hope that that might give us the basis for new initiatives in trying to get to the conference table, because I believe over the long pull there are no military solutions to the economic, social, and political problems of Asia, and that freedom must win that fight over tyranny in the rice fields and not in the battlefields."

In 1968, no longer able to support the military approach, father broke publicly with Johnson's policy. He saw the President's push for a military victory as futile. Johnson, who had thought father would remain a loyal supporter, was furious with the UAW's official statement.

But later that year, when Johnson halted the bombing of North Vietnam, father sent a telegram congratulating him on what he called "your humane and courageous act of statesmanship. . . laying the basis for an eventual peaceful resolution of a tragic conflict for whose end the peoples of the world have been waiting. You can be assured of the unwavering support of the UAW through the taxing months ahead in your efforts to bring about a total cease-fire."

Johnson replied immediately. "I was greatly heartened today to receive both your telegrams endorsing my decision to cease the bombing in Vietnam. My hopes for peace are higher when they are raised up by your encouragement and UAW support. If we have a long and careful way to go, America will travel quicker and to better purpose when we go together."

The National Mobilization to End the War in Vietnam (Mobe) was organizing thousands of demonstrators to attend August's Democratic national convention in Chicago. Mobe's leadership included Tom Hayden, Rennie Davis, and Dave Dellinger. Most of the demonstrators were for Eugene McCarthy, who favored a stop-the-war-now policy, and against Hubert Humphrey, who supported LBJ's strategy. LBJ had dropped out of the race before the convention to devote all his efforts, he said, to finding a solution to the war.

By the summer of 1968, 525,000 U.S. troops were stationed in Vietnam. More than 15,000 Americans had died in the war. Negotiations were at a standstill, with no prospects for peace.

On the eve of the Democratic Convention, the war protesters started gathering at Lincoln Park on Chicago's North Side. Mayor Richard Daley had recently criticized his police force for not being tough enough during the riots following the assassination of Martin Luther King, saying their job was to "shoot to kill arsonists and shoot to maim looters."

Just before the convention, the police had arrested 12 Blackstone Rangers, leather-jacketed advocates of "black power." They were charged with planning to assassinate the Democratic presidential candidates. The police now focused their attention on the 1,000 war protesters, mostly students, who had gathered at Lincoln Park. They drove the demonstrators from the park into the neighboring streets, where they beat them with their billy clubs.

Battered and bruised, the demonstrators regrouped at the park the next evening, now joined by hundreds more. Again the Chicago police charged and drove them from the park. Besides pummeling the protesters, the police attacked 21 reporters and cameramen who were covering the events. Even *Playboy* publisher Hugh Hefner received a blow across the backside from a nightstick.

Inside the convention, father and others were working on a plank opposing the war. Father felt Humphrey had to come out against our staying in Vietnam. Humphrey had long been a champion of the people and had earned a reputation for deciding issues on their morality, not their political expedience.

Father presented Humphrey with a peace plank calling for an immediate cease-fire, an international peace-keeping force, land redistribution and free elections in South Vietnam. He had put together the proposal with Norman Cousins, Clark Kerr, and other anti-war activists.

Humphrey's only objection was that he wanted the North to stop its military action before we ceased our bombing. That was the Administration's policy, and as LBJ's vice president, Humphrey was reluctant to break from it. Though they were old friends, father was unable to convince Humphrey to make that break.

Outside the convention hall, the protesters listened to the debate inside over the Vietnam peace plank. Late in the afternoon, the plank was defeated. Four-letter epithets filled the air. A young protester climbed a flagpole and brought the American flag down to half-mast. The police charged, again bloodying the demonstrators while TV cameras recorded the action.

Some 3,000 protesters, driven from the park, regrouped and marched down Michigan Avenue toward the Hilton Hotel. Before them was a police barricade. The demonstrators shouted obscenities at the police and hurled bottles, rocks, and balloons filled with urine and paint. The police responded with tear gas and mace. Hundreds of demonstrators were injured. Fifty police needed medical attention. Over 600 arrests were made.

John Haslett, an anti-war demonstrator at the convention, described the scene as "the closest I've ever seen to a police state":

> At one point, Dick Gregory was leading a peaceful march. He lived on Michigan Avenue and invited everyone to his house. It was early evening. We were walking on the sidewalk. The police set up barricades and the protesters spilled over into the streets.
>
> The TV cameras arrived and the protesters began chanting "The whole world is watching!" Black kids lit firecrackers, which increased the intensity.
>
> The demonstrators started to pass out helmets for protection. A friend and I each received one. The police fired tear-gas canisters into the crowd. I felt a sharp pain as one of the canisters struck my leg. It went off in my face. I couldn't see anything. All around me I heard people screaming as they were being beaten by the cops. I was helpless. I couldn't move, I was blinded. I imagined that any second I would become a victim of the club-wielding cops.
>
> Just then, a demonstrator grabbed my hand and led me out of the tear gas into an adjoining alley. It was dark. My eyes began to clear. Then we heard helicopters overhead. Searchlights beamed down on us as everyone moved up against the alley's walls trying to avoid the lights. Those who were lit up got hit with tear gas.
>
> Finally, the helicopters left, and we made our way back to

Grant Park [outside the convention site] to soak our handkerchiefs and wipe away the tear gas. As I was washing the sting out of my eyes, the National Guard surrounded Grant Park. They shot tear gas at one end of the park, so we rushed to the other side to get fresh air. Then they fired tear gas at that end, forcing us back. This went on for hours, the crowd like a ping-pong ball being driven back and forth by the canisters of tear gas.

Not all the casualties were in the streets. Mayor Daley had wanted to show the American people he could keep law and order, but the TV cameras had shown something else. Hubert Humphrey's campaign began under a cloud of violence; the Democratic Party was gravely wounded.

Throughout Humphrey's 1968 presidential campaign, father advised him to break with the Administration's position on Vietnam. At one point Humphrey invited father to his Minnesota home to discuss the issue. Father insisted he could not win the election unless he broke with LBJ. Humphrey asked him to write a speech proclaiming the break.

Father returned to Detroit, wrote the speech, and sent it to Humphrey. Humphrey liked it, but could never bring himself to use it. Victor remembers meeting with Humphrey at the White House later during the campaign. "You know, we have been friends for a long time and I have the greatest affection for you," Victor told him. "But quite frankly, Hubert, if you don't have the courage to come out now against the Vietnam War, you don't deserve to be elected." Humphrey was stunned and hurt by his remark but appreciated his honesty. What could he say?

After Humphrey had secured the nomination, father worked hard to unite the deeply divided party behind him. He knew Richard Nixon would not have wide appeal among auto workers, but George Wallace, the segregationist Alabama governor who left the Democrats to run on a third-party ticket, might.

Father campaigned vigorously against both Wallace and Nixon. Humphrey carried the UAW's home state of Michigan by 200,000 votes. But in a close election, Richard M. Nixon became the 37th president of the United States.

CHAPTER FORTY-FIVE

A CHAIR
FOR
PEACE

"Man must realize the insanity of trying to win a nuclear war. The only war we can now fight is the war against disease, ignorance, and poverty. This is the enemy that degrades man and robs him of his greatest potential."
— Walter Reuther, accepting a peace chair
at the Weizmann Institute, Rehovot, Israel.

My 21st birthday was the day of my declaration of independence. It established a new framework for communication with my parents. It was a relief to put some distance between my own life and my parents' compelling concerns.

Working at Pontiac State Hospital was a challenge. The children came from alcoholic parents and broken homes. They were labeled pre-adolescent, though many had reached puberty. Their parents had been unable to discipline them. As I supervised their recreation and took them on field trips, my relationships with many grew close. But setting limits on their behavior wasn't easy, and they often succeeded in tricking me.

One day while my partner was in the supervisor's office, I was on the ward alone with the children. Two little sisters had been upset all morning because they were not going home for a weekend visit. We used home visits as a way of reinforcing positive behavior. Suddenly one of the girls grabbed my keys. She motioned to her younger sister to delay me while she unlocked the outside door. "Grab Miss Reuther, Shirley. Don't let her come near me!"

The younger girl placed a chair in front of the door. She sat on it and kicked me when I approached. I tried to her convince her to let me pass. Meanwhile, the older girl had run outside. Frantically, I phoned the supervisor. They caught her just as she was about to cross the busy Pontiac street.

While afraid for the child's safety, I was also greatly embarrassed by how little control I had over these children. In fact, the whole hospital's control over the children was weak. The ratio of staff to children was low. At any moment the patients might release their frustrations and terrorize an entire ward. One of the girls, Hope, was 14 years old, stood six feet tall and weighed about 200 pounds. When Hope was angry, it took four strong staff members to handle her.

Coming on the ward after a weekend off, I learned that two girls had been put "in seclusion" for pushing around and tying up a night worker. So I didn't like to work the floor alone.

More than anything, the children needed friends. Some had become wards of the court, which meant they might be institutionalized for life. One child, an eight-year-old girl, had no major personality disorder, so one of the nurses decided to adopt her. During the trial period, the child went to the nurse's home on weekends. Those trips transformed the sullen-faced youngster. She no longer vented her anger on the other girls. After six months, the court for some reason forbade the adoption and sent the child to an orphanage in another city! Both child and nurse were crushed.

Time and again I saw how bureaucratic red tape was strangling patients' futures. And for the present, the hospital's small staff relied heavily on medications to control unruly behavior. I often wished we could motivate the children more. Yet within the context of their lives at Pontiac State, there was little we few staff members could offer them. Except our love. By loving them, we tried to help them love themselves.

After I had worked at the hospital for two months, there was a strike. I was not a member of the union because I was working part time to finish school. I told father about my dilemma. Despite the poor working conditions and the demands for higher wages and more staff, I was afraid that "if I don't go to work the children will suffer."

"I respect your concern for their welfare," he replied, "BUT NO DAUGHTER OF MINE IS GOING TO CROSS A PICKET LINE!"

The issue was closed. On Monday I called in sick, and the next day a new contract was signed, solving my quandary.

Father was by now in great demand as a speaker at colleges and universities. He was a "real live reformer," appealing both to students and progressive faculties. At the University of California at Berkeley, the capital of student radicalism in the 1960s, he commanded the largest crowd ever gathered for a speaker (except for Alfred C. Kinsey, the famous sex researcher).

But father found the "SDS kids," as he called them, very hard to reach. A product of the 1960s, the Students for a Democratic Society were known for their radical politics and violent measures for achieving their goals. Their favorite stratagem was to storm a university's administration building, take it over, smash equipment, destroy documents, and demand that the administrators be fired.

Father met with SDS members on a number of occasions. "Violence is counterproductive," he told them, pointing out that the auto workers never destroyed one piece of machinery when they were striking in a factory. He told them about his own protest at Wayne State in 1932, when he fought against compulsory ROTC for men. "We knew what we were fighting for," he challenged them, "and you only know what you are fighting against. You have no moral right to destroy something unless you have something better to put in its place."

Father's support for Hubert Humphrey at the 1968 Democratic convention enraged protesting students, especially when Humphrey refused the peace plank and continued to support the Vietnam War. Speaking on conservation at the University of Michigan, father was interrupted by SDS heckling. Booing, cursing, stamping and hissing persisted throughout his address.

Age was an issue within the union as well. By 1969 about one third of the members were 30 and under. That spring father convened a three-day meeting of young members in Detroit. He wanted them to gain a sense of the history of the UAW so that its original goals would not be lost. It was time for the older warriors to hand the reins to the younger generation, who, father hoped, would keep the UAW a cornerstone of American democracy.

The conference was a great opportunity for younger members to sound off. Father listened carefully. He liked to identify with them. They were idealistic, and though he had known adversity and disappointment, he never lost his idealism. He lived the philosophy that there is nothing to stop the individual from attaining any goal except the limits one sets for oneself.

Ever since I had moved away from Paint Creek, mother had tried to increase our dialogues. "Father and I will be going to Israel in November," she called to say one day, "and we want you to come along."

I was suspicious. Maybe she would try to persuade me to move back home. But after consulting my hospital supervisor about time off, I agreed.

Mother was delighted and proceeded to buy me new clothes, shoes, and accessories. As a member of the Reuther "delegation," I would need a suitable wardrobe. My own income covered only the basics. I appreciated the new acquisitions.

The main occasion for the trip was the dedication of a chair for the peaceful use of atomic energy at the Weizmann Institute in Rehovot, Israel. The chair was established in perpetuity in honor of father. Before our departure, the Weizmann Institute and a 250-person International Committee sponsored a fund-raising dinner, attracting 1,500 persons. At the dinner, Israel's Foreign Minister Abba Eban extolled father's contributions as a social statesman. Ludwig Rosenberg, president of the German Trade Union Federation, added: "It is not incidental that this chair, established for the advancement of mankind has been named in honor of Walter P. Reuther, who has stressed the importance and demanded the full utilization of atomic power for economic and scientific progress, [but] did not weaken in supporting all appropriate means to protect men against the threat of martial use of atomic energy."

We flew to Tel Aviv. After touring the city, we dined at the home of President Meyer Weisgal. The occasion gave father the opportunity to meet political and labor leaders like Becker, Dayan, and Barbour. Weisgal's wife befriended mother and me. Sensing our ongoing confrontation, she told us about her own daughter, who had rejected her father for years. "She embraced Marx and Lenin as her real fathers. Now finally she acknowledges Meyer. On his last birthday, she wrote him a card saying, 'Now I realize you are my only father.' How difficult are these youthful quests."

Sunday, the first of December, the Weizmann Institute designated as Reuther Day. In the morning we toured the Institute and placed a wreath on the grave of Dr. Chaim Weizmann, Israel's scientist-statesman and first president.

The ceremony honoring father started at noon in the small Wix Auditorium. A harpist filled the hall with ethereal notes. Mother and I sat in fascination as her skilled hands cascaded across the strings. Her playing set the mood for the entire program, which was intimate, tasteful and precise.

After several short salutations, Professor Joel Gat read the scroll honoring father, then called upon him to speak. The atmosphere grew solemn and silent. Father moved to the microphone, his lips quivering with emotion. "We hold the future in our hands," he began. "Man must realize the insanity of trying to win a nuclear war. The only war we can now fight is the war against disease, ignorance, and poverty. This is the enemy which degrades man, robs him of his greatest potential."

The harpist closed the program as we were escorted out of the auditorium. That evening we attended a concert of the Israel Philharmonic Orchestra, dedicated to father.

May and Walter Reuther — world citizens.

A playful moment with daddy during our Israel trip.

From Rehovot, we traveled by air for a three-day visit to Jerusalem. For hours we walked up and down the narrow cobblestone streets and back into history. We followed the stations where Christ had carried his cross and stopped at the Wailing Wall, where pilgrims were rapt in spiritual emotion. There was nothing like this in America.

"You know, Lisa," mother said, "people come here just to touch this wall. It is their link with God's mercy and love. The mood here is very mystical."

After stopping at a holocaust memorial, we flew to Haifa and spent time at a kibbutz. The living conditions there reflected the tremendous strain of the wars in the Middle East. Every kibbutz had bomb shelters in the residences. It was common practice to have the children sleep in these shelters, since gunfire was prevalent at night. The nursery building bore bullet holes. Both men and women were trained to use weapons.

"Maybe you should stay here for a few years, Lisa," father teased. "You look like a kibbutz girl, rugged and ready to pull your weight."

"No thanks, dad. I like simple living, but I'm not ready to carry a gun." Still, I admired the people's will to live. To farm despite the arid climate and to raise their children despite the wars.

The second part of our journey took us to Turkey and Yugoslavia. We spent two days in Istanbul, where father met with government officials and mother and I saw the sights.

At 5 a.m. the second day, mother and I left the hotel to join the dawn flow to the mosques. The huge shrines faced Mecca. I sensed the soulful mood of the people, who were pious and poor. The women completely covered themselves, leaving only a small space for their eyes.

"Uncovered" Western women aroused the Turk in some of the men. As mother and I walked arm-in-arm through the dirty streets, I was grabbed several times by strangers. One man grabbed my leg above the knee. I tightened my grip on mother's arm and gave him a good kick. We increased our pace and decided to enjoy Istanbul's charms from a distance.

Yugoslavia was one of the few Communist satellites with a healthy trade union movement. The Yugoslavian Confederation of Trade Unions hosted our visit. Again, father spent his days in meetings, while mother and I toured the art museums and government-run day-care facilities.

In the evenings, father joined us for dinner and more sightseeing. Eager to show us how Yugoslavia was keeping pace with the West, the union delegation invited us to a Belgrade discotheque. Modern paintings lined the walls. Strobe lights pulsed to loud music. The imitation of Western pop culture gave us the impression we were in New York or London. We clustered around a small table, watching the young people dance a sort of Transylvania twist. Soon one of them invited me to the floor. After several numbers I returned to our table.

My dancing disturbed mother. "You're too wild, Lisa. Can't you dance without shaking your head?"

My long, loose hair did look wild when I danced — but that's a style that the late '60s revived. Father was also unhappy about the dancing. He was ready to leave, but I was just warming up. After all our touring, I had finally found a place where I could relax a little, away from the labor-sponsored dinner parties, the ceremonies, the endless show-and-tell. Milan Rukavina-Sain and his interpreter, Mirjana Rajkovic, offered to be my chaperones for an additional hour. Milan had two daughters and said he would be delighted to give me this opportunity to experience Yugoslavia's youth culture.

I glanced toward father for his approval but was surprised. "No, you cannot stay," he said flatly. "I don't like you shaking and carrying on."

Father had added a new plank to his already rigid moral platform. As we rose and walked to the elevator, I pleaded: "Please, father. Let me stay."

"Can't you accept my authority? Can't you *listen*, Lisa?"

By the time we entered the elevator, I was in tears. Milan apologized for causing trouble with my father. He was disappointed I could not stay for a few more dances. But when father said no, he meant it.

After the Belgrade meetings, we toured the Yugoslavian countryside, then flew to Zurich, New York and finally Detroit.

Back at Pontiac Hospital at the onset of a long Michigan winter, I brought all the children at the hospital gifts from my travels. They wondered how other children live, so I told them stories about what I had seen in other countries. Especially the hardships. Troubled as America was, they began to appreciate the many freedoms and opportunities available in the good old U.S.A.

CHAPTER FORTY-SIX

TAKING
AMERICA'S
PULSE

"The Nixon Administration, with Mr. Spiro Agnew leading the pack, continues to sow the seeds of division and polarize America at the very time there is a desperate need for a deeper sense of national unity and national purpose."
— Father, in a letter to
Senator Edmund Muskie,1969

Father was deeply concerned about the arms race. Early in 1969 he said that the country should cut back $20 billion from its arms budget. Testifying before a Joint Economic Subcommittee, he stated:

Our whole value system is cockeyed. It seems to us in the UAW that the time has come for the American people and the Congress to blow the whistle on war-games strategists and their swollen budgets and sweetheart deals with defense contractors, and to demand a mobilization of our great resources on behalf of strategies for world and domestic peace.

Support for the Department of Health, Education and Welfare provided better security for America than military precautions, he maintained. "The Soviet Union needs relief from the arms race as desperately as we do."

Said Uncle Victor: "Walter fully accepted the fact that the nuclear age had made an end to armaments an absolute essential for human survival. He felt international relationships had to be based on mutual trust as well as mutual on-site inspection."

Father felt one key to peace lay in giving people access to life's basics: food, shelter, and medical care. He believed health care was a birthright that government should freely provide its citizens, as it does in England, India, and every other industrialized democracy. He considered the inequities of America's health-care system a national disgrace.

Twenty years earlier, when father's right arm was still mending from the assassination attempt, he had addressed the UAW national convention on anamolies in the American health-care system. He told the delegates about a 28-year-old man who had been paralyzed for one third of his life. He had begun to regain the use of his limbs when he ran out of money and was refused further treatment at the hospital.

"I say there is something wrong in America when, if you happen to be born on the wrong side of the railroad tracks, you lie on your back for nine years because you can't afford the treatment that medical science can give you. I say that is morally wrong. No nation that has an ounce of self-respect or human decency, no nation that can spend $400 billion for war can stand idly by and tolerate a continuation of that kind of double standard."

Then he launched into a *Detroit Free Press* story about GM President Charles Wilson's sick bull. One of the executive's favorite hobbies was raising prize cattle. The bull, the story said, had a bad back, so Wilson had General Electric send a special 140,000-volt X-ray machine into Detroit on a chartered plane. "The bull didn't even have to leave home to get medical care," father marveled. "When they got the X-ray machine out to the farm, they couldn't operate it because they didn't have enough power, so the Detroit Edison Company ran a special power line out to C.E. Wilson's farm."

The story went on to say that medical specialists from around the country showed up to give advice and offer treatment. Why, father asked, did the bull get the best of medical care while millions of young and old people do not? "It is because C.E. Wilson's bull cost $16,000, and you can get boys and workers for free."

At the 1955 Miami convention sealing the merger of the AFL-CIO, father had met with health-care consultant Dr. Edwin Daily to explore the possibility of the UAW setting up its own family clinics and hospitals. Daily recalled the meeting: "He had his bodyguards there. At a nod from him, they stepped to one side and for about half an hour

Reuther and I sat on the sofa talking. He listened closely while I was outlining the basic structure of our plan, and at the end he asked some very pointed questions. Within that half-hour he had grasped all the important aspects. He really wanted some plan that would benefit the general public."

Father's immediate public was the UAW, for whom he established the Community Health Association (CHA). He renovated a rundown Detroit hospital and renamed it Metropolitan Hospital, which became the hub of a system of satellite clinics for union members and other groups.

In the 1960s a friend of mine landed a clerical job with Wayne State University. After completing the employment forms, she was told she could choose between traditional medical insurance and CHA — the Community Health Association. "You probably wouldn't be interested in CHA," the personnel officer said. "It's for janitors and people like that."

But when my friend heard the benefits—the central hospital with satellite clinics, the $2 visit fee, minimal lab charges, a variety of hospital services at nominal cost—she picked CHA despite her white-collar status.

Today, CHA is known as the Health Alliance Plan (HAP) and is Michigan's largest Health Maintenance Organization (HMO). More than 1,600 physicians serve as salaried employees of the association in more than 60 area hospitals and clinics. Costs are carefully monitored and controlled. Patients are encouraged to practice preventive medicine or visit the clinics regularly for health maintenance, before ailments reach the expensive stage.

In 1969, as chairman of the Committee for National Health Insurance, father worked to devise a medical plan "which will be uniquely American and which will try to preserve the good things in our system while overcoming its deficiencies and its waste." In Cincinnati that November, he addressed the 80th Annual Convention of the Association of American Medical Colleges and laid out the facts:

• 24 million Americans had no health insurance
• 35 million Americans had no surgical insurance
• 61 million Americans had no hospital medical coverage

- 108 million Americans had no prescription coverage
- 176 million Americans had no dental insurance

He challenged the members of the medical profession to be the leaders in making "adequate medical care available to all. By defaulting on this responsibility, you force us to make medical decisions in the political arena. Instead of taxing each member of the American Medical Association $25 to fight health insurance, you should be raising that money to supply what you think is a better method."

Health care, father pointed out, was only available to those old enough for Medicare, poor enough for Medicaid, or rich enough to pay the bills. As that left out most Americans, he said a new system should replace the old. "You cannot cure it with a box of aspirin. Major surgery is required. You could throw additional billions of dollars into the system and it still would not function."

In a letter to Senator Edmund Muskie, father wrote that "despite expenditures of greater resources than any nation in the world ($60 billion in 1969), America has a second-rate, obsolete, health-care non-system." How, he asked, could the greatest Democracy in the world live with a health-care system based on one's privilege and income?

Senator Edward Kennedy later stated: "Walter Reuther made the wave of the health care revolution that is now cresting in America."

As President Nixon played out the tragedy in Vietnam, father sponsored full-page ads in the *New York Times* and the *Wall Street Journal* endorsing a demonstration to end the war. I hugged him when he showed me the newspapers. Father had done a lot of soul-searching in the years since his official support of LBJ's Vietnam policy. I admired his ability to change his mind publicly even as others in business and labor still supported the war — a war that would cost over 58,000 American lives.

Nixon's presidency deeply worried father. In another letter to Senator Muskie, dated November 21, 1969, father spelled out his concerns:

I share with many of our friends deep concern about the future as the Nixon Administration, with Mr. Agnew leading the pack, continues to sow the seeds of division and polarize America at the very time there is a desperate need for a deeper sense of national unity and national purpose.

Father told the *Chicago Sun Times* that the Democratic Party needed to "come forward with a tangible alternative to President Nixon." He accused the Administration of ignoring the country's major problems while dabbling in the "outer fringes."

While father was trying to help the Democratic Party get back on its feet, columnist Victor Riesel, who had been critical of father for years, tried to damage his relationship with his lifelong friend Hubert Humphrey. Late in 1969 Riesel wrote that at a committee meeting to give the party a new direction, "one of the first moves by Reuther ... was to tell those in hearing range that Humphrey is out, McGovern is in; older candidates are out; younger men are in; negotiationists are out."

Hubert Humphrey sent the column to father with a letter dated December 18, 1969:

Dear Walter,
   I am sure you have seen the attached column. Just another one of those many efforts that are made to divide us.... The one thing that has pleased and strengthened me in my public life is knowing that I was working on the same team with you. That's the way I want it in the days ahead...
   I don't care what a columnist might say. I happen to think that Walter Reuther is a great man and has been a powerful force for good in our country and, indeed, in the world.
Sincerely,
Hubert H.

Father responded January 5, 1970.

Dear Hubert,
   I had not seen the Riesel column... Those of us who have fought for what we believe to be right have had to live with the many abuses that free speech and free press subject us to.
   Among the things I cherish is the warmth and richness of

friendships that I have been privileged to share, and yours is one of those I cherish most; and I am certain that wagging of idle tongues and irresponsible journalism will in no way weaken or diminish our friendship.

Sincerely,

Walter

Hubert Humphrey and father — lifelong friends.

Father usually spent the first day of September out of town. That was his birthday, but also near Labor Day, a day for a labor leader to be out making speeches. A labor leader's duties on Labor Day weekend seldom included his family.

But 1969 was different. With Nixon in power, it would be years before the government would again sponsor any progressive social programs. So father poured his energy into the Black Lake project. He and mother spent many weekends there supervising final construction.

When father confirmed he would be at Black Lake the weekend of his birthday, I drove up there with my friend, Celia Mitchell. I also brought my cello for a happy birthday serenade.

Arriving at Black Lake, mother, Celia, and I went with father on his grand tour. He proudly pointed out the builders' bites around the edges of the roofs, each making way for a growing tree. "We must preserve nature's delicate balance," he remarked, noting every form's right to live.

The next day was father's birthday. He was up very early with the contractors, but he promised to spend the afternoon with us. Mother and I prepared a sumptuous salad, one of his favorite dishes. I baked brownies for dessert, and we decorated a stack of them like a birthday cake, with candles and blue lettering.

When father returned from his morning with the contractors, mother, Celia and I took our positions in my parents' cabin. As father stepped into the room, I launched into an upbeat *Happy Birthday To You* on my cello as we sang to the guest of honor. Father blushed with embarrassment and delight. It was a kindness of fate that we could celebrate together what would be father's last birthday.

As Christmas, 1969, approached, father yearned for a greater reunion. I was with him one weekend when he called Oskar Stonorov about plans for a holiday get-together. Our families were scattered around the country. Linda was in California; Oskar's eldest daughter, Tina, was in Alaska. It took several calls to confirm the dates, but the day after Christmas we all converged again on Black Lake.

Before the huge roaring fireplace we caroled, and around the silvery snowscape we marched, Oskar and father in the lead. Father proudly wore the red hardhat presented to him by Black Lake's construction workers. It bore the letters CABGF — an acronym for Chief Architect, Builder and General Flunky.

The feasting and laughter we shared were another kindness. Unknown to all, this would be father, mother, *and* Oskar's last Christmas.

Father sharing his enthusiasm during one of his famous Black Lake tours.

One of Black Lake's many architectural wonders, designed by Oskar Stonorov and father.

CHAPTER FORTY-SEVEN

TOGETHER
AGAIN

"To our Lisa: We trust you. Love, Mother."
— Mother's last message to me

In April 1970, I asked father to be the guest speaker at Oakland University's Earth Day. It was the spring of my senior year, and I had just moved back to our home at Paint Creek. My parents and I were becoming close again, closer than we'd ever been. Father said yes, he would speak at Earth Day.

Father had long been a working conservationist — from helping Boy Scouts clean up Paint Creek to advising presidents on preserving America's national parks. He placed Olga Madar, the UAW's first woman Executive Board member, at the head of the union's own Department of Conservation and Resource Development. And he continued to press for a national effort to clean the air, purify streams, replenish wildlife, and expand the national parks.

While preparing for his Earth Day talk, father was arranging for the ecological experts of 17 nations to meet at Black Lake that summer. The seminar would create the foundation for the UN's first worldwide environment conference scheduled for Stockholm the following year.

Earth Day found me giddy with excitement, as if *I* were to be the speaker. Father spoke magnificently. His message of hope received a standing ovation. I was never so proud of him as I was on that day.

The week after I moved back to Paint Creek, my parents moved out temporarily, to the 22nd national UAW convention. The union presented two Social Justice Awards that year, one to former Chief Justice Earl Warren and the other posthumously to Dr. Martin Luther King, Jr. Warren had previously refused to accept any awards, believing "a judge should neither seek nor accept awards for the plain doing of his duty." Now that he was retired from the bench, he accepted the UAW citation with obvious pleasure.

In presenting King's award to his widow, Coretta Scott King, father stated:

> He will stand in history as a giant among the giants. Martin Luther King had great inner strength, a deep commitment to his belief in man and brotherhood, in justice and freedom.... His was like the faith of Mahatma Gandhi, who rocked the British Empire not with the might of armies gathered on a battlefield, but with the power of the belief in the worth and dignity of each human being.

In her remarks, Mrs. King answered:

> I always like to think of the great British Prime Minister Disraeli. One time he was asked by a young man how he could pursue a worthwhile and satisfying life. The prime minister advised him to adopt some good cause, preferably an unpopular one, and then pursue it diligently....'

Father's convention goals included building international worker solidarity and peace.

> The essential and wonderful fact about the UAW is that our union enables each of us to have a say in the world, a say multiplied by the million and half voices our union represents, by the eleven million voices the International Metalworkers Federation amplifies, and often by joining with people of good will everywhere we can raise a great demand voicing the aspirations of tens and even hundreds of millions of people.

Behind every great man, the saying goes, there stands a great woman. Father's home may have been his castle, but his hearth was mother's heart. Mother's quiet femininity complemented father's uncompromising drive. Her approach to life was cautious, gentle, and loving. Her equilibrium and confidence helped father to mature into the powerful world leader he became.

Like father, mother was a thinker, always looking for practical ways to help the world's oppressed. With grace and gentle wit, she moved through widely diverse social circles. Shy and beautiful, she always wanted to improve herself intellectually and spiritually. A measure of self-doubt opened her to others' suffering.

When she was home, she was the gracious, warm hostess, quiet and conservative in her manner. There was not much idle chatter in May Reuther's living room. Mother preferred an exchange of ideas.

She often declined social invitations when father could not or would not attend. "I'm feeling too tired," she would say. She shunned publicity for herself and her daughters: "I feel the girls deserve more privacy."

A long-time "peacenik," mother was unhappy she had not found some way to work more effectively for peace. "There is such a real desire for peace, almost everywhere" she told an interviewer. "We must do more than talk about it."

Asked about her years of marriage to father, she replied: "The whole purpose of our life has been fulfilling. I guess if we had to do it over, Walter and I would live our lives in much the same way."

Some 30 years earlier, on a rainy night in November, father had written her:

The Hotel Hamilton
Washington, D.C.
Sunday evening

Mayichka mine,

Hello — how are you this evening? Since I wrote you yesterday I have had a night's sleep. It is raining and the air is sticky like a hot July night. I am very uncomfortable and terribly lonely. I wish you were here, or I was with you wherever you are — or any place with you would do. I wish I could say that I will never leave you again for one minute and know that board meetings, conventions, nothing would ever make me leave. I am completely lost without you. If I ever say that I can live without you, please don't take me seriously. For it ain't so — I love you and you are mine forever and for keeps. When I am away from our mechanical-like existence, I begin to see why we are on edge all the time. Please let's try real hard to work out a schedule and stick to it. I know I have said this before — we must do something — so we don't keep going like two machines. Living in this hotel and alone every night is driving me mad. The other fellows have their poker and drinks every night. But that lets me out. I'd give a million dollars if you were here now.

Do you know what we'd do? Well, it's 9:45, just time to make a show. After the show, you could have a sandwich, and yes, even a Tom Collins. And then home. I would put you to bed and then I would hold you real close. And tell you how much I love you. And how much I need you. You would love it, wouldn't you? We wouldn't go to sleep all night. We would just "schmooze" all night. You could sleep all day tomorrow while I sit in that do-nothing board. There is no further news except that I am lonely and I need you and love you.

All my love,

Your Dope,

Walter

IRVING BLUESTONE: "The perception of the outside world was that Walter was very busy, a dedicated man with no sense of humor. A kind of rigid personality. That wasn't true at all. He was a very easy person to work with and to be with. He had a good sense of humor and could laugh at himself. And occasionally, when he was excited enough, he would use profanity like anyone else coming out of the shop. There were many times when he and I had great fun.

"Once I asked him, 'Walter, in the 23 years you have been president of the union, what is your greatest achievement?' Without hesitation he replied, 'I think I'm a good educator.'

"Now here was a man whose achievements — as a collective bargainer, as a world citizen — were legendary. But the thing that impressed him was his ability to educate others. And, my God, he was a marvelous educator. He could dream up an idea, then bring the union along by showing the membership what he was trying to do. That's why, for example, the membership accepted a UAW civil rights posture long before the nation realized it.

"Then I said, 'I've got another question. What have you found to be the most difficult task you've had during your presidency?' Without batting an eye, he replied, 'Fighting bureaucracy.'"

Father was a perfectionist in personal habits and in how he ran the union. He was a coalition-builder, able to motivate others into action. He took pragmatic, innovative plans and actualized them, using his political astuteness. Watching so many of his ideas become reality kept him going. Father had a knack for spreading his time and his absolute concentration over many issues. He picked a staff of young, creative professionals and knew how to use their ideas to advance the union cause. Leonard Woodcock described him as "a man of soaring vision, searching for the horizon."

Later in their marriage, my parents had the pleasure of traveling together as ambassadors for peace. To mark their 34th wedding anniversary, father wrote on a plain manila folder this message to mother:

Dear Mayichka,
   Happy Anniversary.
   These 34 years have gone all to quickly, and they were filled with hours of trial and triumph. We have had our problems and our Blessings. May the next 34 years give us both good health and the continuing opportunity to share in the things that are family, the movement and the world. In the years ahead may the pressures be less and opportunities to enjoy the beauty of Paint Creek, Orange River, Black Lake be greater — even a sand beach somewhere in Shangri-La. We have two girls, both lovely like you; both forcefully independent, like me; and we both love them very much.
   After 34 years, I love you very, very much, and I wouldn't trade you in on one of the new models — for you are mine.
   Much love,
Yours,
Walter

Father had addressed the cover of the folder "To May." Mother entered the date of the message on the bottom of the plain manila folder. "Friday, March 13, 1970." Friday the 13th. The same as their wedding day.

Shortly after I moved back to Paint Creek, mother wrote me what would be her last message. It was a tiny gift card with a field of wildflowers on the front. Inside, she had inscribed: "To our Lisa: We trust you. Love, Mother."

Mother's philosophical nature enriched father's idealism.

CHAPTER FORTY-EIGHT

THE
CRASH

"Dearest mother and father, I love you so much. Please know that I love you."
— The final message I wanted to send my parents.

It was early May. I moved quickly around the kitchen, preparing a salad for our evening meal. Salads were my parents' favorite meal, especially as the weather grew warmer. As mother had taught me, I combined crisp romaine lettuce with the velvety leaves of bibb lettuce. Cheese, tomatoes and beets added color and texture. Later I would pour mother's homemade garlic dressing over the vegetables. I enjoyed working in the kitchen above our rushing creek. Preparing nourishment for others felt natural and satisfying. I had learned a lot from my mother. Her fine taste gave flair to her cooking and serving.

After three years, the cold war with my parents was over. Our relationship had matured. It felt good to be living at home again. I knew I was welcome and wanted. Having sorted out my values, I returned feeling more relaxed about myself.

Thinking about my parents over the salad, my feelings overflowed, and a tear dropped from my cheek into the bowl. We had all learned from my breaking away. I had found how to express my deepest feelings and mother had learned to control her over-protectiveness. Father had at last recognized my need to be independent, and I had achieved a new inner freedom that allowed me to be comfortable within the confines of Paint Creek. No longer authority figures, my parents were now my dearest friends.

That evening mother and father were staying late at Solidarity House for some meetings. "Maybe you can throw a simple supper together for us," mother had suggested.

As we ate our supper that evening, shocking news footage appeared on the TV screen. Our own National Guard soldiers were firing on Kent State University students, marching to protest the U.S. invasion of Cambodia. Nine students lay wounded, four were dead.

"Oh, why is this happening in America?" mother cried, and I cried too. But father flew into a rage. "Our leaders have lost touch with reality!" Immediately he left the dinner table and went into the den to draft a telegram to the White House denouncing Nixon's invasion of Cambodia:

> Your decision to invade the territory of Cambodia can only increase the enormity of the tragedy... in that area. Widening the war merely reinforces the bankruptcy of our policy of force and violence in Vietnam. Your action, taken without the advice or consent of Congress, has created a serious constitutional crisis at a time when there is a growing division in our nation. The bitter fruits of this growing alienation and frustration among America's youth are now being harvested on the campus of Kent State University.... The problem, Mr. President, is that we cannot successfully preach nonviolence at home while we escalate mass violence abroad. It is your responsibility to lead us out of the Southeast Asian war — to peace at home and abroad."

That week 400 colleges were shut in protest. Nixon responded by condemning "these bums . . . blowing up campuses . . . burning books." And Nixon's long-time "enforcer" J. Edgar Hoover declared that the Kent State students "invited and got what they deserved."

That Saturday we all arose early. It was the day before Mother's Day so father was taking mother to Mr. Riemann's nursery in Romeo where they would buy more trees for the Japanese garden. After they rode away in the blue Barracuda, I jumped into my old Valiant to buy a gift for mother and a pair of new shoes for myself.

Returning home, I found my parents were already engaged in tree-planting. I showed mother my delicate new sandals. Quite a change from my protester's combat boots. As mother gave me a gentle hug, I smiled. "I'm finally becoming a lady."

Standing on the bridge in front of our house, mother and I watched the tiny minnows swimming near the sandy bottom of the creek. Father joined us on the bridge. The conversation turned to the weekend. Mother and father would be flying to Black Lake. "Just a short trip to check last-minute details before the grand opening."

They asked me to come along. "Please, Lisa," mother pressed. "We enjoy your company and this will be the last free time daddy has before negotiations."

I told them I was going hiking with friends at nearby Stoney Creek Park. The spring semester was over; I wanted to relax with with my friends after final exams. "Anyway, mother, I'll see you both tomorrow night — I'm going to surprise you with a Mother's Day feast."

The afternoon was brilliant, a perfect day in May. After changing clothes, my parents emerged to drive to the airport. "Are you sure you want to stay, Lisa?" I gave them both a hug, promising to see them the next day, then drove off to the state park to join my friends. Mother's pleading had made me restless, but I dismissed it as her way of showing affection.

It was dusk when I returned to our empty house. I found a small shopping list on mother's walnut desk. "Here's five dollars for romaine lettuce and cottage cheese. See you Sunday night. Love, Mother."

In my room I curled up with a book. The day's hike had been invigorating, but as the evening sky darkened, I began to feel lonely. The telephone rang once and stopped. I read on.

Mother and father's takeoff had been delayed. They had to wait for Oskar Stonorov to make a connection from Philadelphia. Visibility was limited that night. Scattered clouds hung as low as 400 feet and the pilots — George Evans and Joseph Karaffa — would be flying into a steady rain. Finally, Oskar arrived — and so did father's bodyguard, Billy Wolfman. At 8:44 they were up and away.

At the small Emmett County Airport in Pellston, a UAW car waited, ready to drive them to Black Lake 40 miles away. At 9:28 p.m., Evans at the controls, reported: "I've got the airport in sight."

Three miles from the landing strip, they began their descent. They were quickly enveloped in a thick fog and relied solely on the plane's altimeter to judge their height. One little instrument...

Suddenly the jet collided with the top of a 50-foot elm tree. Its engines sucked in leaves and branches. The plane crashed into a pine forest and burst into flames.

At Paint Creek I was uneasy. I didn't know why. I had been alone at night many times before. I laid down my book and went downstairs to get a glass of juice. The telephone rang. It was the security guard at Solidarity House in Detroit. His voice sounded distant. "I'm so sorry," he began. "I heard the news on the radio...."

I caught my breath.

"It can't be true," I remember saying, as if my words could change reality. I hung up. Frantically I dialed my parents' cabin at Black Lake. The telephone rang for five minutes. The peace of the night turned to horror. My childhood fears came out of hiding and possessed me — my anxieties about mummy and daddy's safety. For years I had carried a dark image of violent death locked in my mind. I put the receiver in the cradle and sobbed. A few moments later I tried the number again. I was hoping to hear father: "Oh, we were just out watching the moon over the lake." But each ring of their phone thundered the end.

Frantically sobbing, I called the main desk at Black Lake. "Why, I didn't know they were expected here," the receptionist said. "We haven't heard anything."

My heart was pounding. I tried to call my aunt and uncle in Lake Orion. Nobody answered. Again I called the switchboard at Black Lake. No information. "Why don't you know? They're my parents," I cried. "Please tell me something." The stillness was unbearable. Like a nightmare. I phoned a friend and asked her to come keep me company. I kept envisioning my parents' last moments, their terror as the plane crashed into the trees. Did their whole life pass before them? Did their thoughts turn to their daughters? To their mission? I wanted to send them one last message: "Dearest mother and father, I love you so much. Please know that I love you."

CHAPTER FORTY-NINE

THE
OUTCRY

*"Walter and May have not died. They live in the minds and
hearts of those of us who, like them, look not to yesterday but
to the bright tomorrow."*
— Irving Bluestone at the memorial service

My sister Linda flew home from California the next day. We held
each other in our sorrow. It was Mother's Day.

Through all the tears, I saw clearly the person my parents had
wanted me to be. A person who could help others. For 22 years they
had helped me. Now their passing released an awesome metamorphosis. As the fear fell away, I saw them in my heart: *driven by a dream.*
And I, too, wanted to become my brother's keeper.

From around the world the letters arrived, workers and world
leaders alike, expressing their deepest sorrow. They came by the thousands and called father "brother." Linda and I sat together on the living
room floor and read the notes aloud, the tears flowing unchecked. I
wanted to write back to each person and share our love for mother and
father. I wanted to thank each of them for helping to ease our grief.

One of the first tributes came from father's close friend Willy
Brandt, chancellor of West Germany. "Walter was the man to first
offer the hand of reconciliation to a former adversary and help smooth
the path to a democratic and peaceful partnership with the peoples of
the world. His good relations with the leaders of European social
democracy helped decidedly with the improvement and solidification
of relations with America."

Israeli Prime Minister Golda Meir wrote: "The people of Israel will sorely miss a true and devoted friend of our people, whose memory is enshrined in the hearts of all of us. . .."

Swedish Prime Minister Tage Erlander, who attended the memorial service, also sent this message : "The world has lost a great leader; we have lost a friend who had always been a model for all of us."

President Richard Nixon, who had just received father's stinging telegram about the Kent State massacre, wrote: "Walter Reuther was a man devoted to his cause, spoke for it with eloquence and worked for it tirelessly. Mr. Reuther's death is a deep loss, not only for organized labor, but also for the cause of collective bargaining and the entire American process. Even those who disagreed with him had great respect for his ability, integrity and persistence."

Henry Ford II called father "an extraordinarily effective advocate of labor's interest. His tough-minded dedication, his sense of social concern, his selflessness and eloquence all mark him as a central figure in the development of modern industrial history."

Former Michigan Governor G. Mennen Williams: "Walter Reuther affected the lifestyle of the United States like few in his generation."

Linda and I read this note from U.S. Secretary of Labor George P. Shultz: "He believed passionately in the democratic system and the rights of man. His death is a bruising loss, not only to American labor, but to all of us." Even the Engineering Workers Union of the USSR in Moscow wired its "deep sorrow at Walter Reuther's passing."

The UAW proclaimed a week of mourning. On Wednesday morning, May 13, at the Veterans' Memorial Building in Detroit, Linda and I placed a bouquet of white daisies between our parents' caskets. The simple daisy had been their favorite flower. Linda and I saw it as a symbol of their lives. Next to the flags of the United Nations, the United States, and Canada, a flag with the peace symbol was displayed near the UAW logo.

Thousands streamed past mother and father's plain oak caskets over two long days. Father's was draped with the blue and white flag of the UAW.

Walter Cotes, an auto worker, wiped his eyes and told a reporter: "I feel so bad. Nobody can take his place. He had honest guts. He stood up for the people." A railroad worker hesitated at the door. "I'm not in his union," he said. "But I wish I *was*. He left all of us a better world. It's all right if I say good-bye to him, isn't it?"

Politicians, businessmen, executives, factory workers, clergy, street people, black, white, old, young, all filed past. Alexander Cordozo, a retired black Chrysler worker, fell to his knees in front of father's casket and sobbed, "He was the only friend I had in the world."

These days were heavy with sorrow, but Linda and I helped each other. The hardest times were the evenings, when we were alone at Paint Creek, filled with memories. Less than a month had passed since I had moved back home. Mother, father and I were closer than ever when destiny snatched them away.

Before the funeral, Linda and I stood in a receiving line with other family members at Detroit's Pontchartrain Hotel. I stood next to my mother's lifelong friend, Thelma Zwerdling, who gave me the strength to carry on. It was maddening. I wanted to be alone with Linda, but we had to "perform." It was the climax of our lives as daughters of a public figure. Almost in a daze, I shook hand after hand, nodding and speaking and going straight out of my mind. Many people I recognized from traveling with my parents. I shook hands for their sake.

Uncle Victor finally escorted us to nearby Ford Auditorium for the memorial service. As we entered the elevator, I lost control. Tears poured from my eyes. Victor quickly put his arm around me. "It's OK, Lisa." The elevator doors opened as we hit the street level, a warning to regain my composure.

Ford Auditorium, site of the funeral, is a modern black and white structure overlooking the Detroit River. Sitting in the front row next to Linda, I remembered the bitter battles played out between father and Henry Ford in the '30s. Ford had resisted the unions with all his might. But once he recognized their right to bargain, his company turned out to be the most socially progressive of all.

Thirty-four hundred invited guests crowded the hall to pay final tribute. Outside, thousands more jammed the lawns and sidewalks to hear the services over loudspeakers. Leaders had come from around the world. It was the largest gathering of dignitaries in Detroit's history.

The service began in an ocean of grief. I clutched Linda's hand, Grossmutter at my other side. She had lived to endure many losses. Now we, too, were feeling the slam of destiny. Time had brought us together, witnessed our love and dispersed us. I vowed right then to discover why. As the majestic Marian Anderson sang *He's Got the Whole World in His Hands*, flags on city buildings flew at half mast, thousands of truck drivers slowed to a halt, and automobile assembly lines from coast to coast stopped for a tribute to Walter Philip and May Wolf Reuther.

Inside Ford Auditorium, Hubert Humphrey, George Shultz, Henry Ford II, George Romney, and Edward Kennedy bowed their heads in sorrow, along with thousands.

"You didn't have to carry a UAW card to be one of Walter Reuther's constituents," Michigan Senator Philip Hart began. "You were part of Reuther's constituency if you were poor, powerless, a consumer, an outdoorsman, if you were old, if you were sick, if you were weak . . . If the opponents of that senseless war in Indochina ever muster enough political muscle to shut it down, Walter Reuther's name will be in the books as one of the movers."

John W. Gardner, a close friend of my parents and chairman of the National Urban Coalition: "None of us can speak of May and Walter without emotion and without the deepest gratitude. A friend of mine once said that the purpose of a free society is to produce great individuals, and in producing May and Walter Reuther, this society justified itself many times over. When we speak of them as typical Americans, we flatter ourselves . . . They were the good, vital, generous, loving people that many of us strive to be and never quite are...They renewed our faith. They thought better of us than we thought of ourselves, and by thinking so, made us better people."

Coretta Scott King had marched with my parents: "Walter Reuther was to black people the most widely known and respected white labor leader in the nation. He was there when the storm clouds were thick. We remember him in Montgomery. He was in Birmingham. He marched with us in Selma and Jackson, Mississippi, and in Washington . . . Only yesterday, there he was once more in Charleston, South Carolina, the leader of a million and a half workers giving personal support to a strike of only 400 black women . . . He was a big man, so of course he had enemies and detractors. He had the courage to be with the minority when it was right. He was a simple man in his personal life, a rare quality in these flamboyant times . . . but if his ways were simple, his ideas were grand. He aroused the imagination of millions...."

The eulogies soared, but nothing could bring back my parents. I wished someone would wake me from this nightmare. Then Irving Bluestone told us: "Walter and May have not died. They live in the minds and hearts of those of us who, like them, look not to yesterday but to the bright tomorrow."

Next day, Linda and I flew to Philadelphia for the funeral of Oskar Stonorov. We gathered with his wife, Betty, and the children in a small Quaker meetinghouse for a simple religious ceremony. Oskar had a strong influence on me. His love of life showed in his art. I remembered our dialogues — mother, father, Oskar and I sitting in the dining room, blueprints of Black Lake covering the teakwood table. I glanced at Betty. Even in her hour of grief, she was giving herself to others.

The fatal accident drew us closer to the Stonorovs. Oskar and Betty's youngest daughter, Angie, became my soul mate. As young girls we had both been very close to our fathers. We watched them live their values and realize some of their dreams— projects like Black Lake.

In the fall of 1969, Angie had come to study drama at the Meadow Brook School of Theatre near us in Rochester. The next spring, the Meadow Brook troupe was invited to perform Chekhov's play *The Cherry Orchard* on Broadway. *The Cherry Orchard* portrays a family in crisis, struggling with the loss of their father. Angie played the part of Anya, the daughter. As she prepared for the role, the director coached her about "the realization of her father's death." He told of his own experience as a young boy when his father fell from a ship into the sea. He was never seen again.

On Friday, May 8, Oskar traveled to New York to see and celebrate his daughter's performance. He secured a room at the Plaza Hotel for a late-night cast party. The two performances the next day would be the last.

"Tomorrow, let's have breakfast together," Oskar suggested to Angie. She declined the invitation, knowing she had to prepare for the early matinee.

Before the Saturday performance, Angie was in the wings, rehearsing the lines about her father's death. Suddenly her body began to shake with emotion. "I had to force myself to go on," she later told me. "I didn't know what was happening. I thought it was the strain of the past week's activities."

After the curtain dropped, Angie returned to her apartment. Later her mother called and told her that her father had been killed in the plane crash. The strange fear that had seized her offstage had coincided with the death of her real father.

Letters continued to flood our home. People sent poems, newspaper clippings. One from the *New York Times* read: "The death of Walter Reuther is an even more substantial loss for the nation than for the labor movement... The void of his death will be greater still in the realms of idealism and social inventiveness."

And from *Newsweek*: "During his 24 years as president of the UAW, the dynamic Reuther exerted an influence on American life far beyond his role of fighting for fatter paychecks for his 1.6 million members. At the time of his death ... he was working on a plan for mass-produced housing, and was deeply involved in the civil rights struggle, the fight for cleaner air and a legislative campaign for low-cost health insurance."

The *Des Moines Register*: "The death of Walter Reuther has silenced one of the most compassionate and creative voices of our time."

Some days later a member of the UAW brought two small metal boxes to me at Paint Creek. They contained my parents' ashes. Mother and father had specified cremation in their wills. I was asked to keep them until the UAW Executive Board arranged for a dedication at Black Lake. Father had lived for humanity through his work at the UAW. As mother had said many times, "If I had not been interested

352

in the labor movement, we never would have married!" Now even in death their ashes — and their spirits — in many ways belonged to the union. The UAW was our family. And as we continued to share our parents with the world, we entered the greater family of man.

That summer the UAW Executive Board invited a group of staff members to join with the Reuther and Stonorov families at Black Lake for the dedication of the Reuther Natural Sanctuary. It is a lovely rolling hill where trees sent from all around the world are planted in memory of our parents.

In a simple ceremony, Linda and I placed our parents' ashes in two small holes dug at the base of two evergreens. As our hands grasped the metal boxes, we shuddered as hunks of bones and ashes tumbled out to the earth. My parents were more than this dust, I thought. Surely their exuberant spirits were somewhere still.

A plain bronze plaque marked the spot. It is inscribed with father's creed: "There is no greater calling than to serve your brother. There is no greater satisfaction than to have done it well."

Linda flew back to San Francisco, leaving me to manage our parents' estate. I labored out of duty. It all seemed unreal, except the pain. Father's vision, mother's caring — I knew intimately what the world was missing. And I knew the question that was burning in everyone's mind.

Linda (foreground) and I say "goodbye" at the memorial service at Ford Auditorium in Detroit.

CHAPTER FIFTY

THE
QUESTION

"Certainly there can be no better epitaph for a man. He was fighting the fight of the whole world."
— Coretta Scott King
at the memorial service for my parents

The horror of my parents' deaths haunted me for months. I would lie awake at night and imagine their last moments before the crash. Father grabbing mother's hand as the plane smashed into the trees. Their horror as the cabin burst into flames. Father must have walked away unscathed, I'd thought on hearing the first report. He is invincible, beyond pain. Linda shared a similar reaction. It was mother's shock we had felt. Her soft feminine nature burnt to ashes. We wept for her pain and for father's aborted mission — "an eagle fallen in full flight."

At the time of the crash, mother's father had been living in a Jewish old folks home near Detroit. I visited Pop shortly after the funeral and gave him a long hug. Already he had lost his wife; now his daughter and son-in-law were gone.

Sitting down on his bed, Pop looked up at me with soulful eyes. "They finally got him, those bastards."

I caught my breath. "Oh no, it was an accident, Grandfather. Don't think..."

But was it?

That was the question everyone was asking. To some, like Pop, there was no question about it. Granted, father had enemies. The shotgun blast that had put him in the hospital was my earliest memory. So I couldn't dismiss Pop's answer as the paranoid perception of a doddering old man. Some European leaders were privately saying the same thing he was.

Somewhere deep inside me I had always known it would end like this. A few months before the plane crash, the FBI notified Irving Bluestone there was a contract out on father's life. Someone or some group had hired a professional killer or killers to eliminate him. This was nothing new. There were frequent threats and handfuls of ugly hate mail. The FBI itself was constantly investigating father, for reasons best known to its director.

J. Edgar Hoover's hatred of father produced what one journalist called "one of the longest and most extraordinary investigations in FBI history." Between 1935 and 1970, the "father of domestic surveillance" compiled an 8,400-page Reuther file. Some of the documents show that Hoover frequently authorized the illegal bugging of UAW meetings — especially those concerning Big Three negotiations, civil rights marches and labor strikes. He never stopped calling father a Communist — despite all evidence to the contrary — pinning his whole case on a letter forged many times over in 1934. He was determined to smash Walter Reuther. Their ideologies were diametrically opposed.

Early in 1970, the Nixon White House requested father's FBI file. Nixon and Hoover were old friends and fearful that the New Left might join forces with the old. Such an alliance, they felt, would greatly imperil the status quo — the status quo that father never tired of challenging.

It was Egil ("Bud") Krogh (later convicted as a Watergate conspirator) who called the FBI for the Reuther file. When CBS newsman Bill Gallagher recently asked Krogh why, he gave a couple of implausible answers before finally playing his ace: "I don't remember."

Documents lately obtained under the Freedom of Information Act show that directly after the plane crash, the FBI's Detroit bureau exchanged a half dozen telegrams with Hoover himself in Washington. The messages were attempts to confirm father's death. Although the

Information Act stipulates that only names of informers, alive or deceased, or references to them, may be deleted to protect relatives, large portions of the telegrams were blacked out. As soon as the messages had positively confirmed father's death, they stopped.

Extensive investigations followed the accident. "Because of the prominence of the passengers and the inevitable suspicion of sabotage," Uncle Victor wrote, "the safety board took the unusual step of having the chief pathologist of the University of Michigan conduct the autopsies."

A 33-man team from the Federal Aviation Administration and other agencies determined that during its last flight, the plane's altimeter had been "partially upside-down" inside the instrument panel and was giving a faulty reading. Amid the rain and dense fog, the altimeter had been the pilots' only way of knowing the plane's height. Hence the crash.

Earlier that day, singer Glen Campbell had flown to Detroit on the same jet, with no report of a faulty altimeter. But the Lear Jet firm dismissed the possibility of sabotage, saying only its trusted officials could have known who would be on the plane that evening. The trail ended there, but the *question* remains open.

Newspaper columnist Murray Kempton once referred to father as the only man he ever met who could "reminisce about the future," even though that future held the specter of assassination. One summer day in 1969, as I sat with father at Paint Creek, he spoke of his old friends Jack and Bobby Kennedy, Rabbi Morris Adler (who had recently been shot to death in his suburban Detroit synagogue) and Dr. Martin Luther King. "It's a strange feeling, Lisa. All of my friends are being killed." He seemed to be reaching out to me, as if to say, "This could happen to me, too."

A few days after the crash, I rose early to watch the rising sun say good morning to the trees at Paint Creek. Pouring through the clerestory windows, the exaggerated rays warmed my legs as I sat on the living room floor.

Suddenly a flame-red cardinal flew headlong into the bullet-proof glass and dropped dead. I gasped. Then, holding up my nightgown, I ran outside, through the morning dew to where the bird lay. Its lifeless

357

face stared up at me over a broken neck. I carefully placed the little body under the evergreens that served as the family cemetery for birds and animals.

The cardinals had been my parents' special friends. Mother often rose at dawn to watch the cardinals on the roof. They came in pairs and would mate for life. Mother and father had even considered renaming Paint Creek "Cardinals Cove."

As I lay the bird to rest, I sensed the transition. Death was yet another change. The life that flew these feathers and bones had flown somewhere else.

But now another presence filled the sunlit yard, the very familiar presence of mother and father. Their vibrations warmed my heart and relieved my sorrow.

"We know you love us," I felt them say. "We love you, too. Now our relationship is changing. We don't want it to, but we have no control."

I especially felt mother's concern. "Follow your heart, Lisa. Everything will be good for you."

"Mummy and daddy!" I shouted. "I love you!" As the sun passed behind a cloud, their presence vanished. The air became still, and the trees fell into shadows. Though no one could tell me where they had gone, a deep gratitude filled my heart. Life had blessed me with 22 years as the daughter of May and Walter Reuther. The cardinal's death had opened a last communion. I loved them dearly, and they loved me. They brought out the best in people, by demanding the best from themselves.

"Certainly there can be no better epitaph for a man," declared Coretta Scott King at my parents' memorial service. "He was fighting the fight of the whole world."

EPILOGUE

"As the embodied soul continuously passes, in this body, from childhood to youth to old age, the soul similarly passes into another body at death. The self-realized person is not bewildered by such a change."
— Bhagavad-gita

The final communion with my parents convinced me they still existed. Their bodies had exploded with the plane, leaving us a few grey bones and ashes to bury. But even if their remains were delivered intact, we would still be missing them. The irrepressible spirits who had expressed themselves in mother's kindness, in father's vision, in all the transcendent symptoms of life, were gone.

Where did they go? The question intrigued me even more than the unanswered question of sabotage surrounding their deaths. I remembered our lifelong interest in reincarnation — the transmigration of the soul — and turned once again to the teachings of the ancients.

The months following the tragic accident were filled with bewilderment. I looked for something stable in a world which seemed chaotic. After months of mourning, I moved to Ann Arbor where I purchased a house on the old west side. I was planning on enrolling in the graduate program in social work at the University of Michigan. Hopefully, this curriculum would allow me to genuinely help others. However, Providence had its own plan for fulfilling this desire.

One night, as I sat in a local pub, The Blind Pig, I looked up and noticed a man playing the piano. He came over and introduced himself as Willie — artist, wood carver and Rhodes scholar with a

PhD in architecture. Willie was easy to talk to and soon I was pouring out my heart about the crash and about my parents still existing somewhere.

"Of course they're still existing," Willie exclaimed. "None of us ever dies. We simply change bodies."

He started talking very matter-of-factly about reincarnation and quoted greats in both East and West — Buddha, Christ, Plato, Confucius, Emerson, Tolstoy, Ghandi — many of the people I had been reading. I was struck by his conviction, and how destiny had brought us together.

He quoted the *Bhagavad-gita (Song of God)* in which Lord Krishna declares, "That which pervades the entire body you should know to be indestructible. No one is able to destroy that imperishable soul."

My mind was racing. "But what happens to the soul after the death of the body?"

Again he quoted Krishna: "As the embodied soul continuously passes in this body, from childhood to youth to old age, the soul similarly passes into another body at death. The self-realized person is not bewildered by such a change."

Daily we would meet and discuss these mystical matters — ideas that had intrigued me all my life. As he chiseled a piece of cherry wood one afternoon, I asked him about life on other planets.

"Why not?" Willie laughed. "Just because NASA sent men to the moon and found no life, why should we conclude we are the only living beings within the universe? There's probably life right on earth that we don't know about, living beyond the range of our senses and instruments."

Willie based his convictions on India's Vedic literature, ancient Sanskrit texts describing both material and spiritual worlds. Different kinds of beings, he said, inhabit different kinds of planets. Some planets are higher than earth, some lower.

"Kind of like heaven and hell?"

"Exactly. Only they're all temporary. We transmigrate up and down these planets until we learn life's lesson and go back to God."

A week later we drove together to Detroit to visit the Krishna Temple on East Jefferson Avenue, just a block from Solidarity House.

It was late summer. As we pulled up to the temple, a sound from a conch filled the midday sky. I walked through the door into an atmosphere at once exotic and familiar. Sandalwood incense curled upward from a marble altar. Robed devotees took up cymbals and drums, then started singing Sanskrit hymns from the Vedas. The rhythms carried me deep into spiritual India. As the tempo increased, the devotees began to chant Hare Krishna, the same mantra I had learned at camp six years earlier. It was like hearing an old friend. But now those holy names of God moved me even more than they had in the woods. I immersed myself in the chanting. The temple was holy, and it felt like home.

As I began to visit the temple regularly, I learned a lot about the person who had brought the Vedic vision of God as "Krishna" ("all-attractive") to the West. At the age of 69, His Divine Grace A.C. Bhaktivedanta Swami Prabhupada (the same swami my camp friend had wanted me to meet in New York City) had come to America to teach Krishna consciousness. Srila Prabhupada, as the devotees called him, was respected in India as a holy man and scholar. He was a contemporary representative of a five-thousand-year-old disciplic succession of spiritual masters and had translated dozens of the original Sanskrit texts into English. Yet in 1965, he had arrived in America with only a few dollars in his pocket and a one-month sponsorship at a stranger's home. How, in eight years, he had attracted thousands of followers, started scores of temples, and spread Krishna consciousness around the world was beyond me. But as I read his translation and exposition of Krishna's *Bhagavad-gita,* I began to understand. His words spoke directly to my soul.

The Krishna-conscious lifestyle appealed to me. By avoiding illicit sex, intoxication, gambling, and meat-eating, the devotee was free to develop his or her natural spiritual qualities. Qualities like cleanliness, kindness, self-control, and ultimately love of God. Already I had given up meat and, like my father, avoided intoxicants as best I could. For the most part, the yogic disciplines of Krishna consciousness marked a path I was already on. The spiritual path to God. Those who would try to love God purely must transcend the pleasures and pains of the flesh. Every sage and saint in every tradition had taught this. It was up to me to take the next step.

I decided I wasn't ready. More than two years had passed since my parents' death. I wanted to take my newfound knowledge and get away from it all. I took off for South America and soon found myself in the Ecuadorian village of San Antonio de Ibarre. I rented a small house overlooking the Andes for $18 a month. It had dirt floors, no electricity and no running water — a perfect place to meditate. Sitting cross-legged, I would chant Hare Krishna and look out at the mountains. Lickety-split went those holy names, over my tongue, through my ears, and into my heart. There is no place in the world, I thought, where I would rather be.

I chanted a lot — while hiking, swimming, watching the weavers and the wood-carvers, bargaining in the market for vegetables, and then alone in the shanty. The light of the sun, the taste of water, the fragrance of the earth — everything began to remind me of God. As Krishna's *Gita* taught, I started to experience myself as distinct from the body and hear more clearly that inner voice which had been guiding me all these years, all those lifetimes.

After eight months in the Andes, I woke up one morning and thought, "I'm ready to move into the temple." I flew to Amsterdam where I stayed in the local Krishna temple for several weeks.

A bright, burly German named Prithu ran the Amsterdam temple with his wife, Rambhoru. Rambhoru was a spirited poetess, and we immediately became good friends. I confided that I wanted to go to India and meet Srila Prabhupada. I also mentioned that I had a large inheritance from my parents' life-insurance policy. Using this money for the greatest good had become one of my quests.

Prithu asked me to travel to Germany with him to meet Hansaduta, a senior devotee who was overseeing the Krishna movement's activities in Western Europe. I agreed to put off my India trip and away we went.

Hansaduta had Germany buzzing about Hare Krishna. Daily large chanting parties were dancing in the streets, and in the evenings many people were gathering with the devotees to hear the timeless teachings of the Vedas. The Germans had a long-standing interest in India's spiritual culture.

Hansaduta had been eyeing a large castle in the German countryside for a temple. When he heard about my inheritance, he made arrangements to take me there.

The castle was magnificent, with orchards, a large barn for cows, and several smaller buildings that devotees could use for living quarters. Here was a suitable headquarters for spreading Krishna consciousness throughout Germany.

Hansaduta spun a scenario of me donating my inheritance to buy the castle, and Prabhupada flying there for the grand opening. It all sounded presumptuous, to say the least. I respected Hansaduta. He had preached Krishna consciousness far and wide. But who was he to tell me how to spend my money?

Hansaduta advised me to return to Detroit and liquidate my assets. I flew back, burning with anxiety and resentment. Growing up, I had seen many powerful leaders up close — some good, some bad. I wasn't about to be intimidated by someone whose character I doubted.

When I reached the Detroit temple, the devotees were surprised to see me dressed in a sari. Even more surprising was my chanting of Hare Krishna round a 108-bead strand 16 times daily — a devotion that takes a good two hours to complete.

The temple president was a fatherly man named Govardhan. He was not interested in my money and immediately began making arrangements for me to go to India to meet Srila Prabhupada.

What a relief!

A few days later, I received a phone call from New York. It was Hansaduta. He wanted me to follow through with his proposal. I felt as though I were being chased.

"Did you liquidate your assets, Lisa?"

"I'm sorry," I began, "but I am not going to give you the money. I'm going to India to speak directly with Srila Prabhupada."

Desperately Hansaduta tried to change my mind. Images of the beautiful castle flashed by. I was a brand-new devotee and a little surprised I was standing up to someone so senior and persistent. But standing up to my father, persistence personified, had given me plenty of practice. After a while Hansaduta hung up.

It was March 1974. Govardhan and I were flying to India. India! Since father's trip there in 1956, I had wanted to visit this mystical land. But I wasn't going as a diplomat or sightseer; I was going as a seeker. As we descended over the Arabian Sea, excitement and caution splashed the shores of my heart. I had been following Srila Prabhupada's teachings for a year and a half. It was time to meet him face to face.

Seaside palms shimmered in the Bombay twilight. A cool breeze swept aside the evening heat. Govardhan and I found Prabhupada on a dormitory rooftop, addressing friends and followers. We sat cross-legged on cushions and listened as he spoke.

"The real problem," he was saying, "is that we are thinking 'I am this body. I am black. I am white. I am American. I am Russian. I am Hindu. I am Christian.' These bodily designations are a kind of skin disease. The healthy outlook is, 'I am spirit, part and parcel of the Supreme.'"

Prabhupada was clarifying something my father had told me long ago: "Inside, Lisa, we are exactly alike. We are all children of God." I was struck with wonder. What I'd read many times in Krishna's *Gita* —"You are not the body, you are the consciousness within"— came alive as Prabhupada spoke. The implications of this ABC of transcendental knowledge were, and still are, immense. Problems as diverse as war, racism, AIDS, drug addiction, divorce and pollution can be traced to the fundamental illusion that "We are our bodies."

Next day Govardhan arranged for me to meet privately with Srila Prabhupada. Understanding how much the world would profit by reading his translations of the ancient Vedic wisdom, I offered Prabhupada $50,000 from my inheritance to print more of his books.

He accepted the donation as God's grace and asked me about my parents. I told him about the plane crash and the possibility of sabotage.

"Accha!" he exclaimed with widening eyes. "I see."

He spoke with gravity and humility. His smile was childlike, and when he laughed, his belly shook. Though his mission was grand, his manner was simple, without pretense. Prabhupada was no shyster swami.

Returning to my departed parents, he quoted a Sanskrit verse and said, "The consciousness continues to live after the death of the body."

Tears of gratitude filled my eyes. Sitting with Prabhupada I could understand I had at last met a genuine holy man, someone who could teach me the mysteries of life. Providence had been kind after all. Prabhupada's birthday was the same day as father's: September 1. This I took as a wink from God. "Trust him."

A year later Providence winked again when Henry Ford's great-grandson, Alfred Brush Ford, joined the Krishna consciousness movement. Alfred had begun reading *The Bhagavad-gita* while a student at Tulane University. I remember when he first came to the temple on East Jefferson in Detroit. Govardhan came over to me during dinner and whispered in my ear: "Do you know who is visiting tonight? Henry Ford's great-grandson!" I chuckled inside as I watched Krishna unfold His plan. Alfred, known to the devotees as Ambarish, is a sensitive and keenly intelligent man. His perception allowed him to see through the glitter of wealth and fame. He turned to the East and, like his great-grandfather, became intrigued with the concept of reincarnation.

"Ford and Reuther on the same team?" The press played it up and Prabhupada loved it. All material differences, he affirmed, can be reconciled when people awaken to their identity as spirit souls, part and parcel of Krishna, or God.

In 1976 Alfred and I pooled our resources to purchase the ornate Lawrence P. ("Body by") Fisher Mansion in Detroit. Prabhupada asked us to restore it as a museum for Western and Vedic culture, and to feed the poor. He himself never lived in the mansion but requested that we use it to serve the public.

In August 1977, Alfred was the best man at my marriage to fellow devotee Bruce Dickmeyer. When I first met Bruce, I felt we had known each other for years. He is a very loving, conscientious man. Bruce radiates sincerity and Uncle Victor whispered to me at our wedding: "What took you so long, Lisa, to find him?" Now, 12 years later, I appreciate that God gave me not only a loyal husband but an entire family; indeed I am as close to Bruce's parents and siblings as any daughter could be. Bruce and I are soul-mates.

Three months after our wedding, Prabhupada passed away, filling us all with unspeakable grief. The Hare Krishna movement's struggles since Prabhupada's departure could easily fill another volume. It has been hard but always hopeful. Both father and Prabhupada had the vision to build their movements on principles, not personalities. Leaders come and go; truth endures.

Prabhupada hoped his followers would combine the wealth of the West with the wisdom of the East to "respiritualize human society." He appreciated America's belief in the worth of the individual and the freedom that gives us to pursue the transcendental path. Others have not been so lucky. Krishna devotees in the Soviet Union, for example, have been imprisoned, committed to psychiatric hospitals, and exiled to slave labor camps as "ideological saboteurs." Recently, protests by the Krishna consciousness movement and humanitarian groups worldwide have impelled the Gorbachev regime to release many of the Soviet devotees. Despite *glasnost,* persecution persists.

As a mother of three, I am grateful to live in a country that safeguards its citizens' freedom. In their different ways, both Prabhupada and my father saw America as the leader of a spiritual force that could embrace all the peoples of the world. As father used to say, "Let us agree that it is tough to put the world together. Let us remember, however, that when you put man together, you put the world together."

OWEN BIEBER
AND
BOB WHITE
ON
WALTER REUTHER

It is impossible to overestimate the impact that Walter Reuther's speeches and even his mere presence had upon the UAW leaders of my generation.

We were relatively young people when Walter was in his prime during the '50s and '60s. The union Walter shaped was itself young and robust in terms of its self-confidence, which in turn reflected Walter's self-confidence.

You have to remember that working people in America are not used to feeling powerful. We are not taught to think that we have the capability to improve our working conditions and benefits dramatically, let alone to have a major impact on the direction of national affairs.

But with Walter Reuther at the helm, we not only *talked* about the changes we wanted, but we actually went out and *made* those changes. And being part of that forward movement was tremendously inspiring to everyone at the local and regional level. That tradition lives on in our union.

To this day, many UAW leaders and staff people talk about Walter's style. The man had a tremendous sense of style. And while people still express wonderment about the length of some of Walter's speeches, it's obvious that the ideas and even the words in those speeches had a lasting impact.

Walter's example taught me many things, but the most important is that we have to have a program to keep the union in front of the issues. Walter was great at picking the brains of his staff and colleagues. Once he had solicited the views of everyone, he added his own insights and formulated the program. Then when the program was "hatched," so to speak, Walter made sure that everyone understood it and that everyone was prepared to carry it forward.

Walter Reuther taught us all that ideas and strategy are vitally important to the union's progress. I can't imagine a greater legacy or a more relevant lesson for our own times.

Owen Bieber
President
United Auto Workers

I first met Walter Reuther when I attended my first UAW convention in Atlantic City in 1957. Prior to then, I had read about him, as well as seen movies of his involvement in the early days of the UAW. Walter, in his speech to that convention, opened my eyes to his vision of what the union really meant; that the UAW was much more than just a union, it was a social and political force, both domestically and internationally.

He inspired me, as I am sure he inspired hundreds of other local union leaders, to become more active on behalf of working people.

I had an opportunity to meet Walter several times after that convention, including having him speak to a large organizing rally of aircraft workers in Toronto, where I was the organizer.

I remember the night that he and May lost their lives in the tragic airplane crash like it was only yesterday, as several local union delegates attending our Canadian Council meeting in Windsor huddled around our TVs and radios late at night with tears in our eyes. We thought the UAW could not carry on, but it did. It carried on because Walter had built a cadre of leadership capable of facing the challenges ahead.

It is interesting that 18 years later, the Reuther saga still plays an important part in the U.S. labour movement. My guess is that had he lived longer, he would have changed it for the better.

I have a few pictures in my office and one of them is of Walter Reuther. He was and still is an inspiration and an example of what I believe leadership is about.

Bob White
President, Canadian Auto Workers

ACKNOWLEDGEMENTS

I am deeply indebted to many people who have helped make this book possible. For their generous interviews, I would like to thank Victor Reuther, Doug Fraser, Irving Bluestone, Paul Schrade, Angie Stonorov and John Haslett.

There is no way to measure the help and support given by the staff of the Archives of Labor History and Urban Affairs at Wayne State University. My heartfelt gratitude to Dr. Philip P. Mason, director of the archives, for his steadfast friendship and encouragement; Warner Pflug for his hours spent proofreading the manuscript; Marjorie Long for her professional skills as a photo librarian in providing many of the beautiful pictures in this book.

The assistance of the staff at the Walter and May Reuther Family Education Center at Black Lake, Mich., has been greatly appreciated. Sections of this book were composed at Black Lake, whose atmosphere radiates the dreams and aspirations of my parents. I would especially like to thank Chuck Yancey, Prince Moon and Art Shy, as well as the many other people who have helped us at the center.

I want to thank UAW President Owen Bieber and CAW President Bob White for their statements which appear in the Appendix. And special thanks to Arthur Schlesinger Jr. for his comments and suggestions.

The support of sincere friends has given us encouragement along the way. Many thanks to Esther Kratz, the Mary and Scott Mitchell family, Thelma and Abe Zwerdling, Eric and Ann Fromm, Paul and Sheila Allen, Bob Richardson, Sally Rank, Dr. Ted Wietrzykowski, Janet Blair, Alfred Brush Ford, Michael Grant, Dr. Edward Pappas,

Paru Triveti, Rosalie McGlinn, William and Anna Halteman, Bill and Elizabeth Gallagher, John Herling, Robert Lacey, J. Patrick Wright and Lowell Ecklund.

I am grateful to our good friend Richard A. Hall for his editing skills and to his wife, Kate, for her patience. Thanks also go to Jenny King for her help with the original manuscript; Richard A. Wright for his technical assistance; and Dr. Philip O. Spelman, our publisher.

I must extend my love and gratitude to all of the Reuther family; and to my mother-in-law and father-in-law, Darlene and Ben Dickmeyer, and the entire family for their inspirational support.

My deep appreciation to all the Stonorovs for their courage and friendship.

My deepest love to my sister, Linda Ann, who lived this story with me. I dedicate this book to her.

Finally, I must express my devoted love to our three children, little Walter (10), May (6) and Victor (1). They have tolerated a very busy mother and father for five years.

This book would not have been possible without the tremendous help of my husband, Bruce Dickmeyer. Beginning with the historical research at the archives at Wayne State University and working constantly as my guide, Bruce often carried the load of this project when it became too difficult for me. This book has enriched our marriage and increased my respect for him as a dedicated friend.

Elisabeth Reuther Dickmeyer

Photograph on Page 54, courtesy of Tony Spina, The Detroit Free Press; Page 17, The Detroit News; Page 26, AP/World Wide Photos; Page 48, The UAW. The rest, except for a few family snapshots, are published with permission of The Archives of Labor and Urban Affairs, Wayne State University.

BIBLIOGRAPHY

Babson, Steve. *Working Detroit: The Making of a Union Town*. New York: Adama Books, 1984.

Christman, Henry M. *Walter P. Reuther: Selected Papers*. New York: The Macmillan Co., 1961.

Cook, Fred. *The Nightmare Decade*. New York: Random House, 1971.

Cormier and Eaton. *Reuther*. New York: Prentice-Hall, 1970.

Gelderman, Carol. *Henry Ford: The Wayward Capitalist*. New York: Dial Press, 1981.

Gould, Hickok. *Walter Reuther, Labor's Rugged Individualist*. New York: Dodd, Mead & Co., 1972.

Halberstam, David. *The Reckoning*. New York: William Morrow and Co., 1986.

Hareven, Tamara K. *Eleanor Roosevelt — An American Conscience*. Quadrangle, 1968.

Herndon, Booton. *Ford: An Unconventional Biography of the Men and Their Times*. New York: Weybright and Talley, 1969.

Kennedy, Robert. *The Enemy Within*. New York: Harper & Brothers, 1960.

Lacey, Robert. *Ford: The Men and the Machine*. Boston: Little, Brown, 1986.

Lash, Joseph P. *A World of Love; Eleanor Roosevelt and her Friends, 1943-62*. New York: McGraw-Hill, 1984.

Levy, Jacques. *Cesar Chavez: Autobiography of La Causa*. New York: W.W. Norton Co., 1975.

Lewis, David L. *King: A Biography*. Champaign, Ill.: University of Illinois Press, 1976.

Lewis, David L. *The Public Image of Henry Ford: An American Folk Hero and His Company*. Detroit: Wayne State University Press, 1976.

Oates, Stephen B. *Let the Trumpet Sound: The Life of Martin Luther King Jr*. Plume, 1982.

Powers, Richard G. *Secrecy and Power: The Life of J. Edgar Hoover*. New York: The Free Press, 1987.

Reuther, Victor. *The Brothers Reuther and the Story of the UAW*. Boston: Houghton Mifflin Co., 1976.

Schlesinger, Arthur M. Jr.. *Robert Kennedy and His Times*. New York: Ballantine, 1978.

Solberg, Carl. *Hubert Humphrey: A Biography*. New York: W.W. Norton Co., 1984.

Tyler, R.L. *Walter Reuther*. Grand Rapids, Mich.: William B. Eerdmans Publishing Co., 1973.

White, Bob. *Hard Bargains: My Life on the Line*. Toronto: McClelland and Stewart, 1987.

INDEX

COLOPHON

Editorial Consultants: Jenny Lungershausen King, Richard Hall, Bruce Dickmeyer, Richard A. Wright, Philip O. Spelman

Designed and composed electronically by Richard A. Wright in 12-point Times Roman text with Zapf Calligraphic display

Cover design by Hank Van Fleteren and Denny Denel

Union Printed
on 60# Arcata Finch Opaque and bound by Arcata Graphics Kingsport

Would someone you know enjoy this book?

Any history buff or union member would enjoy this intimate account of the dramatic life of America's legendary labor leader, Walter Reuther, as seen through the eyes of his youngest daughter, Elisabeth.

Endorsed by: Arthur Schlesinger Jr.
Doug Fraser
Owen Bieber
Bob White